MONSTER TREK

MONSTER
TREK

THE OBSESSIVE SEARCH
FOR BIGFOOT | JOE GISONDI

UNIVERSITY OF NEBRASKA PRESS | LINCOLN AND LONDON

Library of Congress
Cataloging-in-Publication Data
Gisondi, Joe.
Monster trek: the obsessive search
for Bigfoot / Joe Gisondi.
pages   cm
Includes bibliographical references.
ISBN 978-0-8032-4994-3 (pbk.: alk. paper)
ISBN 978-0-8032-8518-7 (epub)
ISBN 978-0-8032-8519-4 (mobi)
ISBN 978-0-8032-8520-0 (pdf)
1. Sasquatch—United States—
Anecdotes. I. Title.
QL89.2.S2G57 2015
001.944—dc23
2015019927

Set in Minion by M. Scheer.
Designed by N. Putens.

To my sweeties, Betsy, Kristen, and Sarah,
for making family life the best adventure of all.

There are more things in heaven and earth, Horatio,
Than are dreamt of in your philosophy.

—**HAMLET**

That's the trouble with losing your mind; by the time
it's gone, it's too late to get it back.

—**BILL BRYSON**, *A Walk in the Woods: Rediscovering
America on the Appalachian Trail*

CONTENTS

Acknowledgments   ix

Introduction   xi

Prologue   1

1. Ouachita Mountains, Oklahoma   5

2. Uwharrie Mountains, North Carolina   45

3. Southern Illinois   79

4. Green Swamp, Florida   101

5. Northern Wisconsin   137

6. Eastern Kentucky   165

7. Salt Fork State Park, Ohio   201

8. Wind River Mountains, Wyoming   223

Epilogue   251

Notes   275

ACKNOWLEDGMENTS

To alter a pervasive sports metaphor, there's no *I* in *book* (although there is justifiably one in *bigfoot*). Yet there is an *I* in this book. As a journalist, I have been taught to remain neutral, report the facts, and rely on quoted material — good advice to a point. But this is not that kind of book. At first, I *fought* against inserting myself into this story, arguing that this narrative is about people who search for bigfoot. Eventually I realized (thanks in large part to Dianne Aprile's constant encouragement) that every story needs a guide, and that's the role I serve in this book. Like those who search for bigfoot, we all need to expand our perspectives and to take risks. This book, I hope you agree, is enriched by this approach. I have been blessed by having so many people besides Dianne serve as mentors through this project — Nancy McCabe, who helped me develop the opening chapters; Roy Hoffman, who helped me move in a new direction; Richard Goodman, who opened up a whole new approach to writing; and a community of supportive friends and teachers in Spalding's MFA program.

Of course, there's no way I could have completed this project without so many bigfoot investigators bringing me into their confidence, sharing personal stories and thoughts, and allowing me to traipse through woods, mountains, and swamps to follow them in their endeavors. I hope this book treats everyone as respectfully as they very well deserve. Thanks, in particular, to Harold Benny, Donna Cohrs, Melissa Hovey, Don Keating, Jeff Meldrum, John Mionczynski, Matt Moneymaker, Tommy Poland, Pat Rance, Carolanne Solomon, Billy Willard, and Don Young.

Thanks also to Eastern Illinois University for allowing me the time to work on this project and to colleagues who constantly offered support and encouragement.

Thanks more than anything to my wife, Betsy, and to my daughters, Kristen and Sarah, who carried the biggest burden of living with a writer whose mind constantly ventured, whose body constantly sat in an office writing, and whose psyche sometimes zagged. Without you all, none of this matters.

INTRODUCTION

Believing in bigfoot's a matter of faith.

Let me confess: I dig reading about the paranormal — ghosts flitting around old homes, *chupacabras* sucking the blood of goats and chickens in Puerto Rico, Nessie eluding searchers in a Scottish loch, UFOs soaring through western skies. What's not to enjoy? I devoured these stories with millions of other Americans as a kid. I also learned that explorers like Admiral Byrd descended into middle earth from openings found in Antarctica and that lycanthropic people shape-shift into werewolves under a full moon. Did a large, hairy, man-like creature living deep in the Pacific Northwest woods scare hikers, abduct campers, and topple tractors sent to destroy its homeland in Northern California? Duh.

These stories all seemed real, especially to a ten-year-old kid reading them in a newspaper tossed on the coffee table right next to the *Newark Star-Ledger*, the *New York Daily News*, and the *Bridgewater Courier-News*. How could I not believe? How was any of this crazier than the stories in the *Star-Ledger* about men killing store clerks over fifty bucks? Or articles about gangs that raped young girls in the Bronx? Or even politicians taking bribes for favors despite what I had just read in my fourth-grade history texts? The Founding Fathers would have rolled over in their graves. (Actually, that may have been a story in the *National Enquirer*. Can't recall.) None of these news stories seemed more bizarre than those described in the more "mainstream" newspapers, not that I knew the difference back in elementary school.

I blame my mom, of course. It's always easier to blame one's parents for flaws revealed in adulthood. After all, my mom was the one who'd casually grab the *National Enquirer* at the cash register, tossing it onto the conveyor along with the canned green beans, ground beef, and Super Sugar Crisps each week. At home, she'd spend days reading it on the couch, just like she did the other newspapers. So when she'd make dinner or vacuum, I'd put down the sports section and the comics to sneak it up into my room the same way my friends pilfered *Playboy*. Upstairs in my room, I'd read features about the real-life ghost story of the month, check updates on the Missouri Monster, known as MoMo, or determine where aliens had recently abducted my fellow Americans (like Betty and Barney Hill, who had not recalled the probing by small humanoid figures until they were hypnotized!).

In 1973 I had not yet learned that aliens preferred to snag people from trailer parks and rural southern homes. But, doggone it, that seemed to be the case in the *Enquirer*. That same year, Hollywood started producing TV documentaries about Erich von Daniken's books like *Chariots of the Gods?*, which purported that space travelers in ancient times inspired many religious ideas about God and angels—a shocking hypothesis for an impressionable Catholic kid. But enquiring minds, like me and my mom, wanted to know the truth. We couldn't help ourselves. The truth was out there.

As I said, none of this seemed crazier than other reports in the news. In 1974 the president of the United States resigned from office for lying and cheating—something that could get you kicked off our Little League baseball team or sent to the principal's office.

What could be more bizarre than that? That more than fifty people reported seeing a large, hairy beast wondering in the woods that same year? Please. Besides, to an eleven-year-old, the woods seemed much more mysterious and foreboding, especially after reading reports in the "paper."

By 1976 I was watching *In Search of . . .* , a TV show that documented investigations into the paranormal by showing reenactments, interviewing "experts," and offering scientific explanations. Actor Leonard Nimoy, the ever-logical Spock, narrated each show laconically, stating facts as unceremoniously as Walter Cronkite did on the CBS *Evening News*. That summer I also watched the documentary *The Legend of Bigfoot* at the historic Brook Theater in Bound Brook, New Jersey. That's where I saw this mythic creature for the first time (or, should I say, bigfoot looked directly at me) in the infamous Patterson-Gimlin film. Needless to say, I no longer walked alone through the woods to Adamsville Middle School after that.

Even my father, a decorated Korean War veteran, piled on, telling me stories about people seeing the Jersey Devil not far away, in the Pine Barrens of southern New Jersey. My dad, who owned a pool company, sometimes heard bigfoot accounts from clients across the state. But that's not a surprise. Bigfoot are reported across all social, educational, and economic classes. Despite popular opinion, sightings are not just reported by gullible, lazy rednecks with little intelligence (and far fewer teeth). Witnesses include police officers, office managers, lawyers, business vice presidents, soldiers, housewives, teachers, and kids. Most witnesses have nothing to gain, but a great deal to lose. Some witnesses have had their lives turned upside down, ridiculed by neighbors and coworkers for admitting they may have viewed something.

The Bigfoot Field Researchers Organization's geographic database includes more than four thousand reports from every state except Hawaii, along with nearly four hundred reports from

Canada. For the most part, witnesses describe seeing a creature that is six to eight feet tall, weighs six to eight hundred pounds, is covered with brown, red, black, or white hair, and has a face that is human-like. Some report that the face is flat like a gorilla's, the neck is short, and the head pointed. The eyes, for the most part, are unusually large and black—although, at night, some claim the eyes glow red, orange, or white. Most people report that the creature walks on two feet, but several people say it has dropped down on all fours, running on both knuckles and feet. A few bigfoot have been reported climbing or clinging to trees. In Florida, witnesses claim they smell a nasty stench similar to a skunk's emissions—prompting the creature to be called a Skunk Ape. Smell a dead skunk at night and, inevitably, a friend will break out some story about the creature wreaking havoc on campsites or running alongside cars racing down state roads, keeping up with cars going as fast as 45 mph. Bigfoot is far from the craziest thing running around the Sunshine State. But that smell can still cause some anxiety during a late-night run along country roads in DeLand, Palm Bay, and Titusville. Or so I hear.

In the South, bigfoot are described as being lean, whereas witnesses in the Pacific Northwest and the Southwest report bulky creatures measuring eight to ten feet tall. In the South they are also called "boogers," a term derived from "boogey man," probably because the stories from this part of the country tend to characterize a far more sinister or mean-spirited creature. Both the Fouke Monster in Arkansas and the Lizard Man in South Carolina, for example, attacked people and ate farm animals. Not sure if these darker stories are a reflection of rugged pioneers who plowed over mountains and swamps or if we can just blame it all on white lightning poured from large jugs.

Australians call them yowies, a name whose genesis is more challenging to pinpoint. Some reports claim the term harkens to the beasts in Jonathan Swift's *Gulliver's Travels*. The name is also cited in Aboriginal folklore to describe a hybrid beast that is a cross between a lizard and an ant with large red eyes and fangs that emerges from the earth each night to eat whatever it finds — including humans. "Yowie" was also slang referring to an orangutan in Victorian England.

In the Himalayas, of course, they are yetis or the Abominable Snowman, terms popularized by Sir Edmund Hillary after he scaled Mount Everest in 1953. The yeti's image was softened a decade later by Rankin/Bass, those claymation geniuses who brought us the Christmas TV classic *Rudolph the Red-Nosed Reindeer*. Hermey the elf extracted the Abominable's fangs, turning it into a humble Bumble that put stars atop Christmas trees.

Canadians call them sasquatches, an Anglicized derivative of a word, *sésquac*, used by the Coast Salish Indians in British Columbia to describe a wild man. Native Americans across the country have named a wild man living in their respective areas — Esti Capcaki/Tall Men by the Seminoles; Iktomi/the Trickster by the Plains Indians; Tso apittse/Cannibal Giant by the Shoshones; and Kecleh-Kudleh/Hairy Savage by the Cherokees. Native American tribes have more than fifty names that characterize this creature as a cannibal demon, big elder brother, bad luck, stick Indian, devil of the forest, evil god of the woods, mountain devil, wicked cannibal, owl monster woman, and frightener.

More than two hundred people regularly investigate bigfoot in the United States, either as part of the forty-plus organizations devoted to such work or on their own. The Bigfoot Field Researchers Organization (BFRO) utilizes dozens of investigators across the country, making it by far the largest group in the United States. Since the early 1990s, bigfoot organizations have popped up all over the country — Gulf Coast Bigfoot Research Organization, Virginia Bigfoot Research Organization, Ohio Bigfoot Research Team, American Bigfoot Society, Northeast Sasquatch Researchers Association, Mid-America Bigfoot Research Center, Texas

Bigfoot Research Conservancy, Pennsylvania Bigfoot Society, Squatch Inc. Research and Investigative Organization, and the New Jersey Bigfoot Reporting Center, among others.

Many of these researchers and observers prefer to work anonymously. The Ohio Bigfoot Research Team, for example, refused to speak with me, despite several overtures. The Michigan Recording Project, which focuses on making audio recordings at a location in that state, has also refused to speak. "We do honestly appreciate the interest," Paul Willison wrote to me, "but public media exposure is simply not our intent." Media exposure can create problems, he said, by luring other enthusiasts to these areas. That infuriates most researchers, who are as territorial as gold miners. Bigfoot rule no. 1: Do not investigate within ten miles of another person's staked area — unless invited to do so.

Eventually I learned to distinguish real news, working as a student reporter in high school before working for several daily newspapers in Florida, where we moved in 1977. I took my role as journalist seriously. As the years passed, I started to focus more and more on hard news — state budgets, school board policy debates, political election violations, companies spilling chemicals into local streams. I trusted no source, verified all information, and embraced the old journalist bromide: "If your mother says she loves you, check it out." That, I knew. I also knew that my mom now also loved the *Weekly World News*, a paper that challenged the *National Enquirer* for enquiring minds.

At the same time, I continued to read about the paranormal. I bought books about bigfoot, such as John Green's *Sasquatch: The Apes among Us*, and searched on microfiche for articles published in obscure magazines. I even joined the International Society of Cryptozoology in order to get its semiregular newsletters that featured articles on other unknown, or cryptid, species, like the Tongan Skink, Mexican Onza puma, and previously unknown parrots in South America. Really, though, all I cared about were the reports on sasquatches and yetis.

As a teen, I struggled with faith—especially after my mother got breast cancer, my grandfather died, and my father left to live with another woman. In fact, my father had lived with this person since I was six years old, something my parents had covered up. Those events helped shatter my previously held beliefs about the world.

But I had always struggled with faith. As a five-year-old, I'd pepper my parents with questions nobody could answer, not even the pope or Carl Sagan. Who were God's parents? Does the universe end? If so, what's outside that? What existed before the universe was created? These questions still melt my brain. There's no way I'm ever going to get any answers. I want to believe that science and religion can someday answer a few of them, but I'm not expecting any answers anytime soon.

Bigfoot, for me, offer a litmus test of sorts. Searching for bigfoot is somewhat like searching for one's faith. If something as unlikely as bigfoot can exist, perhaps that indicates that other unlikely things may also exist—like heaven and an afterlife. I've never seen a bigfoot, but I've now viewed footprints allegedly left by one. That's my experience with religion. I was not there with Jesus, but I have read the Gospels and Epistles. I guess I am staggering at the promise of God, as Paul states in Romans. I lack the strong faith needed to overcome major challenges.

On a much smaller scale, I imagine if I can find bigfoot, I can more fully believe in a supreme being, heaven, angels—the works. At least, that's my hope, not that I have a great track record. I have witnessed several moments that were nothing short of miraculous. But later I would dissect each moment, questioning what I'd seen. That also happened during my first bigfoot expedition, when I saw a creature kneeling on his right leg through a thermal imager, his head cocked in my direction and looking straight at me in the Oklahoma hills. I can still visualize that image. Only now I wonder whether I actually saw something that I wanted to see, as I do sometimes when I look up into the clouds. Faith is fickle even to those who want to believe, it seems. That's why I'm enamored of those whose faith is unwavering—people who describe experiences so lucidly that I can picture them, those who believe strongly even though they've only seen footprints or read Corinthians, or even people who have merely sensed something at night in the woods or in a pew in the morning. That's all it takes for some people. Me, I need to shake the hand of a bigfoot or weep at the feet of Jesus—if I truly want to believe with my heart and soul.

A few years after my two daughters were born, I worked hard to return to religion, joining an Episcopal church. Eventually I became a vestry member, even though I always felt like a fake among all the other glowing, smiling people each Sunday. One day I asked the reverend, Father Joe, how one becomes a true believer, how one can embrace the Bible as if it were a newspaper report—every fact checked and every idea a certitude.

In a few sentences, I learned more about faith than I ever imagined possible.

Father Joe turned to me under a large oak by his office and paused. "Those are the people who scare the hell out of me," he said. "Faith is about believing in one's heart even when you are not sure. Faith is a constant struggle. But wanting to believe is the most important part of it all."

That was the day I realized journalism and religion were not as different as I had thought. That day I started to look at the world in a whole new way.

So you can call people who search for bigfoot nuts, crazies, loons, batty, daft, screwy, unbalanced, or idiotic. I call them passionate. And I want to know more about how they think, why they act as they do, who they really are. That's the reason I set out with several dozen investigators as they searched for bigfoot, following them into densely wooded areas where bears and cougars lurked, into gator-logged swamps, and into secluded sections of the Rocky Mountains and Midwest where one can get lost for days. Perhaps I'm the crazy one, following people who are perceived to be unbalanced into remote areas at night. But I figured it could all be worth it, especially if, along the way, I could gain illumination — or even something close to it.

MONSTER TREK

PROLOGUE

It was well past midnight in the middle of the north Georgia woods. My bladder was full. But I was afraid to leave my tent. Something was watching. Something was waiting. Many times during the past three days, even at night, I had walked the fifty yards to the outhouse here atop Black Rock Mountain—without so much as a tingle.

It's crazy how one can suddenly freeze in terror for no apparent reason, even when one's spouse and young daughters are a few feet away dozing in their sleeping bags. I'm not one to imagine monsters—or even bears—lurking in the woods. Lurking for prey. Lurking for me! In fact, I often dismiss such notions.

However, I've been known to fall for other people's stories of such fantasies. For example, there was the time a friend claimed a giant snake had slithered toward him from a canal inside Florida's Cape Canaveral National Seashore, a remote area filled with exceptionally large boar, rattlesnakes, and alligators.

From my friend's description, the snake sounded like an anaconda, something we both knew did not inhabit Florida marshes. This intrigued me, so I agreed to go back to the cape with him to see if we could track down the snake and get a good look. We ended up at a canal that opened into a marsh, where, sure enough, we saw a large creature shaped like the tail of an otter, moving along the ground. As we watched, a *Lontra canadensis* dove into the green marsh, doing a headstand as it searched for food in crevices in the lagoon's bottom. When the otter returned to the surface, it floated on its back while holding a mullet in its webbed paws. Oh, but the mind plays tricks.

I listen to as many stories as I tell, but as a journalist, I do not always believe the ones I hear, even when I want to believe them. I'm usually looking for a rational explanation. Years ago, in grad school, I had heard about another strange encounter in the cape, not far from Titusville, where residents are more inclined to believe in life on Mars thirty-six million miles away than in hairy beasts padding around along the Indian River. My friend Darlene reported spotting something big and scary during a camping trip she'd taken with her boyfriend. During the night, while her boyfriend slept, she heard what sounded like a chimpanzee screaming as it rushed through the thick royal palms and tall grasses. Darlene wondered if she had actually heard a wild boar or, perhaps, a hungry black bear. She was an experienced camper, and she had never heard anything like that high-pitched screech. When the screeching stopped, she stayed under her covers, eyes wide open, wondering whether the animal were now standing over the tent, sizing her up, as if she were a rolled-up human burrito. She never used the term "bigfoot" to describe the creature, but I knew—and she knew—that bigfoot was exactly what she believed she had encountered.

I wanted to believe Darlene's story, but she told it to me with too much flourish at a party. Sure, I enjoyed it. Stories like that are exhilarating. The heart pumps, the mind races, and the imagination runs wild. Reality, however, is another matter. I was studying to be a journalist when Darlene told me her story. I was on my way to becoming a trained skeptic.

A true bigfoot believer? No way. Yet, over the years, I became less sure that bigfoot were a fantasy. I read enough about the sasquatch, as bigfoot are sometimes called, and spent enough time researching the ever-growing body of bigfoot sightings in the United States to become capable of imagining, in lurid detail, their alleged behaviors in the wild.

So there I was in north Georgia, atop Black Rock Mountain, camping with my family—paralyzed with fear. My bladder was about to burst, yet I was totally afraid of leaving the tent to use the outhouse not far away. Instead, hands trembling, I unzipped the door flap and took a quick look around, hoping I would not see a creature looking back at me. And I didn't. But I *felt* something watching me.

Suddenly fearful, I fell to my knees, half in and half out of the tent, allowing my eyes to adjust to the darkness. It was close to 3:00 a.m. The stars were barely visible through the trees. The narrow path to the outhouse was impossible to discern. I peered into the woods, expecting to see glowing red eyes or smell musky odors or hear a high-pitched screech—anything to justify my fears, to make me feel as if I were not a scared little child. But the confounding part was that I heard nothing—not a snapped twig, not an owl's late-night hoot, nor a curious raccoon or squirrel rustling in the leaves. It was eerily silent. So I quietly stood to urinate, shooting a stream off to the side of the tent's entrance, far enough away to avoid creating a puddle someone might step in the next morning. I was now especially glad we were departing the next day, before the stench (and questions) would hit me.

Wife: "Honey, did you see one of the girls pee near the tent today?"

Me (waving a dismissive hand): "No, that was me. I was scared that a monster was going to eat me last night so I peed out the entrance rather than risking my life with a trek to the outhouse."

In the morning I walked around the campground but found nothing, save for a few broken branches on the path that had probably been lying there for months and an impression in the earth that was too large for a footprint. But the impression was explained away by another camper who casually mentioned hearing a bear during the night, a common sight in these north Georgia hills. I chalked up my nervousness to an overactive imagination and put the incident behind me.

A few years later, however, I had another experience while hiking through mountains in western Virginia—a moment alone on a trail, less than a mile from my campsite, when my spine tingled and I suddenly (and inexplicably) felt as if someone (or something) were tracking me. Less than a mile from camp. I stopped, paused, and looked deeper into the woods ahead, thinking I must have heard a bear. A few acorns fell from a tree.

Why, I wondered, did I feel the need to turn my head to look behind me every few yards? And why, after turning at a bend in the trail, did I take off running until I reached the edge of the campsite, my heart beating much faster than normal?

Psychologists say fear is a primal emotional impulse, something that causes a flight response. Sometimes, though, imagination gets the better of us—or so I thought. It wasn't until after I had spoken to bigfoot trackers that I started connecting the dots among these two personal experiences and my friend Darlene's story. For the first time, I seriously asked myself: is bigfoot a hoax or a reality?

1 OUACHITA MOUNTAINS
OKLAHOMA

So I'm sitting in a dive, grease spattered everywhere, while Harold Benny chews away on his eggs and sausage and talks about bigfoot. Last night, Harold believes he heard a few sasquatches communicating to him through a process called wood knocks. A few other researchers sitting at Clancy's say they heard howls and yelps, although in southeastern Oklahoma those sounds could easily come from the hundreds of dogs that roam the countryside. The Native Americans who live in the area, mostly Okmulgees and Choctaws, do not believe in putting dogs on leashes, something I learned accidentally deep in the woods the night before. Harold listens to the others tell stories and nods. He scoffs, though, when big Ed talks about the tapes he played in the woods last night, hoping the sounds of house pets would attract a bigfoot. Unlike the other investigators at the table, Ed believes sasquatches eat dogs. To bigfoot, they're a delicacy, Ed tells me. Harold is not the only person who dismisses Ed as a crackpot.

Even among bigfoot hunters, Ed is unusual. He does not wear pricey boots, does not put on wraparound sunglasses, and does not dress in camouflage pants and shirts. Instead, Ed wears blue bib overalls and beat-up construction boots, and he smokes like the proverbial chimney. It's about 7:00 a.m. Five hours earlier, I had returned from my own trek through the Kiamichi Mountains, a night that had left me feeling like an outsider, inept, and a little uncomfortable.

I could tell Ed was an odd egg when we met outside Clancy's an hour earlier. He had leaned uncomfortably close to me and whispered, "Did you see anything last night?" I told him I thought I saw something staring at me through the night-vision goggles. But, I admitted, that was probably an overactive imagination.

"Just because it was your first time doesn't mean you didn't see anything." Ed pulled a tick from his arm, squeezed it, and tossed the bloodsucker into the dirt parking lot outside Clancy's Cabins. "Want to get something to eat?"

Not anymore, I thought, but my stomach rumbled as we walked to the entrance. I really did not want to test the food so far from a hospital, but I needed to escape these chilly winds outside so I could learn more about this expedition.

Inside, Ed quickly digs into the eggs and toast and bacon and coffee and tells me about a life spent as a dive driller for several oil companies off the coasts of Louisiana and Texas. Harold sits across from me. Ed would dive down about 190 feet for up to an hour at a time, welding and drilling and looking for oil, a skill, he says, he learned while serving in the U.S. Army. He even developed his own asbestos helmet, which must have been big enough to hold his thick mane. After he left diving, he drove a truck for three years. At the moment, Ed says he is unemployed ("But I'm not looking very hard," he says). Yet he has enough money to purchase sound-recording devices and he's currently bidding for a bionic ear on eBay. This lightweight device can be used to pick up distant animal sounds, but it's illegal to use the ear to overhear human voices that are normally undetectable.

Bigfoot hunters do not all seek evidence in the same manner.

Some scout out areas to sit and wait, and some trek through the woods with night-vision goggles. Ed prefers to use sound recording to lure them closer to him so he can take some photos. "I spoke with a woman up a ways where there's some activity," Ed tells me. "While she was out in the barn, she said they were mimicking the animals inside. When I went up there, all I caught were some deer and possum and raccoons. Overnight, these people lost about twenty peaches off a tree. Most of them were pretty high up there. Who do you think took them?" There is no skepticism in his voice, nor science in his actions. He's just someone seeking some answers, not unlike me. Ed finishes his breakfast, sips coffee, and watches a few other bigfoot investigators walk in the cabin. He gets up to mingle with a few of them, exchanging stories from last night before heading back to his RV.

Harold and a few others watch Ed depart. I sit down across the small table from them. "Ed just told me that bigfoot and deer are friends," I say. "He said one night he saw a bigfoot with its arm draped over a deer as if it were his pet."

Harold finishes chewing. "The first time I saw Ed," he says, "Matt was talking about that story." Matt Moneymaker is the founder and president of the Bigfoot Field Researchers Organization, which organized this expedition. "Matt said, 'Bigfoot's just carrying his lunch with him.'"

Moneymaker is fairly well known today thanks to his role as host for Animal Planet's *Finding Bigfoot*, which, in its sixth season, has not conclusively found anything yet. Moneymaker created the BFRO in 1995, launching the website and popular database the following year. The BFRO's main goal is to find conclusive evidence, which is categorized as Class A (firsthand contact, like eyewitness accounts) and Class B (secondary proof, like footprints or collected hair samples.) "Experienced" members investigate these sightings, which does not always mean much. Some veteran members have experience in ballistics, anatomy, and chemistry.

Sometimes, though, experience just means going on a few expeditions. Few have scientific experience in related fields. On the other hand, how can one actually study sasquatches except by going out in the woods?

Within the bigfoot community, Moneymaker has many detractors who scoff at his methods for collecting evidence. A few competitors claim Matt is really just collecting money from members. On an online forum for bigfoot enthusiasts, one angry researcher said, "He's really a money maker." Those participating in expeditions like this one in Oklahoma could pay a one-time fee of $300, which secured a lifetime BFRO membership. Members could then sign up for as many expeditions as they liked after paying this initial fee. (A year after the Oklahoma expedition the BFRO changed its policy, requiring everybody except its top researchers to pay an additional $100 per trip.) Patty Lee, an expedition leader, says this fee helps defray some costs. More importantly, she says, this fee limits the number of crazy thrill-seekers. The BFRO organizers say they prefer people who seriously want to search for the big guys. (But they really want people who seriously want to pony up some dough.) I'm not sure I would have been willing to pay had I not decided to write a book on this topic, although I was excited to head out and meet people. I'm just not sure I was $300 excited. Searching for bigfoot is not a cheap endeavor. Thermal binoculars cost about $9,000. Infrared cameras cost thousands of dollars. Digital recorders are at least fifty bucks a pop. Plus, add the cost for rental cars, plane tickets, and meals. We had about twenty-five people here in Oklahoma, which could mean as much as $7,500 had everybody been a new member—but that is not the case here. Matt is rumored to rely on Wally Hersom, a silent benefactor who purchased more than $100,000 of equipment. "There's a lot easier ways to make money than this, I'll tell you," Matt tells me.

That somebody is attacking Moneymaker, though, should not

be a surprise, because conflict rules in a bigfoot community in which many are looking for fame and fortune. Ironically, that does not appear to be the case with the people who sign up for the BFRO expeditions, who are more interested in the adventure. I'm excited to go out later tonight for the same reason, even though I do not really expect to catch a bigfoot. But there could be a chance, I convince myself. Even a minuscule chance can keep us reading and watching mysteries.

Harold, though, is a believer. In his late fifties, he carries more weight than he should on a frame that goes about five feet nine. But he gets around well most of the time — although he would have struggles later that night when I would be forced to lay him by the side of the road before racing down a trail toward a terrified fellow bigfoot hunter. With thinning hair and wire-rimmed glasses, he looks like a professor. He also has the credentials, having earned a master's degree in zoology from Eastern Illinois University before working as a chemist. After being laid off, Harold taught science in high school for several years. Right now, he's struggling to make ends meet, working part-time jobs at a local factory and a photo business where he cleans up old pictures in Photoshop. He suspects he'll have to take additional shifts when he returns home to central Illinois.

Harold says his father, also a scientist, fostered his passion for science and mysteries. He would talk about stories he had heard or about the space race that pitted the United States against the Soviet Union, each one hoping to send the first satellite into space. When the Soviet Union launched Sputnik, ten-year-old Harold sat with his father in the backyard and watched it slide across the horizon at night. "Did you ever see the movie *October Sky*?" he says. "They showed where they were watching that thing. It was not as clear but just like that. You'd see it go across the sky and see the light reflect off it. It was really neat. This is kind of like that kind of thing."

His father also introduced Harold to American Indian legends and news reports that were starting to emerge from all over the country. They read the first reports of the Fouke Monster, a creature in Arkansas that eats pigs and dogs and chases humans. This creature's mythical reputation was cemented in the 1970s when Charles B. Pierce produced a documentary called *Legend of Boggy Creek* that chronicled an attack on a family near Jonesville, Arkansas. In the summer of 1955, eight-year-old Harold probably discussed some of the reports regarding little gray men walking around a ranch in Edison, Georgia, or stories about the man in southern Georgia who fought off a bigfoot with a scythe. Later that summer, Mrs. Darwin Johnson said a creature with a furry palm grabbed her left leg as she swam across the Ohio River. (Remarkably, she did not die of a heart attack right there.) By the following year, the reports started to mount. An Alaskan fisheries boat claimed to have seen a bigfoot at a beach, while nearly a dozen hikers near Georgia reported seeing a seven-foot-tall creature along some roads. I'm not sure what happened to the two people in northern Michigan who claimed a sasquatch carried them off, but that certainly would have led to spirited discussions at dinner for Harold and his father. The next year, as the Russians were preparing to launch Sputnik, two hunters said a bigfoot stood near their hammocks, watching them with glowing eyes for what must have been the longest two minutes in their lives before it walked back into the Everglades at Big Cypress Swamp. And a few months later, in October 1957, when Harold and the world pulled out their telescopes to watch Sputnik glide across the sky, a hunter north of San Antonio, Texas, instead watched through his gun's telescope as an eight- to nine-foot creature moved tree limbs near a lake. Science grabbed the headlines despite the mythic reports across the country. Harold and his father debated both sets of stories.

"In 1957, we didn't have information like this—all you had was Indian legends and old books and stories about a creature here and there," Harold says. "It was about '58 or so when it all started happening. And my dad would run across something and bring it home. I don't even know where it all came from. My dad was a real smart guy and he had an open mind about everything. He believed that such an animal could be there. And why not? Some people don't know the kind of countryside you have all over the country. Patches of wild areas that are scary, like down here [in Oklahoma]—especially at night. He'd believe in the possibility. And I guess he raised me that way. He had a scientific orientation. He worked as a chemist, which I did for several years, too. He read constantly—anything he could pick up, even a label on a soup can to see what was in it. Some people are raised not to believe in anything, and I was raised just the opposite: to take a good look at it all."

In late 1958 bigfoot burst on the national scene thanks to a newspaper report in a California paper. A road crew, bulldozing a new road through the mountainous dense backwoods near Willows Creek, said a large creature continually walked through their camp at night. The crew's chief, Jerry Crew, originally believed pranksters made the footprints through camp, until he traced them to a steep, seventy-five-degree incline where the stride, remarkably, did not change. So he bought some materials and made plaster of Paris casts of the prints to prove what they all saw. A reporter in Eureka (who probably yelled "Eureka!" when he saw he had a front-page story) jumped on these reports, running them in the *Humboldt Times* a few days later. The story (and a picture of Jerry Crew holding the casts) ran in newspapers across the country, prompting people like Harold and his father to discuss the existence of an American Abominable Snowman. Some pondered: is this the missing link?

Meanwhile, people all over the country got caught up in the frenzy. Two boys claimed they shot at a creature near Roseburg, Oregon; two hunters insisted they ran from a creature watching them in British Columbia; two men fired on what they said was a bigfoot that came up to their house near Knoxville, Tennessee; and a police officer in Carroll County, Maryland, reported shooting at a bigfoot that walked toward him. Sheriff's deputies in Washington, game guides in Montana, and Native Americans in Kansas also reported seeing similar creatures. Bigfoot ran beside cars in Oregon, banged on houses in Pennsylvania, and peered at a crowd in West Virginia with eyes like big balls of fire. And an eleven-foot, one-thousand-pound creature called Orange Eyes stalked teenagers in central Ohio. How could young Harold not be intrigued?

An article in *True* magazine also stoked interest in bigfoot. The magazine, which catered to men interested in adventure and the outdoors, featured high-drama stories like one about men working deep undersea, offered advice on ways to start a hunting lodge, and told readers where to find the perfect beer. (Is there an imperfect beer?) *True*, which had the largest circulation of these so-called men's magazines, also did not mind investigating more bizarre topics, like whether aliens were flying saucers across the skies — or whether the creature purportedly lurking around construction equipment in the northern California woods was real. Thousands of young (and older) men were captivated when a respected naturalist, Ivan Sanderson, wrote in *True's* 1959 issue, "Somewhere in the wilds of California there is a gigantic creature which walks on its hind legs, leaves huge tracks, and is scaring hell out of everybody. What is it? Nobody knows — yet." (More than fifty years later, this is still the case, much to the chagrin of researchers and to weekend investigators like Harold.)

Sanderson believed a humanoid creature existed, which is not a surprise considering his other investigations of giant penguins, sea serpents, and modern dinosaurs in Africa. Sanderson also coined the term "cryptozoology," which, translated from Greek, means the study of hidden animals — or animals not currently cataloged by science. Still, the fact that a respected, well-known zoologist believed in bigfoot shocked people across the country. This popular magazine probably helped jumpstart the modern fascination with bigfoot.

Clearly that fascination is evident here this weekend in southeastern Oklahoma, where at least twenty others are eating breakfast in a run-down cabin, sleeping in tents, and living on caffeine after walking through the woods most of the night. But what do they expect to find? And how do they propose to find it without specialized training?

Harold, who has more training than most, earned his master's degree by studying cytology (cellular biology), histology (microscopic anatomy), and histochemistry, which is a hybrid branch of science that focuses on the chemical composition of the cells and tissues in the body. Compared to Harold, I felt poorly equipped for the weekend—although my friend Brian, a nonbeliever, put this expedition in perspective one afternoon. "What training do you need to hunt down a mythical creature?" Brian said. "You know what would be funny? As you guys are walking through the woods, you should point and say, 'Hey, there's a leprechaun!'"

Unlike Harold, most of us do not have any scientific training. Instead, most are like me, people who love an adventure but who are clueless when it comes to tracking down a creature that has eluded people for thousands of years. The group includes a restaurant owner from Memphis, a sixty-five-year-old outdoorsman, a retired data processor, a bar manager, a musician, a pharmacist, and a chief operating officer for a financial services company. Tom Ruh, a retired university physiology professor, is one of the few trackers who have relevant scientific experience. He says he has always been interested in bigfoot. "This all started in 1960 when a sasquatch tried to intimidate me in the coastal mountains of Oregon," Ruh says. "Not knowing what it was, I came close to throwing a rock at it." (Which, if he had done so, might have prevented us from hearing this anecdote.)

Troy Hudson, a man in his early thirties who grew up near Honobia, organized the current expedition. He's now a ballistics expert in Dallas, where he says he works with the FBI and U.S. Navy. Troy, like the others, defers to Matt Moneymaker. Harold respects Matt, as do most of the people who take part in investigations that detractors call setups, unscientific, and fakes. Part of the attraction can be the opportunity to spend time with others who share the same values. Part can be that the presumptive leader takes the time to speak with those still learning, acting like a teacher. A few kind words here and there, and a student will give even a poor teacher a great evaluation. Harold shoves aside his plate. "Matt's a real good guy," he says. "I've come across others in these searches along the way. The other day I told him, 'You're a class act.' As a matter of fact, on the first trip I was ever on they all wanted to stay another day. He asked me to stay another night and I thought about it. I told him, 'I could but I'm dead tired and I have a thirteen-hour trip.' He talked with me for half an hour before I left. He spent that time with me. That was pretty good, I thought."

Matt Moneymaker had come to my rescue along a narrow, deserted two-lane road the previous night. After carefully following the directions into the Kiamichi Mountains, I was unmistakably lost and two hours late after driving for twelve hours. It was already eight o'clock and too dark to read any signs. Few people drive in these hills at night, so every road felt like it was either abandoned or going in the wrong direction.

My eleven-year-old daughter, Sarah, called: "Are you scared?" She thought her papa was crazy for heading *toward* monsters that live in the woods. She offered to let me have her baby, a tattered, pink, cloth doll that she clutches when she's upset. Before I could answer, I lost my cell phone signal. And I continued to lose my way, driving up and down the two-lane road. Being a man, I did not ask anybody for directions, not that I had much choice. Few homes sat along the road leading up the mountain. The road was unlit and the woods were dark and silent, except for a few people sitting on a porch at a cabin home. Not sure where to go, I pulled into their driveway.

"Just go back up to the dirt road and head back toward the lodge," a young man said. "That's where you'll probably find your friends." A teenage girl giggled.

That road, though, was barely discernible in the pitch darkness. Tree branches scraped against the side of my Mazda Tribute, large rocks smacked against my tires, and potholes induced my axle to slam down hard. Did I mention it was eerily silent and blindingly dark? So I put the car in park, turned off the lights, and rolled down a window, hoping to hear the other investigators happily bantering around a fire — maybe even singing campfire standards like "Oh! Susanna" or "On Top of Old Smokey." Within seconds, though, I felt uncomfortable. I could not turn the car around, could not see more than a few feet in front of me, and did not know why in the hell I had turned off the lights. I did not hear a thing, which made me worry all the more that something might be in the woods. I could imagine a beast suddenly leaping out, fierce orange eyes.

Really, though, I was worried about a far more dangerous creature. Why had the folks at the cabin sent me down this narrow road, knowing I could not turn my car around until after it was too late? Why had the girl laughed and looked at her friends? At the moment, I thought of the movie *Deliverance* — "He's got a real pretty mouth on him, don't he?" — which was enough to prompt me to keep driving over the rocky road. Lights on, I found a spot to maneuver through some trees and turn back toward the blacktop road. At the top of the mountain, I turned on my Midland two-way radio to channel 3, as directed earlier that night. Every once in a while, I heard a muffled or staticky voice. I called out, "Is anybody out there from the BFRO group?" Then I hit the call button that sent beeping sounds across the airwaves. Certainly that would grab someone's attention. Ten minutes later, Matt called back, telling me to sit by the road until he reached me. Only later did I learn that my beeping had become an irritant to those already out in the woods.

Matt arrived in a midsized rental car a few minutes later, asking me to follow him to the cabins where he had asked the group to meet him. Matt told me that bigfoot did not like bright lights, so we'd have to drive through the hills without lights. "I'll keep my lights on dim. Just stay close to my bumper." Thus began the scariest drive of my life, one made all the more frightful the next morning when I saw where we had driven. We drove up, down, around, and through washed-out dirt roads, where large rocks smacked against my axle, scraped across my bumpers, and punched deep into my tires. I drove along the edges of precipices where the car would have smashed hard ten to thirty feet below. At the time, I could barely see, relying on Matt for direction. But I could hear the scrapes and thuds against the Tribute. After about ten minutes, we reached a flatter area near a ridge. The car nearly bottomed out in a pothole before we parked.

"That was pretty good driving," Matt said. "We need to sit here for a while and see what happens." Other investigators were already in place. Over the walkie-talkies, Matt asked someone to create some wood knocks, emulating what some researchers believe is a communication method used by these creatures. Apparently, they knock on trees to indicate locations. The knock sounded a lot like a bat smacking a ball, a sound that, at first, was comforting in the middle of the woods. But the sound also sounded eerily reminiscent of the sounds I'd hear while hiking through the Ocala National Forest and Hontoon Island State Park, something my wife (who is a biologist) would dismiss as woodpeckers even though the knocks reverberated—and were deeper and more resonant than a bird's bill could produce. Matt handed me thermal-vision binoculars, which can detect heat radiated from animals.

Trees emanate heat at night to a lesser degree after days when the sun has beat down. Matt leaned against his rental car, lit up a cigarette, and listened to the night. "Let me know if you see anything move," he said. Imagination is a delightful, but vexing, element. As soon as you imagine something, your brain tries to make it so. So when someone points to a cloud shaped like a dragon, you can see it clearly. A friend tells you John Mayer sounds like Bob Dylan—heck, you hear that as well. And if someone hands you some thermal-vision goggles in the middle of the woods and tells you to look for bigfoot—damn it—you see one of those, too. And he was looking straight at me.

My hands shook. As a journalist, I did not want to jump to conclusions and admit I saw something—especially during my first minute with the binoculars. I did not want to sound like some crazed person who claims to have seen something he had not. Yet there it was—a cone-shaped creature kneeling on one leg, left arm resting against a tree, staring right back at me, as if to say, "Yeah, I see you as well." The creature did not move, satisfied to keep a watch on me. Matt also seemed comfortable, leaning back, exhaling smoke, and watching the bright stars overhead. I turned to Matt, unable to hold back my curiosity. I tried to soften my tone, not allowing him to see the rank amateur that stood before him. My voice cracked: "So what does a bigfoot look like?"

Matt straightened up and tossed the cigarette aside. Clearly, I needed to work on my acting ability. "What did you see?" he asked. "Did it move? Did it look bright? What was it doing?"

"I'm not sure. I thought I saw something by the trees over there."

Matt took the thermals. "In what direction? Move the binoculars in that direction." Nothing appeared.

He offered the thermals back. "See if you can see anything." I tried in vain to see what I believed was a bigfoot—or even any evidence of a tree bent over and twisted that might look like a kneeling creature. Either I could not find the location or my imagination allowed it to dissipate like a fleeting cloud. Or else—gulp!—it had quickly dropped to the ground to hide. A woman at the cabin would tell me the next night, "You know, bigfoot is sneaky. They can crawl on their belly really well and get really close to you without a sound." I scanned a wider area but saw nothing. "I guess my imagination got the best of me. I should have known better than to think I would see something the first time."

"That's not impossible," Matt said. "Let's go walk down the road and see what we can find."

The dogs appeared to come out of nowhere—barking and snarling and whelping and nearly circling us. In the dark, we could not determine how many dogs there were at first, but we suspected it was a good-sized pack. How I did not run, I don't know. My instincts told me to sprint back to the car and leave Matt to his fate. My athletic training would come in handy this night. Sadly, this would be a painful lesson that Matt should stop smoking if he wanted to live out here in the wild.

"Don't run," Matt said. "These are not wild dogs. Most of them probably live with the Indians in the area. They don't believe in leashes or fences so the dogs wander around at night. Just walk back slowly."

The Choctaws settled this area in the mid-1800s after being removed from Tennessee. Like the Muscogees, Seminoles, and Cherokees, the Choctaws settled into reservations in eastern Oklahoma after completing the murderous Trail of Tears. Many Native Americans lived outside the reservations, moving to rural communities like Honobia.

Matt and I walked backward for about thirty or forty yards,

facing the dogs, before they eventually lost interest and departed, looking for something far more interesting than two guys who could use a shower.

Matt recommended we take our cars down the road with us, parking them a little closer to the woods. Matt then directed several groups to work together, orchestrating two groups to time wood knocks and another individual to release a deep-throated (and hair-raising) howl. After a while, Matt ducked into his car and rolled down his windows.

"Stay out there and let me know if you hear anything."

In Oklahoma, a mid-October night can get chilly, so I zipped up my jacket and leaned against my car. Almost immediately, Matt started to snore. Oh, how I hoped that sound would not attract anything. Without the thermals, I could not detect a creature peering at me nor see a bigfoot crawling on the ground in the weeds just ahead. No, the only thing I could detect was a shivering torso and a shaky hand. I moved away from the car, worried that something would reach out and grab my feet—yet that moved me closer to the tall grass and the tree line. Holy crap. I had lost all ability to think rationally. I was no longer a skeptical journalist. Instead, I was scared, a believer in creatures that lurked through the night. I squinted until my head hurt, swiveled my head to see behind me, picked my feet up high enough to avoid outstretched hands, and generally acted like a stupid, scared kid. I decided I could act just as scientifically inside my car—although I did close the door gently, not wanting Matt to know he had invited a wimp out to this expedition. I rolled down the window and listened.

Someone's Midland beeped. "Did anybody hear that?" a voice crackled over the radio. "Thought I heard a wood knock." Nobody heard anything. Matt sat up. "Okay, let's head back to the cabins for the night." I had not distinguished myself this night. I felt more than a little sheepish but was still excited to head deeper into the woods the next night, when I would act in a far braver manner, racing back to help a fellow investigator facing the scariest night of her life.

Troy walks into Clancy's restaurant just as I finish talking with Ed. "Has anybody seen Pam?" Troy is worried that one of the crew has not responded since last night.

"Did anybody see her after we got back last night?" I ask.

"She was out with us until after one," says Troy, the leader for this expedition. Troy grew up in this area. He knows the mind-set of the people, the challenges of the terrain. He also loves researching. At five foot nine, he is probably only about 160 pounds. But he is formidable in the woods where he grew up, ambling over rocks, reading maps, and able to discern sounds in the woods. He still spends considerable time searching for bigfoot in northern Texas—more than 1,250 hours by his count. ("I'm lucky to have a location within forty-five minutes of my home," he says.) Troy readjusts his cap that reads IJAWA and sips on a large coffee. "Last time we talked she was on her way out. I had just asked her if she had heard a hoot."

"Maybe her radio is not working, or she went to get gas," Harold says.

Pam Porter, a thirty-five-year-old financial officer, likes to camp away from the bigger group. Instead of bivouacking next to the cabins, she had set up camp in woods a few miles away. Normally, someone going off alone is not a concern, but this area is known for its bigfoot festival—something that attracts youth who like to pester groups like ours. The festival had ended the week before. The area also holds much wildlife, which is not surprising since we are along the edge of the Ouachita National Forest, a 1.8-million-acre tract that rolls across Arkansas and Oklahoma. The Kiamichis, a subrange of the Ouachita Mountains, extend west.

Troy starts reading aloud, citing animals that live in the

area—panthers, rattlesnakes, coral snakes, skinks, alligators, bears, panthers. "Oh, yeah, and water moccasins," he adds.

Like Indiana Jones, I hate snakes of all kinds—even after hiking through trails and swamps in Florida for twenty years. I'm hesitant to touch the rubbery skin of small boas held by guides at places like Busch Gardens or the St. Louis Zoo. I don't even like fake plastic snakes. There's nothing I hate more than snakes (well, except spiders—especially the big, hairy ones, not that I love the long-limbed banana spiders that weave webs across walking paths in woods or the jumpy wolf spiders that leap on you—or bite and leave welts—as you sleep). Even my wife, who once saved a rattlesnake from a construction site by emptying luggage so she could place the six-footer inside and drive it nearly two hours north from Apopka to Gainesville, Florida—and all the while *not* checking her rearview mirror in case it escaped)—hates water moccasins, easily the most aggressive snake around, one that will chase you through the woods and into your boat. As a state biologist, Betsy and her colleagues had little regard for the thousands of alligators they moved among while collecting water samples and replanting tall grasses in central Florida's lakes and rivers. But these biologists did avoid walking through canals that might house an underwater nest of moccasins—which are highly venomous—dreading a deep drop-off where a dozen or so young *Ancistrodon piscivorus* might be nestled together.

My wife and I have been fortunate in our encounters with mocs. Freezing temperatures saved me the time I carelessly walked through DeLeon Springs State Park, never a smart idea in any wooded Florida area. Snakes are usually not aggressive unless you step right on them. That's what I nearly did that morning on the trail where a fat, angry water moccasin had coiled, its cottony white mouth open and hoping for brief contact with a warm body so it could get enough energy to bite into me. Fortunately, these cold-blooded creatures cannot move when the temperature plummets to near freezing, as it had that late morning in central Florida.

What saved my wife from severe swelling, decaying skin, and infection caused from a moc's bite one afternoon in Lake Apopka? Perhaps pure luck guarded her from the debilitating effect of necrotizing fasciitis, which literally means "flesh-eating bacteria." (Did I mention that cottonmouths latch on after biting, injecting more venom as you struggle?) Chest-deep in water, Betsy walked through tall grass and cattails with a colleague in a restored marsh area, slugging through the mud in waders to check whether plants had taken root in a previously dead lake. As she pushed aside some cattails, she saw it—or rather, it saw her—lounging on an otherwise lovely floating hyacinth whose broad, glossy leaves coiled onto themselves to form a floating bed. Biologists hate that these invasive plants impede water flow and block sunlight to native plants. Mocs love that they offer a place to rest and gather energy in the sun, usually coiling themselves around a single stalk of lavender and pinkish flowers that are otherwise pretty. Betsy, who has faced sixteen-foot gators in central Florida lakes before, stopped immediately, appreciating the far more dangerous creature now six feet away. For some reason, the snake uncoiled, slid to another hyacinth, and allowed Betsy to turn and depart. "Maybe it had just eaten," Betsy said later. "Maybe it was lazing in the sun. Thank God, either way."

Troy says he read about an eight-foot gator found in a river not far from our camp, something that does not worry me. Gators are plodders, unable to move to their left (a lot like me on the basketball court) or to run for more than about twenty yards at a time. They can be relatively easily avoided, unlike spiders that slip into homes like ninjas and snakes that languidly hang out everywhere else. To put it simply: do not go swimming in any lake or river in the Sunshine State. Instead, go swim at the beach, where there are only sharks, jellyfish, and stingrays.

The woman who runs the restaurant brings out eggs and sausage for a few late-rising campers. "You know," she says, "bears often steal food from the trash bins out back. Who knows what else is getting in there." She hints that something else might be reaching into the bins at night. "You ought to put some cameras out by the garbage. That area keeps getting messed up. I don't think coyotes can reach in there."

"You don't think so, huh?" Troy offers a wry smile. "A few days ago, we did some calls back there. Something was already near the garbage cans. We heard 'thunk-thunk,' as if someone fell in and out of the bin. It could've been a bear. It could've been a hobo who is living under a bridge."

Matt decides to go check on Pam.

"Maybe she went a wrong way or got a flat tire or something," Matt says. "Who knows? Maybe she got super freezing last night and tried to find a hotel. You know what happens with tires here: they go flat." (Amazingly, I had not popped a tire the night before while following Matt on that drive reminiscent of Mr. Toad's Wild Ride.) Matt knows Pam is not one to panic or to get lost. In fact, she has become one of Matt's favorites, a woman who has proven herself in the face of several exciting encounters, including one where bigfoot allegedly harassed her in northern Michigan. Matt clearly admires Pam, later telling me about her personal adventures in southwestern Ohio, where she regularly heads out to secluded areas cited in BFRO reports, something employees at her financial institution might be shocked to hear. Nothing, though, would ultimately be as jolting as her experiences tonight in southeastern Oklahoma, which would force her to visit doctors.

In Honobia, bigfoot investigators are as common as deer and hardwoods, drawn by regular reports from the people who live in this remote and sparsely populated town that sits in the midst of 130,000 acres of commercial timberland. They are also drawn to

Honobia thanks to savvy marketers who created a bigfoot festival. The third annual event concluded the week before we arrived, which meant locals still had sasquatch on the brain—and many of them have stories to tell, some more plausible than others. News of any investigator is sure to attract attention even in this sleepy, backwoods area. That's why BFRO members were told to keep the location quiet and why reservations were not made under the organization's name. But, Honobia being a small town (about thirteen hundred people), everybody knew we were there.

Residents are forced to drive more than an hour to the nearest grocery store, which makes Clancy's Cabins a popular spot. Inside, residents can purchase essentials like milk, bread, and butter as well as weekend essentials like beer, chips, and soda. A fair number of people drive down U.S. Highway 144, part of the last unpaved highway in Oklahoma. A car rolls by every few minutes. Residents must be vigilant when driving, though, because the nearest gas station is at least twenty-five minutes away, something I found out nearly too late one afternoon.

Several BFRO investigators are enjoying some down time on the porch, a rustic enclosure that includes chairs, worn tables, and a barrel. It's a beautiful day: temperatures hover in the low sixties, the sky is clear, the sun is shining.

Randy Scott is settled into a chair across from me. He is quiet, hesitant to speak. Randy looks like a mountain man. At about six feet one, he is slightly taller than me, but he's burlier, with larger arms and broad shoulders. I bet Randy could handle himself in a bar fight. His thick, gray beard adds to this romantic appearance. But Randy also seems to know how to handle himself intellectually, something I notice by the questions he asks others and by the way he reacts to stories in the cabin.

Pam, who had driven into town for something to eat, is curled up in a chair next to Randy, legs folded under her. She does not understand the concerns for her safety. "I'm not used to checking in with anybody. Even my family doesn't worry unless they haven't heard from me for at least two days." Pam seems eager to talk about her experiences. She smiles frequently, speaks softly, and loves to laugh when others tell jokes — even bad ones. Not the type of attitude one would expect from a chief operating officer for a stuffy financial services company that tracks electronic checks online.

Eventually, a few others come out to the porch. Greta, who is part Cherokee, lights up yet another cigarette, letting it dangle in her right hand. Kenny, the cabins' cook, stands against a rail, puffing from a Winston between sips of coffee. In between, he talks incessantly, glad for companionship after being stuck alone in the kitchen. "Heard that story about water moccasins," he tells me. "Maybe they just want to be left alone, perhaps like bigfoot."

Pam appreciates water moccasins and gators, having grown up northeast of Naples, Florida, when that area was filled more with reptiles and wild boars than condos and shopping malls. "I learned how to outrun an alligator before I learned to cross the road," she says.

Greta says gators and snakes don't bother her. "I have never been afraid of the woods and of things I can't see, like ghosts and bigfoot, but I am afraid of bears and cougars and wild boar. Wild boar *are* in this area. And they're mean. They'll attack and attack and attack. When I go in the woods, that's what I'm scared of. If I'm watching for something, I'm watching for something we already know about. Spiders get to me, though. Last winter, I rented room number five since it had a little kitchen. The gal I brought with me, Shelly, pulled her blankets back and screamed. She found a big old black tarantula under the sheets. We slept on the couches that night, which were leather. The owner said tarantulas are not venomous and wouldn't get us sick, but the fangs may hurt. Anyway, the owner killed it and put it in a baggie. She then went inch by inch, cleaning the whole place." Greta lights up a second cigarette. "But I will never stay in number five again," she says, laughing. "I guess that's the moral of the story."

The conversation eventually turns to bigfoot. A few years earlier, Greta's thirteen-year-old nephew (a boy who, Greta says, is "not afraid of the devil himself") saw a creature in central Oklahoma while he was riding his motorcycle. "It's a full moon, he has no shirt on, and he's driving a motorcycle through the trails at midnight. 'Just messing around,' he told us. And then this bigfoot steps right in front of him—walks right over the bike, plants his feet, and turns to look down at him. Matthew said its eyes were like glowing red lights. And then it turned back, stepped over a tall fence, and took off. Matthew said, 'Aunt Eta, my heart was in my throat.'" (At age forty-four, I wonder if my own heart would even be beating.) Greta shakes her head and lights another cigarette. "Yet that kid still rides the woods on that motorcycle at night."

Pam recounts a trip to Michigan's Upper Peninsula a few months earlier that included several alleged encounters. Pam believes a bigfoot ran past her. On the trip, Randy says, another bigfoot zapped him, sending electromagnetic impulses that buckled his knees. At first blush, this all seems crazy. But numerous animals use both infrasound and ultrasound. Infrasound involves low-frequency waves, between three and twenty hertz, that human ears cannot detect. But we can feel them, the way the bass from a Tone Loc or Sir Mix-A-Lot song sucker punches us from a car stereo. Ultrasound involves sound waves significantly higher than twenty megahertz. Dolphins use ultrasonic vibrations to navigate and to stun prey. Humpback whales use it to drive herring to the surface, where the small fish can be scooped up and eaten much more easily. African elephants use ultrasound to communicate over ranges of up to ten kilometers. Giraffes, rhinos, and bats also use ultrasound to varying degrees. The U.S. military has even developed infrasonic and ultrasonic weapons—canons, grenades, mines—to incapacitate or injure enemies. In rare instances, they can kill. Infrasound can cause disorientation, increased blood flow, nausea, drowsiness, and even respiratory problems. Many bigfoot researchers now believe bigfoot use infrasound in much the same way. The thinking: causing harm like this enables bigfoot to scare off intruders in a safer manner. This leads to an equally controversial belief: That bigfoot are also imbued with great intelligence. Therefore, bigfoot know that killing humans would draw more people to their territories. Cliff Barackman, best known for his work on Animal Planet's TV show *Finding Bigfoot*, believes infrasound blasts are used by bigfoot to disorient deer and to repulse humans.

Randy is a quiet, reflective man whose interest in bigfoot was sparked by the film taken by Roger Patterson in 1967. In the film, a large creature walks across an opening, swinging those powerful arms and looking back a few times. Like Randy, I watched that footage as a kid, hiding my eleven-year-old face when the creature looked back at Patterson, whose spooked horse reared and caused the camera to move about at first—something that made this whole film all the more realistic and scary. The directors of *The Blair Witch Project* used this technique to create an equally scary story years later. But, Randy says, then life happened. He joined the U.S. Army when he turned eighteen, married, and started a family, claiming he never gave bigfoot a second thought. But that was not true. Bigfoot was always in the back of his mind.

"I would tell my kids, 'One of these days, when my ship comes in, we're going to go and look for bigfoot,'" Randy says. "At which point I would get a polite, 'Yeah, sure, Dad. One of these days we'll have to do that.' Usually I would just get the eye roll."

A year earlier, Randy had stumbled upon a television show about bigfoot while flipping channels in a hotel. "What did I see but a show about looking for bigfoot in Texas," he says. "If that don't beat all. Prior to this, I thought bigfoot was only in the northwest part of the country. I didn't know he was all over the place, but then again, I suppose when you think about it, *big*foot and Texas do go together. Anyhow, it sure was exciting to see other people doing what I always wanted to do ever since I was a kid."

A few months later, Randy headed to a Barnes & Noble to look for books on sasquatches. He checked throughout the store but found nothing in sections featuring hiking, camping, and mountains. "I can't find anything on the big guy, so off to the information desk I go. 'Excuse me, where do I find books on sasquatch?'"

A puzzled clerk replied, "Let's look on the computer. How do you spell it?"

"I don't know," Randy said.

The girl's associates shrugged, indicating they did not know either.

Undaunted, Randy said, the girl tried several spellings, to no avail. A few customers suggested alternative spellings before another clerk walked up with a book, *Sasquatch: Legend Meets Science.*

"Thanks. Where did you find it?" Randy asked.

"In the paranormal-occult section," she said matter-of-factly.

"'Oh, great,' I think to myself. I'm forty-six years old, lurking around the paranormal-occult section of a bookstore, looking for information on a cryptid animal-monster thing." A little later, Randy tracked down the Bigfoot Field Research Organization site, talked with founder Matt Moneymaker, and booked a trip to Michigan's Upper Peninsula, where he joined others in a similar quest—perhaps to find a monster, perhaps to solve a mystery, perhaps to feel like a kid on an adventure. In Upper Michigan, Randy got hooked. "This is so exciting," Randy says. "I feel like a kid who gets to go to Disneyland."

Still, Randy does seem wary around me, the self-professed writer on safari with these big-game hunters. I suspect he does not want to be painted as a fool, satirized as a crazy monster hunter. He has not been impolite, but he has not said much, content to sit back and evaluate me as I speak with others throughout the morning.

Pam, on the other hand, appears more extroverted. She is composed, tranquil even — a condition that is as foreign to me as rooting for the Boston Red Sox. Unlike Pam and Randy, I have rarely felt at ease or content. I've spent most of my life looking for this feeling, pushing myself to find it through accomplishments, relationships, and travels — and all the ironic while, I've started to believe, pushing myself away from any chance of serenity. This quest, I'm hoping, will help show me the way to the ultimate serenity — spiritual faith, something I've struggled with my entire life.

As a kid, I scoffed at the notion that an omniscient being had created the heavens and the earth, that a single being watched over us. Even more so, I rejected organized religion as a method of control for those in power. Why would God care if someone attended church, tithed, or attended Sunday school? This was all crazy talk. As an adult, several events have forced me to reconsider my earlier views — recovery from a physical condition I had thought would kill me, the birth of two beautiful daughters, and marriage to a lovely wife who has endured my restlessness.

A year before this trip, my father sent me the strongest sign that life existed after death — or so I thought and so I want to believe — the day after he passed away. Exhausted and feeling guilty for not having been there by his side when he died, I sat in a car watching my daughters play soccer. At first I wondered if I were imagining the vision, like when you see halos around lights after a day spent swimming in chlorinated water. I looked up again. Two rainbows bent over the horizon, both as richly hued as any I had ever seen before. They arched lower and wider than usual, prompting more than a few people to stop, point, and stare. I pulled off the side of the road to take it all in. I have always teetered between faith and skepticism, something my father clearly would have known. A single rainbow is a coincidence.

Two vibrant rainbows arching overhead, side by side, is a clear sign. But that feeling, unfortunately, dissipated with the rainbow.

Greta, who says she saw a bigfoot as a kid, struggles in much the same manner. "It's in my head and I know that it happened, but I still think, well . . . maybe not."

"But you know it was," interjects her sister.

"If an alleged myth like bigfoot can exist," Greta continues, "so can most anything."

That Michigan's Upper Peninsula would have some bigfoot activity is no surprise, especially if you believe bigfoot exist. Like the area around Honobia, the landscape there is remote, a place where both trees and deer are abundant. The U.P. houses only about 3 percent of Michigan's total population, even though the land area makes up nearly a third of the state. The peninsula, which juts out east from Wisconsin, is surrounded by Lake Superior, the St. Mary's River, Lake Michigan, and Lake Huron. Too far north and too rocky for agriculture, the area relies more on logging but has a history of mining thanks to abundant copper, nickel, iron, and silver deposits. Winds blow cold and sharp through the long winter, bringing at least twenty feet of sometimes blinding snow during long, cold periods when daylight may last but eight hours. Not surprisingly, the peninsula houses five state prisons. Where else would you send hardened criminals than to a remote, unforgiving region? In winter more than a few people must feel imprisoned themselves. Still, more than three hundred thousand people live on the peninsula, which is a little larger than Maryland; many, no doubt, are loners attracted by this remoteness — as well as the chance to play in an area that has considerable charm in the summer.

Researchers like Matt Moneymaker also believe the area has attracted a large bigfoot population. Matt interviewed several residents near Marquette before scheduling an expedition that attracted more than fifty people. "I'm not a believer," Matt told the *Detroit News.* "I'm a knower. You'd have to be in total denial to think none exist." Not everybody in the U.P. agreed, with some calling the expedition a farce while a few others tried to consider the possibility that the creatures exist near their towns.

That was Randy's first trip, Pam's fourth. Pam says she tracked a group of bigfoot while walking with the expedition's main guide, the outdoorsman Don Young. "Don just happened to turn around and look behind us. He said, 'I see two floating basketballs.' I said, 'What? What are you talking about?' So I looked through my thermals. They must have been coming up a hill because he just saw their heads. I thought they were people. They were just walking. You could see their arms, you could see their legs. They looked like people walking in the road. We watched them for a while. Don said, 'They're not people. They're too big.'"

Randy cuts in: "With thermals, you're all kind of blind. You're all screwed from the lighting so you cannot always see well when you put them down."

"The group then split in two," Pam continues. "Sometimes they would walk just on one side of the road, then they would cross over or go off into the woods. And they'd come out in different places. We couldn't tell if it was the same two or if there were different people (and I was really thinking they were people at this point). They were going back and forth until they looked at us and went right into the woods. So we decided to walk down to where they were. When we got down there, all hell broke loose. Branches snapped, trees shook. We were both huddled in the middle of the road looking out our thermals. We did not have anything thrown at us, but they were all around us."

"The shakes," Randy says.

"Yeah, shakes," Pam says. "It was all of a sudden. We felt surrounded. And we were both faced in the same direction when something passed behind us—probably within five feet. Whatever it was, it was big. If I ran across gravel, you would hear my boots. It felt like a rush of wind as it went by. We both turned at the same time and said, 'What the hell was that?' We were blinded by the thermals and could not see anything. At that point we stood back-to-back. We were really scared.

"That wind scared me the most. It was close enough that we could both feel it and hear it, yet it was quiet. We knew something passed even if it didn't make a lot of noise. So we stayed there for a while and it got quiet. Then we saw two more coming off the road from another direction. These two showed the same type of behavior, snapping branches and shaking trees before they went into the woods. Then we'd see heads peak out and go back—on both sides of the road.

"Eventually Matt and another investigator [Jim] came out and went down to the place where we last saw them go into the woods—and Matt looked like a stick figure compared to those things. Matt thought we saw deer. Matt asks me, 'Are you sure you did not see the sides of deer?' But when Jim turned to walk, you couldn't see the definition in his legs. The legs were probably twice as wide as Jim's, and he was about six feet and athletic. These things were also about a foot taller. Don said, 'I told you. I told you.' Don was hilarious. All he kept saying was, 'There's a goddamned village out there.' We must have seen four to six of them out there. We lost count as they kept coming and going into the woods. It was pretty amazing, pretty interesting, pretty intense."

Pam says she felt strangely excited and exhilarated in Upper Michigan, far differently than she would feel tonight when she would suffer both mentally and physically. "I was really scared when something passed between us [she and Don]. That was the scary part, the part where we felt totally, absolutely surrounded. You know, I believed Don that what we were seeing weren't people but, at the same time, the reality of it did not seem right. Until I saw Jim down there, I was convinced we had made a mistake and there were actually people in the road. But when I saw Jim down there, I knew."

"There were more than one," Randy says, "because they were whistling to one another."

When Don had heard the whistling sounds, he had beelined it out of the woods and toward the road with Pam.

Pam says, "The whistling had a different range."

"It comes from deeper in the throat," Randy says.

"Not like it comes out of your mouth," Pam says.

"It's much deeper," Randy says.

"It sounds like a bird but you know it's not quite that," Greta says.

"I could squeal through my vocal chords to make this sound," Harold says.

"He [Don] came out to the road and a few minutes later we pulled up," Randy says. "He was all shaken."

"When I met Don almost exactly a year before that in Wisconsin," Pam says, "he would not go out in to the woods by himself. He had already had five encounters."

Randy shakes his head. "They were eating his cats."

"He grew up living in those woods," Pam says. "He was a hunting guide for his profession. But his last sighting scared him so much that he got a job at a factory. He did not go out in the woods for a long time. When it got dark that night in Michigan, he had his night-vision goggles on and they did not leave his face. He was a totally different person when I met him in Michigan. He was not afraid to go out in the woods. I think he's learned so much more about them. They'll display aggressive behavior but they're not gonna hurt you." (Or so I hoped and prayed.)

I mention the story told by Teddy Roosevelt in *The Wilderness Hunter* of two fur trappers that supposedly took place in mid-1800s somewhere in the Bitterroot Mountains between Montana and Idaho. Bauman, a grizzled woodsman, returned to camp one night to find his partner sprawled on the ground with his neck bitten in half. Alone in the middle of the Rockies, the trapper decided to skedaddle out of there, leaving everything behind. "I think of the Teddy Roosevelt story, too," Randy says. The story always gives me chills.

Harold isn't helping to calm my nerves at the moment. "Bigfoot have been shot at around here, so the attitude might be a little different."

Greta dangles a cigarette over her knee. "From what I've learned, if you get aggressive, they will do the same."

"If you are going to kill one out in the woods," Harold says, "you'd better have a lot of bullets."

"With all the rocks that they've thrown that we've heard through BFRO," Pam says, "they surely could hit someone if they wanted to."

"There was that gal in Michigan," Randy says. "When she was little, her friend was hit in the head with a rock. That's the only one I heard of."

"I was hit once, with a little pebble," Pam says. "So if they're going to hit you, they'll use a smaller one." She laughs.

A week earlier, Patty Lee, an East Coast investigator, had told me that bigfoot threw rocks at their group during an expedition in West Virginia the previous year, and one even appeared to charge them. I share this story with the group.

"I have not had a bluff charge through the woods," Pam says. "But they will charge at you like a bear."

"Like a silverback," Randy says, "rushing, crashing."

Says Pam, "I would like to experience that."

"I can't imagine how shaky my body would be," I say. Or how loose my sphincter would get.

"I always keep a hatchet in the tent," Randy says. "That way you feel safe in your tent." Only a Paul Bunyan–sized hatchet would help, though, if creatures exist that are as strong and large as those in the reports.

Greta says she would stay up as late as necessary to disprove her own doubts. "I was eight, nine years old the last time I had an encounter. I want a fresher point of view."

Doubt is tough to dismiss, even among those who want to believe. There's more doubt than belief among these seekers. They want clearly substantiated proof more than anyone. "Afterward, you think, 'maybe it was a bear,'" Greta says. "Afterward, you rationalize and go, 'Oh, Greta.' So I want to see it one more time or hear it one more time before I die and know I wasn't crazy."

Randy and I stand in the parking lot, waiting to drive and scout a location we would investigate later that night. It's late afternoon. "I was intrigued by your comments about bigfoot and faith," he says.

"Hope you didn't mind that I've been asking so many questions," I tell him.

"I look at asking questions in the old way—that's how you learn and get wisdom." A man who loves the Socratic method is always a friend to me. "I've never been one to worry about what or how other people think. I can't wrap my mind around the fact some people do."

He does not really have a good reason why he's seeking bigfoot right now, he says. Besides intellectual curiosity, that is. "What's your reason for being here?"

"I want to believe in God and Jesus and an afterlife—and not believe this is all there is." Not that I have many complaints in the here and now. "So I want to believe bigfoot exist, too. That may help me believe these other potential 'myths' are true as well."

"That's a funny reason," he says. It does sound odd, but it's the truth.

"I've been struggling with faith issues even more since my father died a few years back."

Randy nods. I get the sense that Randy is not one to judge others too harshly.

A little later, Randy helps a severely overweight woman get

off a medical van and into a wheelchair, showing her the same compassion one would show one's mom. We are drawn to a house across the street by a woman screaming hysterically about her weight and her pain from recent surgery: "Just let me be. I'll never get into that house. I can't do it." Within minutes, Randy calms her. "It's okay, Patricia, we're going to get you into the house," he says. "It's okay. You'll be fine." And he lifts her into the wheelchair, wheels her into the house, and gives her a hug.

I can see why people sign up for these expeditions. My adrenaline pumped as I plowed my Mazda Tribute through more deep holes, scraping the axle over rocks and generally trying to keep up with a caravan rolling over washed-out logging roads. Matt was in the lead, smashing his rental car into areas where I'd be afraid to drive a Humvee. Yet, we were all driving just as recklessly through narrow roads miles and miles from the nearest auto garage. I couldn't recall the last time I'd had such an adrenaline rush. This drive started to feel like several moments rolled into one—the game-winning hit that clinched a league title, hiking along the Appalachian Trail, the first time I read Ernest Hemingway, and the fumbling first sexual encounter with my wife. My hands tingled, my eyes widened, and my imagination went wild with possibility. Hell, this will be the night we were going to catch a damned sasquatch. Slam. (Who needs an axle?) I'd bull-rush one myself if needed, running into the woods to tackle anything stupid enough to get that close. Scrape. (It's only paint.) We'd trick those elusive bastards. We had the thermals, we were learning the terrain, and we had the desire. Pop. (Now, that didn't sound good.) I could tell this was going to be the beginning of a wonderful relationship. Me and the rest of the bigfoot crew, we live for adventure. Bring it on.

The trails were much darker at nine o'clock. The moon was new, which really meant it was hidden, so I could barely see my hands, much less Troy in the middle of the forest. The night was eerily silent save a few hoots from an owl. Troy said it sounded more like mimicked calls from a bigfoot. He told us to space ourselves twenty to third yards apart as we hiked deeper into the Ouachitas—far enough apart that we were nearly invisible to one another without night vision. I imagined several bigfoot crawling in the underbrush, quiet as ninjas, ready to snag my foot and drag me into the woods before anyone else noticed. ("Hey, where's Joe? Wasn't he up ahead? I guess he got excited and ran off into the woods after a squatch.") I asked Randy if I could walk near him for a while. "That's fine," he said. "We can share the thermal." Clearly my adrenaline had worn off.

We walked like this for about forty-five minutes before reaching a bridge over a small stream. We all assembled around Matt's car and heard the plan. He and Troy said they heard bigfoot calls and saw bigfoot images in thermal imagers that revealed we were being followed on both sides of the road, something called "paralleling." Bigfoot were following us on hidden paths about fifty to one hundred feet off in the deeper brush. To lure them in, he decided Pam would set up a tent about fifty yards past the bridge, which, he hoped, would antagonize any bigfoot in the area—sort of like pulling off the interstate and popping up a tent on some stranger's property. Somebody, either the cops or the owner, would be out there talking with those crazy sons of bitches at some point, and hopefully without a loaded gun. Matt says bigfoot are much more likely to respond to a person alone in the woods than a group, even more so if that person happens to be female.

"It's a cat-and-mouse game," Randy said, wary of the whole adventure. "But a cat doesn't just play with a mouse."

After Pam set up her tent, we would trick the local bigfoot by walking back along the path as if returning to our vehicles. In reality, though, some of us would sneak off the path, where we'd listen to Pam's comments over the walkie-talkies. Troy settled in about twenty yards away. Harold, who watched the woods through a thermal, walked back across the bridge by himself. Randy and I ditched into the woods about two hundred yards away. The others retreated to the vehicles.

Within minutes, Pam said she heard rustling in the woods. Branches snapped. Then she heard growling. "I'm having trouble breathing," we heard her say over the walkie talkies.

At that, we all took off running toward her. Randy and I sprinted down the dirt road, somehow dodging large rocks and ruts in the road. We nearly knocked over Harold, whose vision was blurry from looking into a thermal imager for an extended period. We quickly helped him sit down in some brush before racing on. Pam sounded scared, her voice far from the one that had told me calmly about squatching in Ohio. Within twenty seconds, Troy reached her. Within two minutes, Randy and I arrived.

Pam's body shook, her pulse raced. Someone said she had been zapped. Pam could not stand on her own so she settled into a car's passenger seat. As we huddled around her, Troy returned to the site, which was about twenty-five yards away, to poke around. That's when he saw the two large red eyes, while taking a leak near a gulley.

He leaped back and called to us, but we did not see anything. He later estimated the eyes to be at a level of about eight to nine feet above the ground, based on measurements at the site the next afternoon.

As we waited for Pam's pulse to slow, Randy walked to stand beside a tree near the stream. That's where I found him about five minutes later. "I've been hit by a few pebbles," he said quietly, pointing to a bend in the stream. "I think they're coming from that direction."

Nothing hit him while I stood there. So we stood and looked out over the scene: the stream slowly rolling past us, Matt and others huddled around Pam, and stars shining brightly amid a clear sky. It was all so peaceful, yet rushed, so realistic, yet sci-fi. Surreal sounds so haughty or artsy. But that's how it all felt.

Several hours later I fell asleep in a dingy cabin room, trying to make sense of the night's event. Had this all really happened? Had the journalist been hoaxed in a carefully orchestrated scenario? Had Pam really been zapped? By 3:00 a.m., I was too exhausted to care.

A soft breeze flows across the covered porch at Clancy's General Store. At 10:00 a.m., most of us are either eating breakfast inside or smoking and drinking coffee outside. Wary of eating the greasy fare, I snack on a nutrition bar and cranberry juice outside while relaxed in a wooden rocking chair. Matt Moneymaker sits next to me.

"So I heard you talked with Tom Biscardi," he says. "What was that like?"

Matt hates Biscardi. I know he wants me to trash the guy. As a reporter, I've learned to be circumspect, revealing only general ideas and offering positive responses about others. Rumors spread quickly. A reporter's reputation can be destroyed by one inappropriate comment. So I tell Matt that we had a nice conversation, that Tom offered to let me travel to a location next spring, and that Biscardi seemed like a nice guy. You never when you're being tested. If I spoke harshly about Tom and revealed insider info, who knows if Matt could trust me with anything he said. Like Biscardi, Matt is constantly attacked. On websites and forums, Matt is called vindictive, cowardly, malicious, arrogant, and a fraud — and those are just the more respectable descriptors. The BFRO has been tagged BS-RO. And Matt's last name gets considerable play among those who believe Matt's interest is financial, not scientific. Ironically, Moneymaker is not Matt's given last name. One longtime researcher who knew Matt before he started the BFRO believes Matt selected his new name in order to flaunt his success.

Journalists also ridicule Moneymaker. Six months earlier on Fox News, for example, a TV reporter had laughed and smirked while interviewing Matt, acting more like David Letterman than Dan Rather. At one point, the Fox producers displayed a photo on-air of a man standing beside the statue of a giant monster, one that looked a lot like bigfoot. It looked silly. It was an attempt to make Matt look ridiculous. It was a chance for the TV hosts to share a laugh with viewers. The replica did look as though it had been created for a sci-fi Hollywood movie. In reality, the photo reveals a reconstruction of *Gigantopithecus blacki*, an extinct genus of ape that existed until about one hundred thousand years ago, created by special effects guru Bill Munns, the man standing beside it. Munns designed the makeup and effects for movies such as *Swamp Thing, Beastmaster,* and *Return of the Living Dead*. He also constructs replicas of living primates and sculptures of human ancestors based upon actual skulls. The replica shown on the air had been featured at a conference for the Association of Physical Anthropologists. But that did not matter to the impudent Fox News folks, who laughed and chuckled and smirked. That's Matt's view of journalists—flip people asking impertinent questions and writing audacious, smart-alecky stories.

So I shut up, listen, and observe. Matt unleashes on Biscardi, calling him a "bullshit artist" and a "sham." "He takes advantage of people," Matt says, a cigarette in his right hand. "He's just using people to promote himself." Inside the BFRO, Matt is idolized. Outside of the BFRO, this is also how Matt is viewed—as a self-promoting, arrogant asshole.

Finding dirt on Matt or Biscardi or any bigfoot hunter is relatively easy, especially on forums dedicated to the paranormal. There's far more mud-slinging in bigfoot research than in politics.

Jealousy plays a part in these personal attacks. Unlike other bigfoot research organizations, the BFRO is funded by a wealthy philanthropist named Wally Hersom. Unlike other researchers,

Matt does not have to work another job full-time. He allegedly receives a salary to run the BFRO, reportedly around $100,000. Nobody knows for certain, but that doesn't squelch the rumors. Unlike other field investigators, Matt does not have to scrimp to purchase high-tech equipment. The BFRO has more than a dozen thermals that cost about $10,000 apiece. Hersom made his fortune developing technology for cell phones, way before anybody thought it necessary. In 2000 he sold his company for a reported $100 million. Now Wally devotes his time to finding bigfoot with Matt.

Biscardi can't match the BFRO's resources either.

Still, Matt appears a bit envious that Biscardi recently won an award for his latest movie, *Bigfoot Lives*. No doubt, he says, Biscardi manipulated the people who run the Poconos Mountains Film Festival into giving him the award for best documentary. "He *must* have paid someone for that award," Matt says.

That seems plausible given Biscardi's history. Biscardi promotes fuzzy photos and murky videos as real evidence that bigfoot exists, on radio shows like *Coast to Coast AM*, a late-night program that focuses on topics likely to include paranormal phenomena, conspiracies, and alien abductions. Biscardi frequently charges viewers for checking out these pictures. In a few years, Biscardi would help promote a hoax that received national attention after he claimed to have verified a bigfoot carcass found by two Georgia men. Says Matt, "He's disingenuous and doesn't have much class or tact."

Matt pauses, wanting to let me know about a TV show he's developing with National Geographic, where he'll bring a crew out on several expeditions like this—only he'll limit these expeditions to investigators he likes best. This was right before *Monster Quest* and *Ghost Hunter* hit it big on the History and SyFy networks. This idea eventually led to the creation of *Finding Bigfoot* on Animal Planet. Matt clearly likes the attention he receives from running the Bigfoot Field Researchers Organization. But Matt also clearly believes that the woods hold many secrets. He talks about will-o'-the-wisps, eerie lights allegedly seen near bogs, marshes, and swamps. Will-o'-the-wisps are cited in folklore across Europe, South America, Asia, and the eastern United States. In British folklore the lights are malicious, luring travelers from paths into the middle of marshes at night before extinguishing. In Irish culture people can follow these lights to treasures. In parts of England the will-o'-the-wisps steal children, while some tales say they can guide a traveler if the spirits are treated nicely. In Brazil, the wisp is called Boi-tata, a native Indian term for "fiery serpent." This serpent moves at night, thanks to glowing eyes that can see through the darkness (but not during daylight). Matt says the wisps have frequently been spotted during bigfoot sightings, leading him to speculate whether there's a connection. Perhaps these wisps serve as sentinels, protecting bigfoot, he says. Or maybe bigfoot transforms into a wisp, allowing it to travel so quickly and to evade trackers. Of course, he cautions, this is only a wild theory. Yet he does consider it. "When you talk about the paranormal, people think you're not a legitimate organization," he says. "But if you talk about something that exists in ten languages, whether it's this or ghosts or UFOs or bigfoot, you have to at least pause and think about it."

As always, I straddle the world of what could be and what is. At times I want to bust out laughing when I hear people talk about the paranormal. (Spirits floating through the woods? What next—characters from Middle Earth, hobbits and elves?) At other times I feel sad and uncomfortable as people confess their beliefs and sightings. Ultimately they all want to believe in something. Like me. Who knows what the world holds? Species are discovered every year. In the past several years, scientists have uncovered tiny lichen clinging to Yosemite's granite face and have chanced upon a new breed of red foxes in California's Sacramento Valley.

It would be easy for me to dismiss Matt's comments as zany, wild, and dumb. On the other hand, it's just as easy to embrace Matt's ideas, telling others that I am truly open-minded. Either way, I could win with readers who can laugh along. But I could also lose for helping to erode these people's dignity. I know the world loves a decisive person, regardless of the outcome, but I prefer to investigate first. While these folks are searching for bigfoot, I'm hunting for stories. I want to know why these people are doing what they do. What drives them? How can a former law student like Matt toss aside a legal career to search for bigfoot? How can a person who studied law, who relied on facts and evidence, devolve to suppositions and theories? *Black's Law Dictionary* sure doesn't supply many explanations, devoting just a few lines to the idea of truth, whatever the hell that really might be: "1. A fully accurate account of events, factuality. 2. Defamation. An affirmative defense by which the defendant asserts that the alleged defamatory statement is substantially accurate." In bigfootery, the truth is frequently blurred, often elusive, and rarely simple. The more I hear from people like Matt, Harold, and Pam, the less I know for certain.

Several hours later I was driving on State Road 271 through the Ouachita National Forest, sad that I had to leave. I coach my daughter's travel softball team, which had a game scheduled the next day. In order to stay, I would have had to leave around midnight and drive twelve hours without sleep to make the game in mid-central Illinois.

Later I'd learn that Harold saw, in a thermal imager, what appeared to be a bigfoot hiding behind some trees, nor far from Pam's encounter the night before. Away from the group, Harold said he saw the creature's head and shoulders rise above some brush and look directly at him from only fifty feet away. Harold froze and peered into the viewfinder, trying to believe what stood before him. A broad-shouldered creature ducked down, then popped up again in a new position before moving back near the original spot, like a boxer bobbing and weaving. Left, right, bob. Left, right, bob. A minute later he radioed Pam and Troy, who were about fifty yards away. In the viewfinder, Pam saw a large animal from the waist up, trying to hide behind a small tree. Matt and Randy arrived several minutes later. By then the creature was no longer visible. But they all could smell a strong, rank odor, a blend of unbathed dog and dead skunk. As they departed just after midnight, Harold said they heard a distinct wood knock. As tired as I would have been, those moments would have probably seemed like a dream to me, one I could more easily discount.

On State Road 271, a sign for the Family Restaurant proclaims, "Home of Big Foot Brew." It's the only building for miles on a ridge that overlooks thousands of acres of pines, mixed oak, and tall grasses packed into rolling peaks and valleys. Out here it makes perfect sense to talk about creatures hiding in areas where few people have walked and to discuss wood knocks, glowing eyes, paralleling, bull rushes — and, hell, even will-o'-the wisps. But few people are going to believe a word I say when I get back to Charleston, where people are more averse to radical ideas — and where the only monsters are the damned Democrats in Washington DC.

2 UWHARRIE MOUNTAINS

NORTH CAROLINA

John Smith noticed something strange as he fished for crappie in a pond not far from his home in a heavily wooded town in central North Carolina near the Uwharrie Mountains. Birds, which usually flew haphazardly while foraging and building nests, no longer scattered through the sky like black glitter. Instead, John observed, they appeared to fly in unison, moving in a single group from one tree to the next, gradually heading farther away from him.

Earlier he had smelled something like the odor of a wet dog emanating from a thicket of cattails. John had thought some hunting dogs must have gone through there the night before looking for deer.

Just beyond the tree line, John heard something walking—probably a deer foraging for food on this spring morning. Still, John felt strange, as though something were watching him. Next, a limb broke, snapping loudly. Out of the corner of his eye, he saw something large move off to his right. Okay, he thought, time to get the hell out of there. So he gathered his tackle box and walked back to his car, certain that something was now watching him. (He was so scared he forgot about the pistol in his pocket.)

When John reached his car several minutes later, he saw it—a large, human-like creature, covered in black hair and bent down on one leg, looking directly at him from about twenty yards away. The creature's large eyes petrified him. This was absolutely not a bear nor a gorilla nor some idiot dressed in an outfit. John knew that instantly. John tossed his fishing gear in the car and drove off quickly, uninterested in learning more for the sake of science—and certain he would not tell anybody about this, knowing they'd laugh pretty hard at this ridiculous tale.

North Carolina has more than fifty reported bigfoot sightings, according to the Bigfoot Field Researchers Organization's national database, a number that would almost double within a period of six years. That makes the Tar Heel State about the twenty-fifth most active state for bigfoot, if one is to believe these stats (or that these creatures exist). North Carolina, which is the twenty-eighth largest state, has far fewer reported sightings than Washington (nearly five hundred), California (four-hundred-plus), and Oregon (two-hundred-plus). But it has far more than Delaware (two), Rhode Island (four), Vermont (six), or Connecticut (eight). Incidentally, Massachusetts, which introduced Americans to witches and goblins several hundred years ago, remarkably had only fourteen reported sightings as of 2009. Perhaps the Northeast has fewer sightings because these areas are more heavily populated and have fewer wooded areas—or because its residents are not as crazy. It all depends on your perspective.

North Carolina has a rich cultural, geographical, and paranormal history, one of many reasons I am traveling to the Uwharrie National Forest, not far from the location where John Smith reported seeing bigfoot nearly twenty years earlier.

The Uwharries boast of being the oldest mountain range in North America, one with peaks that once rivaled Mount Everest as the tallest in the world. Peaks in the Uwharries once rose twenty-thousand-plus feet, growing to twice the size of those in the Rocky Mountains thanks to a chain of volcanoes that were active about five hundred million years ago. Through time, these volcanoes stopped spewing lava, no longer building mountaintops. Instead, wind and rain started eroding these once-majestic peaks, whittling them down to the one-thousand-foot high, undulating hills now visible in central North Carolina. People have thrived in the area for more than ten thousand years thanks to abundant food and building resources. Today the area has a large number of archaeological sites, perhaps more than anywhere in the Southeast, where fellow researchers pan for history.

Still, I was surprised when told we'd be researching this piedmont area, not the Pisgah Mountains about two hours west, a far more rugged place that seemed a significantly better location for finding sasquatch. And a locale where I'd spent considerable time hiking and camping during the previous twelve years. That's where I thought we'd be headed when North Carolina was mentioned as an expedition site. After all, the Pisgah Mountains are much more furrowed and craggy (and dangerous) once one gets beyond the trimmed, flat trails built by park rangers. One could easily get lost or hurt trying to explore away from the trails in this five-hundred-thousand-plus-acre hiking wonderland—especially at night, when bigfoot hunters prefer to lure in these allegedly nocturnal creatures. Did I mention the area has brazen black bears? Over the years, several have entered my camping area during the night.

Plus, Pisgah could be a paradise for bigfoot, holding large stashes of blueberries and blackberries, squirrels, raccoons, rabbits, and all sorts of other edible small animals and plants. Pisgah is expansive and nearly impenetrable in many areas. The mountains slope down into deep, large crevasses before eventually rising up to another peak several miles (or more) away. Steep cliffs abound. I've always imagined how long it must have taken early settlers to cross this area. But I could just as easily have imagined how long it takes modern hikers to trek between areas like Frying

Pan Gap and Black Balsam Knob, areas that have changed little during the past two hundred years. Experienced hikers still move slowly, needing a day or two to reach an area that birds could flit to in about twenty minutes. Trees are densely packed, trails can decline sharply, and rocks can create slippery footfalls.

The Uwharries, on the other hand, are much more accessible, boasting some of the state's most heavily traveled trails and attracting thousands of people to its lakes, hunting grounds, and campgrounds. That's not to say that one can't find remote areas within the relatively small, fifty-thousand-acre Uwharrie National Forest area. City slickers may be overwhelmed by the Uwharries, but the area is generally a walk in the park for more experienced hikers.

The Uwharries have a curious place in American history. A discovery by a twelve-year-old boy started the nation's first gold rush, which sent thousands of people into this otherwise unexplored part of the nation at the turn of the nineteenth century. Once Conrad Reed discovered a seventeen-pound gold rock, the rush was on. Gold's price is volatile, but that huge rock would be worth about $250,000 today. Conrad's discovery changed the face of several states. Thousands of people feverishly descended on central North Carolina and northern Georgia. In 1799 few people lived in the piedmont near the Reed family's farm in Meadow Creek.

John Reed suspected they could find much more gold on his property. The next year he started a small gold-mining operation that soon yielded a twenty-eight pounder. Soon farmers all over Montgomery and Stanly Counties put aside their plows and hunting rifles for picks and pans. The gold rush would really get going two decades later thanks to veins of gold unearthed in northern Georgia. Still, Conrad Reed's discovery was substantial. More than fifty thousand ounces of gold would be mined in Montgomery County, North Carolina, during the next hundred years. That's more than $45 million worth of gold in today's currency. More than thirty mines developed around what is now the Uwharrie National Forest. People descended on the area in much larger numbers, and they panned rivers, dug tunnels, and sent water sluicing down ravines.

Eventually the mines yielded less and less gold—or at least not enough to recoup the cost of recovering it. As a result, most of the mines closed down, people left the area, and buildings were left to rot. The people in the Uwharries once again became fairly isolated. You can still see wooden homes falling and bending into themselves along both dirt and paved roads. Decades of neglect weigh heavy on wooden walls and tall grass drives through warped planks on the floors. These buildings soon prompted ghost tales. With scary buildings, you usually get scary stories. And on the porches of backwoods homes, the locals loved to tell them. Some ghost stories served as a warning to looters—stay away from any gold inadvertently left behind or in the mines. Civil War soldiers still fight battles in the woods, goes one story. In others, a corpse saves a poor peddler from being butchered by a demented farmer, while a corrupt magistrate still gallops along a road every night on a horse as penance. Fred T. Morgan, who was raised in the area, collected enough ghost tales to fill seven books.

As I drive closer to the Uwharries, I realize why the area evokes ghostly tales. Besides being sparsely populated, the place is full of craggy trees reaching out toward roads, creeks, and rivers. Instead of large malls and superstores that serve more than six hundred thousand people, the small towns west of Charlotte offer few shopping opportunities beyond the occasional convenience store or gas station. McDonald's, Taco Bell, and Burger King are strangers to most towns in Stanly and Montgomery Counties. Albemarle, roughly thirty minutes from Uwharrie, is an exception, boasting a modest mall. With a population of fifteen thousand, the town is the region's hub, servicing residents living in tiny towns like Plyler and Millingport, whose populations are not even listed in my Rand McNally road atlas. The county's other towns, such as Porter (30 people) and Red Cross (761) are tiny, just like those across the river in Montgomery County. Uwharrie, Wadesville, and Eldorado each boast 150 residents, while Ophir, which sits a few miles up the mountain from our campsite, has only 30. Troy, with 3,269 residents, is the biggest town in the county. Not even the stately homes along the Pee Dee River that divides the two counties can stave off the feelings of isolation.

Bob Jordan Highway carries me over the river and into the outskirts of the Uwharrie National Forest, a reserve that stretches across three counties. I nearly miss the turn a mile up the road, where I pull up to the convenience store to gas up and to purchase snacks. I also grab two packs of strawberry licorice and that day's edition of the *Montgomery Herald*, in which I learn that storms had just ripped up trees and damaged vehicles.

I then drive a two-lane road toward Uwharrie just a few miles ahead. Lately I've fallen into a really bad habit, one that is both ridiculous and dangerous. As I drive, I scan for bigfoot in the woods instead of looking ahead for cars, deer, and sharp curves in the road. As if it were that simple to glimpse bigfoot bent over a creek, walking among pine trees, or standing in an open meadow. Stupid, I know, but also mesmerizing. So I gaze off to the side of the road instead of at it, even when it curves into S-turns. That's how I notice the area is not as remote as I had first imagined. New residential communities like Carolina Shores and Holiday Shores are rising close to the river. Several white Baptist churches serve these residents. In the woods, I see a few homes through denuded trees. Winter is waning. Spring would take over in a few days.

White flowers burst from dogwoods near one new home, but the trees fall in a straight line, unlike nature intended. Still, they are absolutely gorgeous, so much that I nearly drive off the road, kicking up small rocks and dirt as I regain my proper lane. As always, I don't see the yellow signs that warn of winding roads until it is too late. Dusty Level Road seems appropriately named, though. The windows are dirty enough that my girls could easily draw "Wash Me" on them with their fingers. Off to the east, a weather-beaten home is falling into itself amidst pine and tall grasses after probably decades of neglect. How long does it take for a house to decay and fall into itself? Why doesn't someone just plow the building? Does it have a use? Highway 109 merges with this road at the Uwharrie business intersection that houses a small family-owned convenience store and a fire department. There I head up the mountain road to the campground two miles ahead.

On group expeditions like this, the plan is usually the same. Initially everybody camps together at a staging area—in this case, the West Morris Mountain Campground. Then some people set up camp in more remote areas or head out to primitive sites where bigfoot may feel either less threatened by a lone camper or more upset that someone would remain in their territory overnight. Either way, the organizers try to investigate areas where activity has already been reported. But they also encourage campers to explore new locations. Organization varies depending on who plans, or leads, the expedition. In North Carolina, the trip was casual. Individuals, like myself, investigated areas out of curiosity and not because of some detailed plan. These trips rely more on enthusiasm and camaraderie than science.

On this trip, we were asked to explore four main areas—the campground itself, the Zoar Cemetery, the Yates Place Camp, and Dark Mountain. The Uwharrie Trail goes right past the campground. Bigfoot, we're told, take this trail at night. People frequently feel as though they are being watched from the woods at Zoar, a family cemetery whose inhabitants date back to the mid-1800s. This site yielded a sighting back in January when a researcher saw two human-like creatures illuminated through his thermal scope, following his fellow researchers down the dirt road. The Yates Place, at the base of these hills, has also yielded some activity, I'm told, probably because it is at the bottom of the Uwharrie Trail. Dark Mountain is Tommy Poland's favorite location, mostly because that is where he lost his sasquatch virginity, so to speak. Tommy has been researching for about two years. Last year Tommy heard a very loud wood knock early one morning atop Dark Mountain—proof, he said, that bigfoot exist. Researchers believe bigfoot communicate with one another by hitting trees with either sticks or large rocks, letting one another know where they are. On Dark Mountain Tommy smacked a tree with a baseball bat to mimic the sound. A quarter mile away, Tommy heard a responsive thwack, which was all it took to pop his skepticism. He believed he had made contact with a bigfoot.

The mountain also yielded the area's first cast footprint, something Tommy displayed at his picnic table during the trip. Ghosts apparently haunt Dark Mountain as well, according to local lore. The family that once owned it scares off potential trespassers. People report having rocks, pinecones, and sticks thrown at them. Sometimes a spirit follows hikers through the woods, especially at night. Last summer something (certainly not a weak-wristed ethereal spirit) dragged two large trees across the forest service road leading up to Dark Mountain. That was proof enough for Tommy. "It made a pretty good visual statement," he said. "Bigfoot only past this point."

People who sign up for these expeditions typically roll in at all times of the day and night. There is no rush, nor any deadline. When I arrived at five o'clock Wednesday, five tents had already been set up in the area closest to the Uwharrie trail. This campground is completely surrounded by woods. After setting up my tent across the road, I joined them, ready to learn about that night's planned foray into the woods.

Tommy Poland, a thirty-five-year-old information technology specialist for a Fortune 500 company, walked over to greet me; my small hand felt lost in his. Tommy looks like a young John Candy, the Canadian comedian known for his work on *Second City Television* and for movies like *Uncle Buck*. Like Candy, Tommy is a big man—about six feet five and 325 pounds. That's a bit more than when he patrolled Korea's demilitarized zone. Still, he is pretty nimble for a large man—and also very friendly. Tommy loves to laugh. When he does, Tommy sounds just like Candy, offering a joyous, booming exhalation whenever someone makes a joke, or even a slightly funny comment. Like the lovable Canadian, Tommy enjoys life no matter how infuriating or problematic. And he clearly enjoys his role as a field investigator for the BFRO. He has even taught his four-year-old son, Elijah, to do a sasquatch whoop. Elijah argues with his fellow preschoolers that bigfoot are real—a true apologist for the cause, Tommy says proudly. Tommy also enjoys a good meal, which is clear from his size. In a few minutes, he said, we would head out to the Eldorado Outpost on State Road 109, a place that is part convenience store, part fishing store, and part restaurant.

I suspected the food there would be mediocre at best. But Tommy's enthusiasm was infectious so I agreed to go along. Those deliciously brittle nutrition bars and flatulent, bold and spicy baked beans would have to wait. Tommy seemed eager to please us all as the expedition's host. He patted me on the back, told me to follow him down the highway, and repeated, "This place has the best fried chicken around." You know, I almost believed him.

At the store I met Stan Courtney, whose recordings of bigfoot calls and wildlife sounds are posted on a website that is well known in the bigfoot community. Stan likes to joke, but his humor is much drier, his laugh far more reserved than Tommy's. He's a thin man in his midsixties who had retired a few years earlier from doing X-rays at a hospital in north central Illinois. He wears a baseball cap that covers a bald head. He looks like a professor in his wire-rim glasses. He acts like one as well, keeping his focus when he speaks. Stan will not be diverted from his stories—even when others interject comments or ask him questions. The stories are almost always about bigfoot. That's his life now. He goes into the woods near his home, an area he calls very active, and he goes out with others across the country. This year Stan plans to search for bigfoot in each of the contiguous forty-eight states. North Carolina is state number five.

By the time I reached the table—back behind the camouflage jackets, fishing lures, and beef jerky—to eat with the group, Stan had already launched into a story about his first encounter with Matt Moneymaker, the Bigfoot Field Researchers Organization's founder, in an Oregon swamp. Matt, apparently, had dashed into a swampy area where a bigfoot sighting had been reported. Stan, not nearly as nimble, did not follow. Instead, he walked back to the cars parked along a dirt road. Within an hour, night had descended and Matt had lost his bearings, unsure whether he was headed toward the coast or back to the road. "But he's always in radio contact," Stan said. "At one point Matt said, 'I just heard a tree go over. It's really dark in here. It's really getting dark in here and I'm up to my waist in water.'" Stan and some others honked car horns so Matt could get back. Along the way, though, Matt kept nervously looking around him. "It was very interesting to listen to his voice, to hear the terror in it as he's walking," Stan said.

Some people think Matt creates sounds and stories to encourage more people to join the expeditions. Bigfoot researchers not associated with the BFRO consider him a shyster, an unscrupulous schemer who wants to find ways to make money off the bigfoot frenzy, even if that means fabricating events or hoaxing people on expeditions. At $300 a pop for newcomers, a trip like this could generate about $5,000. But BFRO investigators are very loyal to Matt, glad that someone is directing research efforts. Matt seemed gracious and candid during our talk in Oklahoma several months earlier.

"I think he asks for the fee in order to keep out the crackpots," Tommy said, "or the people not serious about doing some research."

Stan broke back in as if Tommy had never spoken. On his second trip with Matt, Stan said they encountered several angry bigfoot on an Indian reservation in New Mexico. "We had three or four Class A incidents," Stan said. "They [bigfoot] came down and screamed at us. They threw rocks and I got my first footprint after I had been there only thirty minutes. Afterward, all of this is on the net, see, but critics say nobody can have activity like that. So it's jealousy is what it is. People are jealous of Matt."

Class A sightings, as you might recall, are those where someone visibly and unequivocally believes they have seen a bigfoot. Those where people hear wood knocks or see eyes reflecting in the woods are categorized as Class B.

I'm jealous of people like Stan, whose faith is bolstered by firsthand encounters—or by the belief that they have faced a bigfoot. In Oklahoma the previous fall I had wanted to run out into the woods—if only I had not been worried that I would really face something.

Stan met Pam the week after the Oklahoma trip during a private excursion in southwestern Ohio. "She was still talking about it," Stan said. "There's an aspect of this that happens a lot. It happened to the group in New Mexico. A lot of these people say they're being told to stay away and to get out of the woods. They believe bigfoot is sending mental messages. My wife told me, 'You guys are getting too strange.' And I said, 'Honey, some of these people are getting zapped with infrasound and it's scrambling up their brains. They're sincere, but it doesn't mean they really are hearing voices.' But they believe they do."

Tommy said researchers need to sit down and talk with one another to determine who can be trusted, retaining their skepticism. Tommy used his friend Barry, a graphic designer who lived in Virginia, as an example. He was there for the weekend, wolfing down some of the world's best fried chicken right across from me.

"I use Barry as a litmus test," Tommy said. "He is pretty sound. If Barry says he saw something or heard something, Barry saw it. I know how he's going to react."

"You need to be comfortable enough with other researchers that you can say, 'Hey, I've got a real bad feeling. I feel really bad,'" Stan said.

Stan had a bad feeling—in fact, he was terrified—during a trip to western Pennsylvania the previous year. He had brought along his Karelian, a pugnacious dog breed known for chasing bears, and his friend Robert, a large, strong man. But that did not prevent Stan from acting like a scared little child when he walked out into an open, grassy area. "I suddenly felt really scared," Stan said. "I felt as though I wanted Robert to carry me. I felt like I was a little kid—two or three years old." The group laughed. "That's how I felt," Stan continued. "And I'd stop and look around and not see anything anywhere. Once we got across that area, maybe two or three hundred feet, the feeling just dropped off. I didn't think about infrasound or anything, and he [Robert] didn't feel anything. And then about thirty feet from there we heard a huge branch break across the creek from us. We couldn't see anything, but they were really acting up across the creek. That's one of the few times I've heard anything like that. I did feel there was evil out there."

To keep the story going, I asked Stan, "Evil? How so?" What I really wanted to know was, how could an animal be evil? But I was worried about looking too much like a cynic, an outsider. Besides, we all give creatures personality traits. For instance, I despise raccoons, especially after those thieves stole my grilled chicken dinner one night in the Florida Keys, leaving me with an empty bun and a Pop-Tart. Water snakes, meanwhile, are mean-spirited, sometimes changing direction to slither toward a person innocently floating down the French Broad River on a perfectly sunny day and causing this person to nearly flip the boat while standing up and smacking the damn thing. In the real world, animals are just trying to survive, preying on even cuddly creatures. Foxes eat rabbits. Robins eat butterflies. Polar bears eat seals. That's life, even if we don't always like it. Scientists do not see this as cruelty. Instead, they push aside their personal biases and rely on empirical facts. Scientists won't take sides, even if, say, a crab spider kills and eats a cloudless sulphur, no matter how iridescent green the butterfly. After all, the little eight-legged guy has to eat, too. Scientists accept life as it is. But bigfoot hunters approach life as they'd like it to be.

Tommy said he felt the exact same way last spring when he heard a wood knock nearby. "It was that fight-or-flight feeling, but it was more a feeling of excitement, that something was really happening. Like when you go fishing for the first time and you get a fish on the hook. It kind of scares you a little bit, but you're excited. I had that kind of sensation. I was more upset that I could not see anything more, because it was out there."

Barry, though, said he did not feel intimidated when he saw two figures through the thermals at the Zoar Cemetery a few months earlier. Barry always seems calm—perhaps that's the result of fifteen years in the army. This weekend was his fourth bigfoot expedition. Barry is from North Carolina, which is clear when he speaks in a strong twang, words rolling and slurring into one another. His *I*s often sounded more like "ah." He also hit his *R*s hard, avoiding the pattern more common down in South Carolina, where words like "door" are spoken as "doah." Speech pathologists would probably call Barry's dialect South Midland, a pattern common to areas along the Blue Ridge from Virginia to north Georgia. But the South, like other areas, is a wonderful mixture of constant, and ever-changing, speech patterns. Anybody who has lived in the South long enough can discern the differences between people from Mississippi, Tennessee, and North Carolina. Even the central, inland parts of Florida have a clearly distinctive southern dialect that runs counter to the more northern brogues spoken around cities like Fort Lauderdale, Tampa, and Orlando. It is easy to tell who is a Florida cracker and who just moved from Michigan or New York. I wonder if bigfoot speech patterns also vary in different regions of the country.

In thermal imagery, the camera detects radiation in the infrared range of the electromagnetic spectrum. Radiation is emitted based upon temperature, meaning the cameras can discern variations in temperature. A human emits much warmer temperatures than cars, rocks, and trees, as do deer and other mammals. Ideally, researchers want to record a bigfoot walking through some the woods, capturing its movement to analyze later. Several researchers have posted thermal video on YouTube and other websites, but nothing definitive has been proven.

Like many people, I believe only a body, dead or alive, will prove the existence of bigfoot.

In the thermal at the Zoar Cemetery, Barry saw figures that had large black dots for eyes and a mouth. He saw a third figure lying on the ground, crawling close to his fellow researchers along the dirt road.

Tommy broke in, "They also do belly crawls. Or spider crawls."

A shiver shot down my spine. I did not want to imagine a large creature lying by my feet. That scared me more than the thought of one walking behind me, which seemed more natural and less premeditated. Less evil, I guess. "They kind of looked like if you put your hand under your shirt and push it out like this," Barry said. "The third figure didn't look quite right. It didn't move, so I was convinced it was absolutely nothing. Then it started to move."

"They have the uncanny ability to sit like statues for hours," Tommy said. This point is documented in reports by many researchers. Each story like this makes me wonder whether I actually viewed a bigfoot that first night in Oklahoma. The picture of an ape-like creature leaning on one knee, his arm draped over it and looking straight at me, is burned into my memory.

"A friend of mine saw one that was near a tree and slithered away into the grass," Stan said.

"They use their fingertips and crawl," Tommy said. "If you listen to what Jeff Meldrum says with the foot casts, they have a metatarsal break. The physiology of the foot allows the foot to bend easily. The bones are hooked-in weird, so maybe it could tippy-toe. Could also help them grasp a rock and go up a cliff. There are reports of these things climbing up the side of the mountain that would make rock climbers pause. Which explains the physiology of the animal. That's how I look at it."

We finished up our meals and headed back to the campground, where we would soon address some of the biggest questions related to bigfoot, such as why they don't attack.

Tommy piled on several logs, causing the campfire to leap up. Within ten minutes the fire was waist-high. It was that time of the night when campers can relax, let their food settle, and enjoy being outside. I found it was also a good time to ask everybody some questions that had bothered me for years. So, I threw out, how can bigfoot get so large by just eating berries and small animals?

"They eat a lot of things," Stan said. "In the Northwest they talk about them eating elk. They eat deer. That's a lot of lean protein. So they can put on some mass, but at the same time they are leaner in the swamp areas of Louisiana and Florida and east Texas. But if you go up to the Appalachian chain, they look bulkier. They are more massive. The biology of the animal is based upon the terrain as well as the food source. The problem is we never really know what we're looking at, whether we are seeing juveniles most of the time. How many times did we see Daddy instead?"

Okay, but why do you suppose they do not attack? They're clearly much bigger than we are—and much, much stronger. Bears attack when threatened, as do some smaller animals. But we never hear about bigfoot killing anybody. (Of course, we never hear about elves or leprechauns killing anybody either.)

"Matt had a good theory," Tommy said. "Matt's theory is that they don't attack people because they know if something happens, more people will come out. I buy that. That makes sense. If we're out camping and all of a sudden Jeff and Barry are missing and chopped up to pieces, we'll scream, 'Aaaaaahhhhh!' And the police will come out. And somebody may say, 'It looks like some big animal did this. This is terrible. All kinds of families camp out here.' And then they'll come out in force."

Stan cut in: "If they kind of look at us as squatches, they probably don't interact with each other by killing each other. They interact and scare off one another with territorial things. Like with rocks and stick throwing."

"I think violence is a last resort," Tommy said. "From what I understand, and from hearing Matt, they ramp up. They start with intimidation, thrown rocks, shaking trees. And then it goes to the light in the eyes and the zapping. Then, after zapping, may come physical face-to-face confrontation where they come up to you and bull-rush like a gorilla."

Stan said bigfoot avoid violence by using telepathy, essentially by sending strong mental warnings: do not go any farther or head in another direction. He said his friend felt this anxiety while deer hunting one afternoon. The friend told Stan he felt he shouldn't head down a certain path, so he turned around for no logical reason. Stan, though, has never felt warned. He even keeps his home and car windows open at night so he can get more sound recordings. "My wife thought she saw a handprint once," he said. "And we've had the tree twists. I get the wood knocks from my open bedroom window."

Tommy laughed. "You have an open bedroom window? If I heard a scream at night, I would not keep it open. No way."

"Here's what my thing is," Stan said. "I have heard four mountain lions in Illinois in the past three years. My wife saw one. I saw one behind my house. I saw two in the night with night vision and then I saw one at the road before I got here. And the state of Illinois says they do not exist. Now, I've been in that place a hundred and fifty times. I'd never heard a cat there. With the squatches, I hear them all the time, but I never *see* them."

Stan believes bigfoot are drawn to campgrounds like this. "You want my speculation, which is unproven? We're a country that has campground squatches. I think they go through all of these campgrounds. In Illinois we find footprints between campsites. Between the tenting and the camping areas. Here's my opinion: most of our campgrounds have campground squatches and the eastern part of the U.S.—and I can't prove it, nobody can prove it. And I believe every drainage system has a family. The thing is, since I'm in an organization, I get a lot of calls, but people won't fill out the form. They tell you stuff, but they won't report it."

He cited a report on a site in Champaign, Illinois, where some people saw several bigfoot walking near a windmill farm, between two drainage systems. Stan said when he moved to Illinois only fifteen reported cases existed because most had not been investigated. Now Illinois has more reported sightings than Wisconsin, Iowa, Missouri, and Kentucky.

Stan has several other theories. Bigfoot do not need to live in the middle of the woods. Instead, they sleep in pine thickets. They also shepherd deer like we do cattle. But they do not take deer out of their resident group. Bigfoot also love to eat cats, but they avoid dogs. "I had a friend who had some Great Pyrenees that would go in the woods for a few weeks and would stink when they came back," he said. "They would go out and hang around the squatches for a while."

Tommy couldn't believe his ears. "They eat cats?" he said, laughing.

"Oh yeah," Stan said. "That's one of the common things when people think they have them around. They lose their cats. One of the guys in New Mexico has a sighting where it was chasing a cat."

Even though Stan says he has heard bigfoot, he has never seen one. He has heard wood knocks more than thirty times, viewed six footprints, and seen rocks thrown into his camp. Yet he says he's partially skeptical, which was a shock to me. Stan asked if I believe. I told him I am skeptical about most things—religion, politics, and salesmen. I feel the same way about bigfoot. "Until I actually see one, I won't fully believe," I said.

"I think with religion there's a more faith aspect to that, though," Tommy said. "You have to have faith to see God; it's believing without seeing. That's the strength of religion. But with an unknown animal, there's some physical evidence that you can probably go and get. God asked for faith. Bigfoot doesn't. You're probably not going to get that solid miracle either way."

And even if I did see a miracle, I probably would question it, just as I had several times in my life. Like the time I had vertigo so badly for six weeks that I could barely walk, sleep, or work. Convinced I was dying, I prayed to God, telling him I would do anything to be healed and to watch my girls grow up. I promised to act more faithfully and to give up caffeine. (Lest you think this was a small sacrifice, try going cold turkey yourself.) For months I had strong urges to grab a Coke late in the afternoon or to pour some java in the morning. I reached for soda cans that were no longer there, like the man who tries to scratch an arm that has been cut off. That was ten years ago. Several weeks later, the nausea departed as quickly as it had descended. I was healed. I believe that may have been a miracle.

I can't even cite all the times I did not turn at an intersection or, remarkably, stopped for a yellow traffic light only to see a car flying through the red light. Small miracles happen to all of us. But faith frequently wavers.

"What you probably need more than a sighting is a really, really good footprint," Stan said. "You know what's good about a footprint? When I first got involved with this, my wife's family was very nice to me. They laughed, but not very loud. Had a nephew, told him I'd show him a footprint. My nephew said, 'Do you really want me to come see it?' I called him on Super Bowl Sunday and showed it to him. I got members from each side of the family involved. They all came and looked at the footprint. My nephew asked, 'What color is it?' And I said, 'You can't tell from a footprint.' But they believe now. They don't laugh at me anymore."

Tommy said he loves footprints. He can sit there and look at them from several angles. He can get other people involved.

"When I got that first footprint, I had a rough time for a couple of months," Stan said, "because all of a sudden something is real that we've been told is not."

It was nine o'clock. Several more people popped into our camp, glad for the warmth as the temperature dropped to the upper thirties. Chris Peterson, an administrator at a Veterans Administration hospital, offered his theories about sasquatches and waterways. He believes creeks and streams are their true roads. He loves to pull out maps to illustrate his point when someone asks for more details. Chris believes "biggie," his favorite term for the creatures, uses waterways to travel. As eager as he is, Chris is the first to dismiss others' alleged sightings as "bullshit." He'll roll his eyes when someone claims to have seen eyes shining at night. He does not want evidence that cannot be clearly seen—and believed—by others, not just by bigfoot hunters.

Gwen Barr, a paramedic from Virginia, also arrived. This was her first expedition. A sighting in southern Virginia, not far from Washington DC, prompted her to come on this trip. Gwen's husband, an avid hunter, had a more frightening encounter. Hunting in Virginia one night, he heard something unlike a deer or other large animal move around him. Tall grass grew thick and to his waist between the tightly packed spruce pines. The moon was a sliver, and the woods were pitch-black. Visibility: about ten feet. He lowered his shotgun, not wanting to scare off any deer. Then he heard another noise, a heavy footfall moving toward him. He waited for a few minutes before he started smelling something rancid. He said, "Okay. I'm done"

Gwen's husband usually ties a string between trees to find his way back. So he started putting hand over hand along the string. But something started following him. Was it an echo? "No no no no," he thought. "Not at all." He would take a few steps and stop. Then the other animal would take just one. The hair on the back of his neck just stood up. "Fuck the string," he said and ran. A few minutes later he went off course, losing his way but still hearing footfalls. He gained his composure, found the string, and followed it to his truck.

There's always that pause when you try to unlock the car in every horror flick.

"Yeah," said Tommy. "You get the arm on the shoulder and hear, 'aaaaaahhhh!'"

But Gwen's husband, fortunately, kept the truck unlocked. So he leaped in, turned on the truck, and screeched off, not wanting to look behind him, not wanting to see a face peering at him.

"I knew there was something wrong when he got home," Gwen said. "I asked, 'What happened?' He said, 'I don't want to talk about it right now. Ask me tomorrow.' The next day he said, 'I've been hunting my whole life and never have I got the heebie-jeebies like that.' We went over what it could be. He said, 'Honey, there is no way in the world that a bear could have been doing that. The brush is so thick that it had to be on all fours, and this thing was not on all fours.' 'Could it have been someone screwing with you?' I asked. He said, 'Nobody knows that I hunt back there.'"

As I mentioned, I was never a big fan of hanging out in grave-yards—especially in abandoned ones late at night in the middle of the woods, far from anyone who can hear you scream when the undead grab your ankles, wrestle you to the ground, and drag you into their graves. Not like I wouldn't have it coming. Even as a kid, I knew the ramifications of hanging out with the undead, ghosts, goblins, and all other sorts of monsters. Bother them and you would die a horrifying death. I hated driving past graveyards for other reasons as well. They reminded me of my own mortality. Even as a child, I lamented death. I cried in Mrs. Antwine's first-grade class, not because she yelled at me for talking during reading group but because I felt my life as I knew it was over. No more playing in the woods all morn-ing. No more being a free spirit. I was getting old. Soon life would pass me by as well. At age six, I lamented the end of my days. But graveyards also affected me viscerally. Walking near one gave me the heebie-jeebies, sent shivers down my spine, and raised the hairs on my scrawny (but scrumptious to the undead) arms. I knew bad things happen in a graveyard. After all, I had watched *Creature Feature, Night of the Living Dead*, and countless movies featuring Dracula, Frankenstein, and the Wolfman. As a kid, I knew the bounds of reason—where smart started and stupid began, at least when it came to taunt-ing the undead.

Yet that's where we went that first night, six of us walking across the street to Zoar Cemetery, an area walled off by a strand of trees on all sides, the north side leading back into deeper woods. Inside the woods, the tombstones are placed in eleven rows along a slightly declining hill. Nobody's been buried there for some time. In some respects, the cemetery has died. Most of the bones entombed below us belonged to people who lived during the 1800s, as early as Jesse Millinix in 1808. Many people died during the 1880s and early 1900s, including months-old infants, small children, and child-bearing women. They were all buried below our feet. In the later 1800s Uwharrie was far from medical care that was decent even by contemporary standards. Today we rush our kids to the emergency room when they have a slight fever and physicians deliver babies in tech-driven hospital rooms. When all you have is cod-liver oil and some worn blankets, luck and hardy genes play a larger role in survival.

Some names are worn off the headstones. Some older headstones are unmarked, perhaps because families could not pay an engraver. Now these loved ones linger only in memories of a grandson or a great-niece. At one time this cemetery was relevant, giving comfort to those who returned to talk with sons and mothers and uncles and cousins. But nobody has been buried there since 1951. These people are mostly forgotten except by those who come on dares—or by those who seek bigfoot.

So why were we sitting in the middle of an abandoned grave-yard at 10:00 p.m. on a moonless night? And why had Tommy, Barry, and Jeff been walking around a graveyard several months earlier? Because some researchers believe there's a connection between bigfoot and cemeteries. Few places offer a more protected setting at night, notwithstanding the occasional vandal. Those wails and screams in many ghost stories may actually be sounds from a squatch. I have heard varying reasons for this—among them that bigfoot know people fear walking through abandoned graveyards, especially at night.

Some Native American legends claim bigfoot are guardians of the dead, sort of skinwalkers that can shift shapes into any living creature. You can also find many reports on databases like the BFRO's. In one Pennsylvania cemetery, a bigfoot-like creature called the woollyburger mutilates nighttime visitors. Near Fort Chiswell, Virginia, a "hell hound" allegedly prowls a graveyard near a church.

Tommy is drawn to this location. He absolutely believes they saw bigfoot during two previous trips here. A few months earlier, he is certain, he saw bigfoot walking down the path we just took.

"Your guess is as good as mine as to why they hang out at cemeteries," Tommy said. "Maybe they like to freak people out!"

Unfortunately, we did not hear, smell, or see anything. At first I sat alone in an old open-air tabernacle, where outside funeral services were held fifty-plus years earlier. As Tommy made some knocks and offered a few whooping calls, my eyes adjusted and I realized the tree line was only about twenty yards away, close enough for something to quickly yank me into the woods before the others noticed.

So I walked back out to the hill, where Barry peered through some night vision and Jeff listened to a parabolic microphone. Tommy, who had just unleashed a low, rumbling howl, was in good spirits despite being unable to lure in anything.

"That's okay," he told me. "Tomorrow we can head out to Dark Mountain. That's where I heard my first wood knock, less than forty yards away." That sounded exciting, but I still did not fully understand, the same way it was when my friends talked about sexual encounters during high school. When they offered the titillating details, all I could do was smile and imagine. Perhaps tomorrow will be the big day when I finally break my bigfoot cherry.

Early the next morning, Mark Lange wanders into my tent site, set in a stand of tall pines. At 8:00 a.m., people are stirring in the campground, clanging pots, closing car doors, and walking to the outhouse. About twenty yards away, Tommy cooks bacon—and lots of it. That's something I'd already learned—bigfoot researchers like to eat large, filling their bellies with bacon and eggs and burgers and fried chicken and all kinds of greasy, fattening fare. Like searching for a large hairy creature, eating is an adventure. I'm sitting in my chair, writing notes from the night before and eating a bowl of Honey Cheerios and drinking some orange juice.

Mark has just arrived from Winston-Salem, about an hour north, where he works for a pharmaceutical company. He has a doctorate in analytical chemistry, has studied biology, knows how to collect and preserve evidence, and has backpacked across Colorado, Utah, and North Carolina. A green military hat covers close-cropped black hair. He is slightly built and a few inches shorter than I am, at five feet ten. Mark wears green army pants and a rucksack. He is a good conversationalist but talks in a reserved manner. At age forty-eight, he wants to know if a creature like bigfoot exists, because, frankly, he has never seen one. Like me, he is intrigued by the notion. As a scientist, he requires empirical data.

As fellow skeptics, we decide to head off on our own. Michael Greene and a few others are headed to a slaughterhouse, hoping to bring back buckets of blood and cutoff animal body parts to scatter in the nearby woods. I hope that does not lure the police out this way.

Mark and I drive to a more remote wooded area about twenty minutes away. To get there, we have to drive about five miles down a dirt path that is rarely used except by loggers or the handful of local residents. Along the way we see large sections that have been clear-cut, leaving wide, open areas filled with stumps and brush. The place looks ravaged, like the Rohan countryside in *Lord of the Rings*. No ents live here, for sure. Nor will any mature tree for at least a few decades.

A few houses dot the side of the road. Many are run-down, including one ramshackle white home that looked like those in slasher movies. Closed curtains? Axe leaning against cords of wood? "No Trespassing sign" posted on front lawn? Basement windows painted black? Beat-up car on blocks near the shed? Check, check, and check. Psycho killer peering through the curtains at us? Not checking.

The victims in slasher movies tend to be young, attractive, and flirtatious, so I should be safe. Still, if my car breaks down today,

I will take my chances with bigfoot and walk through the woods alone instead of knocking on that door.

A few more miles down the road, we drive into a dirt parking lot and head down a path, not sure where it leads and uncertain what we'll find. Mark is highly skeptical. "I'm not sure of some of the people back at the camp," he says. "They believe everything is evidence."

A mile down the path, Mark and I find an area where trees have been twisted and bent in all kinds of directions. Ordinarily, I would not think much about this. But we both know that researchers believe bigfoot build stick structures to either hide or to mark their territory. Some of these trees fell into one another, probably from strong winds several years earlier. Through time, other trees grew through and around them, creating the appearance that someone twisted them together. In other spots, several trees and branches fell into one another to create a canopy. Mark walks around these trees, eyeballing possible angles and measuring whether the heavier branches could have fallen into their locations on their own. It is odd to see so many possible stick structures in one spot, but, we know, it's possible.

Even Mark can't explain two very healthy trees that had been broken in half. Usually strong winds will snap older, dying trees. But these two trees appear healthy. The wood and pith are still elastic, not dark and brittle. Nature can do some extraordinary things. Tornadic winds can embed wood splinters into bricks and strip road pavement. And tornadoes can even bounce, leaving a home unscathed on its destructive path. But I'm not sure how nature could cause a tree to twist and bend like this.

An hour later, deeper in the woods, Mark and I find another stick structure that is even more intriguing. Several branches extend about forty feet up against a pine that is significantly taller than that, creating a sort of teepee or lean-to. Not sure why anybody would stack tree limbs against a tree, especially out here in the middle of nowhere. On the other hand, I cannot imagine why a bigfoot would do this either. (A Vietnam vet later shared that Viet Cong soldiers hid easily behind structures like this. It does not take much for someone to blend in to the background.)

After about two and a half hours, Mark and I return to the parking lot. We would share what we found but downplay it as much as possible.

Back at camp, we mention the stick structures to a group who had returned from another location a little earlier, prompting a series of questions. Were the tree ends bent? Were the branches tucked between trees? Was any bark peeled off the trees? After fielding these queries, Mark and I agree to guide a group back out in the late afternoon, forcing us to go on another four-mile hike.

Two miles into another hike, we reach the end of the path where the woods thicken, obscuring sunlight, and the silence is eerier. After walking six miles, my body is tired—but my mind is racing. Adrenaline flows. There are few things I like more than a walk in the woods, except for being part of a team in action. I can see why others are attracted to these group expeditions. It is a chance to catch up with old friends, make new ones—and bond like there's no tomorrow deep in the woods.

John Hines is more fascinated than scared. A thirty-four-year-old environmental scientist from urban Chicago, John restores wetlands for a small company. He got hooked after reading an article on bigfoot several years earlier, eventually reading a few books and watching some documentaries—not that he'll tell his coworkers. His scientific colleagues think it's odd that he would discount overwhelming empirical evidence and head out to search for a nonexistent creature. "But I don't come out here as a scientist," he says. "I come out because I'm curious."

A year earlier he went on his first BFRO expedition, to Michigan's Upper Peninsula.

John thought it odd that a species like bigfoot was not having health issues. "How could the populations be big enough that they're not in-breeding?" he says.

"Let's be honest here," says Jim Sorensen, a fortyish man who owns several businesses near Jupiter, Florida. "You've seen the women here in North Carolina. There's plenty of women for them to hook up with. You can't keep screwing your sister forever."

"Yeah," says John, "they have to have the same rules as other animals. It would be a hard rule to get around."

A minute later, John posits another theory, but he's not sure how to develop it. "Wouldn't you think every once in a while you'd get one that is . . ." He pauses to consider the best way to hypothesize.

"Is what?" asks Jim.

"I'm looking for a better word," John says. "Well, that is retarded. Or one who is sick or messed up in the head. That doesn't mentally know what to do."

Perhaps they do what we did hundreds of years ago, I say. Maybe they kill them before they can mature.

"But that's not something they do here even with the people in North Carolina," Jim says. "Seriously, you should see some of the people I've seen at Quickie-type marts around here. It takes three of them to get a full set of teeth."

John laughs.

I smirk. Not because this was funny. I am amazed how someone who keeps an open mind about bigfoot could close it when it comes to people.

Like Mark and me, John and Jim are equal parts skeptical and hopeful that the branches and limbs leaning against the tree had been piled, not windswept. I want so badly to believe. After all, why (or how) could six or eight branches find their way against a tall pine, and why would two trees be bent back down to the ground in opposite directions to look like twin mini–Gateway Arches? On the other hand, why would anything bother to do this? Can't see how these branches would provide much cover either. Yes, something could hide partially in there, perhaps allowing deer to move close enough to jump on. Or these piled sticks could be some sort of marking, I guess, serving as a sort of posting that tells others this hunting ground has been claimed.

When we return, still others insist they get a chance to check out the stick structures. That's why we're headed out through the woods a third time around 9:00 p.m.

Before we left, Tommy joked that those long branches leaning against the tall pine might be very long skewers, so I'd better watch out if I see a fire out there. Like Tommy, many bigfoot researchers are self-effacing. They make jokes about potential evidence, what they do, and what would happen if they actually came face to face with an eight-foot, five-hundred-pound, wide-shouldered beast like a bigfoot. The general consensus — they'd shit their pants, pass out, urinate, or hyperventilate. They also mock colleagues who see evidence everywhere or who believe bigfoot is really an alien or paranormal being, knowing ridiculous claims like these make them all look absurd. In some ways this is a self-defense mechanism — better that they scoff at their own efforts than hear derisive remarks from someone who does not believe.

Still, many researchers are more dire, believing their mission to find bigfoot is akin to finding the Holy Grail. I chuckled that night in the Uwharries when two veteran researchers tracked a house's night light through the trees, believing it was an approaching bigfoot. After this had been pointed out, they did not laugh, instead offering excuses., The light, they said, shone through the trees in such a way that it appeared to be two glowing white eyes.

At first I had been breathless when they said a bigfoot was walking toward me. Finally, I would see this being — on only my second real expedition.

"Here it comes!" Olof Siemen had said while looking through

a third-generation night vision device, the same level used by the U.S. Army, that nearly turns the night as bright as day. "It's walking toward us."

Looking through his own night vision, Dave Pardue exclaimed, "I see it!"

I was barely able to contain myself. "Where?!" I dearly wanted to see it, too.

"Between those trees!"

"Which ones?"

Dave gave me the night vision and pointed me right at it. "Right there. See? I just saw some more eye shine. It looks pink. You don't even need night goggles to see it."

"Where?"

"Right there, near the two large trees!" Dave said.

"I just saw it move to the left," Olof interjected. "It's moving toward us!"

Where!? I couldn't see a damn thing.

"Right ahead of you," Olof said.

"Point it right there," Dave said, steadying the night-vision goggles.

But I saw nothing except house lights in the distance, something Mark and I had noticed several hours earlier. At first I believed I could not see because I was not experienced. Unlike the wise tracker, I was unable to recognize the subtle blinking from an elusive creature, unable to discern the slight shine on their eyes from the moon or local ambient light.

Perception plays a big role out in the woods. Olof and Dave *wanted* to see something, so they did. Earlier, Mark and I had assumed we'd see nothing and we didn't. Is there a middle ground? I'm not sure. But Olof and Dave eventually recognized the light from the distant home.

"But something was out there between the trees," Olaf said, indignantly. "There is definitely something out there."

Later, a pinecone landed on a backpack while we rested. "Something was just thrown at me," Olof whispered to us. "I heard something."

The pinecone rolled off the bag and onto the dirt path. "See. There's the pinecone."

Dave said a bigfoot once threw an apple so hard against a tree near him that it mashed the fruit into sauce. But there was no way in hell a pinecone, which measured about two inches high and weighed a few ounces, could travel more than about ten feet, even if Peyton Manning had thrown it. That meant a bigfoot would have to be standing relatively close to the path to reach us. That seemed improbable. There was very little brush under the tall pines—certainly not enough to hide a hulking creature. Plus, we could see nearly clear as day with the night-vision goggles. I did not see the reason a sasquatch would toss a pinecone at us.

"You know, they like to throw rocks and other things at people as they walk at night," Dave said. Several months earlier, rocks were thrown at a large group of researchers in West Virginia, he said, as if to herd them out of the area.

Yet here the bigfoot were acting more gently by tossing tiny, light pinecones to drive us from the woods. Wind rustled through the pine trees, prompting them to sway. A few cones fell to the ground around us, one hitting my head. I said nothing.

The next morning Gwen Barr excitedly tells everyone who passes her campsite that she had an encounter the night before. She's luring folks in by making sausages, brats, and bacon—a meatatarian breakfast worthy of any true squatcher. Last night she and Sally Ramey had felt as if they were being watched. Ramey is a forty-six-year-old public relations practitioner from Virginia. As a youth, she claims, she saw a bigfoot. Now she wants to verify what she saw.

Neither Sally nor Gwen actually saw anything the night before but they heard footfalls through the leaves farther back than the campfire could illuminate. Something kept pacing, moving from one side of the site to the other. After a while, Gwen felt nauseous and Sally suffered a severe headache—further evidence, they both believed, that something had been out there.

About thirty yards out in the woods, they show me an area near where several enormous tree trunks had been piled; two are so massive and wide, only an offensive lineman, or Shaquille O'Neal, would have been able to drag them even a few feet. Several other tree trunks and branches are piled on top of these, leaving a few open areas for someone, or something, to survey both Gwen's campsite and the main driveway into the campground. It looks a great deal like the barricades and redoubts built by soldiers at battles near Fredericksburg and Vicksburg during the Civil War. In addition, bark has been torn from a nearby tree, another alleged habit for the big guys.

"There is absolutely no way these trees fell like this," Sally says. "This was constructed."

Would be hard to argue otherwise, but who would have done this? Certainly not any kids on a weekend camping expedition. Why would any adults build a wall like this? Hard to imagine.

Meanwhile, down the campground road, Michael Greene talks about the image his camera captured a few months earlier at a spot not far from where we're standing. He's sitting at a picnic table, where several investigators are bent over to look more closely at the photo of what appears to be a shaggy hand moving past the lens. Unfortunately, the lighting at night and the angle of the camera don't allow for a clear view. Plus, the one-second delay in these cameras is enough to just miss fast-moving animals.

Since moving from Pennsylvania a few months earlier, Michael has been researching this part of the Uwharries, using items like candy bars, squeeze toys, and a small bathtub to lure bigfoot closer to his state-of-the-art infrared camera, a Raytheon PalmIR250 that costs more than $10,000. At six feet five, Michael is nearly as tall as the alleged creatures he seeks. By nature, he is skeptical, having dealt with cons and criminals for most of his life. He was chief of the Criminal Fraud Bureau for the state of New Jersey, where he evaluated court testimony and forgeries. He also has a master's degree in psychiatry, having written his thesis on, ironically, mass hysteria.

That Michael insists the picture is a bigfoot's hand should not be too surprising, given that he admires Carl Jung, a psychiatric pioneer who spent his life studying the unconscious. Jung believed that people in modern societies should look more deeply into our spirituality to better understand the world around us. Natural science, he argued, could not explain everything. That's why he investigated alchemy, astrology, and countercultures. As a result, Jung has not been fully embraced by academics and social scientists. Today you are more likely to study Jung in a humanities class than in a psychology course. Jung is considered an outsider among some scientists, just like these researchers huddled around the photo. Like Michael Greene, Carl Jung would probably very much want to investigate bigfoot. Michael believes his experience as a social scientist helps him understand how bigfoot think. But not everyone is convinced about the hand. Like most bigfoot visual evidence, this picture is more Rorschach than taxonomy.

Internet sites like YouTube offer many bigfoot videos—a mixture of ridiculously bad hoaxes, clearer parodies, and a few honest claims. None are convincing. The most entertaining are those produced by Jack Link's beef jerky, where people "mess" with sasquatch by putting a sleeping bigfoot's hand in warm water, which causes him to fire a thick, strong stream of urine into the perpetrator's face. Two other pranksters track a bigfoot to a cave's entrance, where they place a flaming bag of animal feces that the bigfoot stomps on to extinguish. Sasquatch retaliates by tossing this bag into the face of a fleeing man. There are several other installments in this series of TV commercials where people try to dupe sasquatch—two men reflecting light into the eyes of one grabbing fish in a brook, two others taunting a tired old bigfoot by alternately slowing down and picking up speed as he tries to walk up to the car, and three enterprising fellows who put shaving cream in the big guy's hand before gliding a weed over his face. When the bigfoot uses that hand to brush it away, the cream slaps into his face. Each time, though, sasquatch outwits the pranksters—by either tossing a passenger out of a car, by throwing a large fish at another man's crotch, or by flinging a man into the woods. The slapstick commercials are backslapping fun regardless of whether you believe in bigfoot.

Researchers realize they can't ever sneak up on bigfoot because something that lives in the woods is always going to be more attuned to its surroundings than some weekend warrior more accustomed to driving down paved streets, eating prepared food, and otherwise watching hours of television. Even squirrels and rabbits know that paying attention to one's surroundings is essential to survival. Humans are way too removed from nature to be able to sneak up, or outwit, even a small-brained mouse, much less a creature that may have a more fully developed intellect. So the lack of real evidence is not so shocking.

At the same time, no evidence can also be a sign there's no bigfoot. How could creatures presumed to be so large remain so elusive? In the thick forests of the Pacific Northwest, bigfoot may be able to remain hidden for a little while longer, much like the gorillas of central Africa did for centuries. But how could a bigfoot hide in woods that are not so dense and in areas more heavily populated—especially with today's evolving technology? Easily, argues Matt Moneymaker. First of all, humans are predictable. We usually remain on paths and roads, rarely blazing new trails through woods and forests. Second, we have very poor vision at night. Third, we do not know our surroundings.

In addition, we do not really know ourselves, something Jung understood. Interpretation is essential to knowing, and understanding. That means we need to understand how we think. Based on Jung's research, we have the Myers-Briggs test that measures psychological preferences, revealing how we see the world by using dichotomies — extrovert or introvert, sensing or intuiting, thinking or feeling, and judging or perceiving.

For example, I am an ENFJ, meaning I am an extroverted person who intuits, feels, and judges. Or in psychological terms, I am a benevolent pedagogue who uses his charisma to manipulate others (but in a good way, of course). We're dreamers, helpers, and enablers. Like Franklin D. Roosevelt, Martin Luther King Jr., and Abraham Lincoln, we prefer to see the big picture. In short, we're pretty damned awesome.

We're likely to sway others about our beliefs, unlike ENTJs, who have great difficulty in applying subjective considerations and emotional values to their decision-making process. Tell that to Richard Nixon, who falls in this category.

Clearly, there's more than one way to view the world, something that is difficult to accept for us ENFJs. And there's more than one way to appraise bigfoot research. If nothing else, the collection of folks on these expeditions proves that easy assumptions and generalizations are inadequate. Ultimately, life is how you see it — one large Rorschach test.

Still, some types of evidence are more compelling than others, as I later learned in both the Shawnee National Forest and Florida's Green Swamp.

3 SOUTHERN ILLINOIS

Imagination frequently clouds judgment. Just ask any of the people searching for bigfoot. Witnesses conjure all kinds of outlandish stories, researchers envision large hairy beasts throwing rocks and pinecones at them in the middle of the night, and skeptical reporters see a bunch of idiots traipsing through the woods and creating absurd stories about a nonexistent animal. We all envision what we want to see. How else to explain the popularity of the PT Cruiser, the Jonas Brothers, Keanu Reeves, or Taco Bell?

In daylight or at home, it is easy to disbelieve in bigfoot.

In the middle of the deep woods at night, disbelieving is more challenging.

In a crib, though, monsters appear everywhere for a toddler who awakens in the middle of the night. They lurk under beds, in closets, behind doors, and, sometimes, below Mom and Dad's bed. Or so that's what my oldest daughter, Kristen, believed. Even as a two-year-old, she'd climb the protective bar, rappel over the side, and race to our bedroom, dragging along stuffed Barney, Baby Bop, and BJ for protection.

On these nights Kristen learned a great deal about perception —

especially on that first night, when she just stood beside our bed at about eye level with someone resting her head on her pillow, who did not expect to wake up to see Kristen staring straight at her and have her heart palpitate. Needless to say, Kristen was sent back to her bed. "There's nothing in your room," Betsy said angrily. "Just close your eyes and get back to bed."

Obviously, Kristen thought this was easier said than done. That's why she returned to my side of the bed, whispering in her toddler babble, "Sleepy Papa." I rolled back the sheets, allowing her to slide in before Betsy could hear anything—and we both fell back to sleep rather quickly.

Through the years, Kristen learned to come to my side of the bed whenever she had a nightmare. Eventually, she lured her younger sister to sleep in her room or would just slip into Sarah's bed uninvited. I always felt my role was to comfort and protect my girls. So what was I thinking when I invited her to a bigfoot expedition in southern Illinois? Was it so she'd enjoy an adventure? Was it because she enjoyed hiking and camping in the mountains? Was it because she was bored at home during summer break? Was it because she'd be great material for a new chapter? Tough to say. Really, really difficult, in fact.

On the other hand, what if we encountered a bigfoot? And what if that creature grabbed Kristen, carrying her off in its strong, hairy paws, peering down at her with devilish red eyes while the moon glinted off sharp fangs? That would not merit Dad of the Year honors in anybody's book, no matter how frequently I had allowed her to escape the monsters in her room.

At age fourteen, though, Kristen really wanted to tag along down in the Shawnee National Forest. She loved to hike and camp. Through the past twelve years, Kristen had changed somewhat, aligning herself mentally more with my no-nonsense wife on most matters and sounding like Betsy in both tone and logic. Like my wife, Kristen thought bigfoot did not exist and that those who searched for them were foolish. "I'd say I'm about 100 percent against believing right now," Kristen said a few days before the trip.

Betsy is a New Englander by birth and a skeptic by vocation, having worked as a wildlife biologist in Florida before moving to nursing. As an environmental specialist, my wife drove boats through remote areas, slogged through wetlands to collect alligator eggs, and even saved that angry, eight-foot rattler. As a scientist, my wife required empirical proof.

Born in Rhode Island, Betsy steadfastly disbelieved anything that could not be proven through common sense. Ironically, Rhode Island was the only state without a single historical account attributed to bigfoot in John Green's encyclopedic *Sasquatch: The Apes among Us*. Since the book's publication, Rhode Island has recorded five sightings, the fewest number for any state in North America. Either bigfoot do not want to bother the Yankees living in Rhode Island or those sensible New Englanders refused to believe that those late-night shrieks or fleeting sights could be anything but a fox or an owl.

My home state, on the other hand, boasts the Jersey Devil, a winged, cloven-footed creature that has eviscerated cows, carted off family pets, and scared the bejeebies out of folks in the heavily forested Pine Barrens of southern New Jersey for more than 250 years. Or so the story goes.

As a thrifty Yankee, Betsy also did not like that I had wasted money on even a low-end night-vision monocle or that I had blown $1,000 driving across the country in order to talk with people who had squandered sometimes more than $10,000 on high-tech devices. None of this made any sense to her. This was akin to buying a surfboard when you reside in the Midwest or purchasing snow skis when you live in Florida. It was all a bunch of malarkey, a term she throws at all kinds of foolishness.

Years ago, for example, my wife decided she wanted to swim across a lake in Orlando, a little more than a half mile. A former athlete, my wife would have had little trouble completing the trip physically. But, logically, it was a dumb plan. Gators patrolled every single waterway in our lovely state. On even smaller lakes, you'd find several large killer lizards. Wildlife officers routinely remove gators from ponds near homes, even though, they know, another will eventually move in, no matter how small the water hole. The effort makes neighbors feel good for a few weeks or until an even more ornery gator moves in and snacks on someone's poodle.

Gators, Betsy knew, really want little to do with humans. Nearly 1.5 million gators reside in Florida, about one gator for every twelve people. Yet, gator attacks are infrequent—about six to seven a year on average—and fatal attacks are equally rare, seventeen in the past sixty years. That did not stave off my fears, because Betsy could easily come across a large, hungry gator. She saw more than her share on Lake Apopka and the chain of lakes that extend across central Florida. Ever the self-reliant Yankee, Betsy said she would not get attacked because she would not allow it.

Betsy also dove out of an airplane that was still capable of landing safely. Skydiving is even more dangerous than swimming in a reptile-filled Florida lake, causing anywhere from fifty to seventy deaths per year on average. While she leaped backward out of a plane, I sat at home with a self-induced fever, too fearful to watch her splat onto the macadam. Betsy dismissed these fears as malarkey as well.

What else can be bunched as malarkey? Fears about my ten-year-old daughter walking through a stretch of woods to her friend's. Life forms from another planet visiting earth. My daughters clambering near the edges of cliffs on hikes. And, of course, bigfoot.

So Kristen did not fear monsters snatching her away. More so, she worried about temperatures expected to reach one hundred degrees, scorching heat that is unusual for the Midwest. Some summers we may face ninety-degree temps only once or twice back home in Charleston. But that would not be the case later in Shawnee, three hours away, where the weather would be as hot as I had ever faced in Florida. The heat sucked the air from my lungs and sapped the energy from my soul. That afternoon we felt as though God had shoved us in a microwave. Damn, it was going to be Africa hot.

Southern Illinois has a rich history of phantasmic folklore. Ghosts haunt restaurants, former slave houses, factory buildings, and libraries in towns like Carbondale, Chester, and Equality. Apparitions run along State Route 3. Tourists hear unexplained voices in state historic sites. Night janitors get locked in closets, where chairs then wedge under doorknobs. Chandeliers in old homes swing unexpectedly and ghostly figures later appear in photos. In addition, headless horsemen and four-armed, three-legged aliens travel through small towns near the Shawnee National Forest, probably the legacy of a strong oral tradition that has served two purposes for generations—to chronicle historic events and to entertain listeners with chilling stories. Authors have collected many of these tales in books like *Weird Egypt: History, Haunts and Love of Southern Illinois*, *Haunted Illinois*, and *Weird Illinois*.

Bigfoot sightings have been reported in the Land of Lincoln as far back as 1912, when Beulah Scott said she spotted several hairy creatures near her home in Effingham, a ninety-minute drive north of Murphysboro. In 1929 locals reported a huge gorilla in northwestern Illinois, near the Wisconsin border. And in 1941 Reverend Lepton Harpole, a name straight out of a Jane Austen novel, came across something that looked like a baboon while hunting squirrel in Mt. Vernon, an hour north of Murphysboro. Then Lepton proceeded to act like someone straight out of a *Rambo* movie by striking the creature with his gun and then firing a shot at it. The creature, clearly pissed off, later returned to the area to harass several people, allegedly even scuffling with one fellow. Then, in 1968, a couple spotted a monstrous, ten-foot tall creature that inexplicably threw dirt at their car not far from where we now camped.

The most bizarre report involved a short, three-legged creature that allegedly had two arms extending from its abdomen. In the 1970s UFO fever hit rural areas here in Illinois, Kentucky, and Ohio more than others.

No story is more unsettling to locals than that of the Murphysboro Mud Monster, the large, hairy beast that terrified residents in June 1973. Murphysboro, now a town of about thirteen thousand, sits forty-five miles directly west of Harrisburg, where Kristen and I would be heading to do research in the Garden of the Gods. The Murphysboro creature, by all accounts, fits descriptions of bigfoot, except this one may have had white hair. While rare, white bigfoot have been reported in other parts of the world. In southern Illinois, hunters will occasionally report seeing white-haired raccoons or deer. And hundreds of albino squirrels run through the woods near Olney, a small town in east central Illinois.

This white hair frightened, and confused, the creature's first witness, Christian Baril. The four-year-old, chasing fireflies in his backyard, caught a glimpse of a large, light-haired creature peering at him through the bushes before running into the house to tell his dad, "There's a big ghost out back."

A few minutes later an eight-foot creature terrified Cheryl Ray and Randy Creath, teenaged sweethearts who had been sitting on a front porch breezeway in the same neighborhood. Randy heard some noise in the woods, so they walked over to it, like so many victims in slasher movies.

"Come here," Randy told Cheryl. "I heard something."

At that moment the creature stepped from behind some bushes and looked down at the two wide-eyed teens for about thirty seconds—although it felt like an eternity to Randy and Cheryl. The stench was nearly intolerable, but they did not cover their noses or eyes. They just stared back from about fifteen feet away, close enough that Cheryl noticed the creature's white fur, which was long and shaggy like a sheepdog's. The creature was stocky, like a high school football player, she thought right before it turned and walked back into the woods. The teens heard branches snapping as it increased its pace.

Everybody had been on edge already. The night before, a light-colored creature streaked in mud had lumbered from the river toward a young couple parked near the boat ramp. The woman, though married to another man, was so horrified that she immediately reported the incident to the police, disregarding the shame that would result. Midwesterners, like those in Murphysboro, are not easily excited. But even plain folks can get electrified by gossip about a married woman canoodling with a lover—possibly even more so than by a story about a monster roaming the town. When police arrived to investigate, the officers found large footprints pointing in all directions, as if someone large were drunk. Then they heard a loud, shrill shriek from about one hundred feet away. An officer was so startled that he dropped his gun before running out of the area.

Even carnival workers, accustomed to seeing oddities, reported seeing a bigfoot eyeing the tied-up ponies used to give young kids rides at an event by a riverside park. They feared their animals might become a snack, so they sat by them for several days, afraid to call police and scare off potential customers. They waited until they pulled up stakes ten days later to report how one creature appeared by the tree line, peeking its head out to check on the smaller horses from time to time.

The town's police chief, Tony Berger, ordered all fourteen of his officers to search for the creature that first night. They found a new, rough trail through the brush, snapped branches, and gobs of black slime, probably sewage sludge tracked into the woods. At one point the department's rambunctious eighty-pound German shepherd tracked something to an abandoned barn. But then it yelped and backed off. The dog's owner shoved the dog into the barn, but the usually aggressive shepherd crawled back out, whining. Quickly, fourteen police cars arrived, but they did not find anything.

Creath, now a Baptist minister, says he feels blessed to have seen the creature that night. "It reinforced my belief that humanity is not nearly as intelligent as we think," he said twelve years later. "Our system of natural laws is not really as fixed as we would like to believe. We don't know nearly as much about the world as we pretend."[1]

The police chief was also convinced that a bigfoot-like creature had wandered through their town. "A lot of things are unexpected," Berger said, "and this is another one. We don't know what the creature is. But we do believe what these people saw was real. We have tracked it. And the dogs got a definite scent."[2]

But there may be another theory as well. Mass hysteria. Charles Pierce's mock documentary *The Legend of Boggy Creek* had been released the previous summer, raking in an amazing $20 million for a story set in neighboring Arkansas. Later that same summer, a bigfoot-like creature allegedly tormented Louisiana, Missouri, about a three-hour trip upriver from Murphysboro—and about twenty-five miles southeast of Hannibal, Missouri, the boyhood home of Mark Twain, who lived for these kinds of stories. In July 1972 the Missouri Monster, aptly abbreviated MoMo, frightened parishioners at a Pentecostal church, unnerving even churchgoers accustomed to hearing people shriek in tongues during services. MoMo later chased hunters and dug up dog graves, prompting a twenty-man posse to search for it. A spokesman for the international UFO bureau even claimed aliens had left this "large, hairy biped" behind to scout us—eerily similar, the spokesman said, to bigfoot left in more than three hundred other locations. Clearly the first step toward an invasion, a Wellesian war between worlds.

For more than a month, MoMo was spotted up and down the Mississippi River, prompting one radio deejay to write a song in honor of the Missouri Monster and inspiring thousands to tell taller and taller tales. Mark Twain would have been proud.

More than forty years later, the Murphysboro incident remains one of only two unsolved cases for the Murphysboro police department. This case also remains the department's most requested, and most copied, police report.

Harold Benny, the researcher I had met in Oklahoma, was far more worried about Kristen than her own reckless dad. He was in charge of this expedition. Harold knew she would behave properly, but he was concerned about her psyche. A few weeks earlier, Harold had sent an email: "Is she mentally ready for a possible encounter? I've seen people's minds melt down. She has to understand that this is serious business and she could easily get scared to death out in the dark forest. Have her think real hard on it. It will be too late to change her mind once she's out there. We know the animals are out there because of an 'A' class encounter last January a few miles from the campground."

It is clear that I'm growing more skeptical because I am not concerned about Kristen's psyche in the slightest, at least when it comes to having her mind blown upon seeing a large monster in the middle of the woods. Unlike Harold, I do not accept testimony by witnesses as absolute truth, even though I frequently want to believe them — and even though, as a journalist, I use such comments, since there's often at least a little truth in such testimony. With some people, there's even less truth. On these trips, I have met people whom I wouldn't trust to tell me the color of the sky or grass. Conversely, I have met people who believe they really saw something; however, there are a people, such as Pam, whose unadorned stories make me pause. Harold falls somewhere in the middle. He is a trained scientist, a keen observer, and a generous, kind person. Harold can also be skeptical. But I worry that his relationship with so many investigators and the BFRO could readjust his scientific approach. It's human nature. Hang out with a like-minded group, such as professionals like teachers or police officers or lawyers, and you'll start to think like them. Little did I know at the time, but a rift was growing between Harold and the BFRO, whose expedition leaders, he told me, did not like that he questioned so many reports. So far, I trust Harold's inferences and assessments. But that doesn't mean I won't do my own reporting as well.

Rachel and Mark Luffman arrived at our camp right before dusk. By seven o'clock, we had ten people in camp including this father and daughter, who had reported seeing a bigfoot on an observation trail near the Garden of the Gods, roughly a twenty-minute drive away. Rachel, at age twenty-one, worked in the family restaurant not far from Harrisburg. Her father, Mark, ran the restaurant in a nearby town. At age forty-six, he had spent a great deal of time in these woods, although he had rarely slipped out over the past fifteen years, the restaurant sucking up most of his time. Recently, though, they had devoted some time to squatching, looking for bigfoot during an expedition in Missouri the previous fall, the trip that had gotten me excommunicated from the BFRO. The trip's organizer realized I had never signed the organization's draconian nondisclosure agreement that essentially gives Matt Moneymaker the right to censor anything anybody writes without offering a reasonable explanation. Here's part of the agreement sent by Matt's secretary, Dorota Plazewski:

> Mr. Moneymaker will have the right to censor anything (or everything) that he decides is too sensitive or inappropriate or unfair, etc.

The NDA [nondisclosure agreement] will give Mr. Money-maker the right to strike out things related to the BFRO (directly or indirectly) for any reason or for no reason.

The NDA will also show that you agree that substantial damages will need to be paid to Mr. Moneymaker if you disclose any unapproved writings related to the BFRO (directly or indirectly) regardless of our ability to show actual damages due to your breach.

I fired off several emails explaining my refusal to sign. The language in the agreement made me feel uncomfortable. Just as Matt may have suffered at the hands of some journalists, so too have my students suffered from administrators at schools who have sought to suppress their efforts to report responsibly. I am indeed a First Amendment zealot, believing a free press should act independently. I also believe in many other journalistic statements offered in the Society of Professional Journalism's code of ethics. For example, journalists should seek truth and report it, should minimize harm, should act independently, and should be accountable. In any profession, the blunders of a few hinder the efforts of the whole. I am angry whenever journalists act inappropriately, perhaps because they were lazy or inexperienced. But I am angrier when individuals or organizations use these errors as an excuse to suppress free speech.

I had always been candid about my purpose on these trips, telling everybody that I planned to write about bigfoot researchers. I did not slink around, acting as though I was just someone interested in field research. I always introduced myself as the guy writing a book about bigfoot researchers and explained that I was attending in order to learn more about them (and not to demean or ridicule their efforts). In one case, I deleted from a chapter all references to a person worried that he would be ostracized professionally were anybody to learn he searched for something as crazy as bigfoot. This investigator continues to send me insights into research, knowing I won't ever name him. I promised.

Ultimately, being banned from BFRO proved helpful. I was forced to seek out other researchers in Florida, Wisconsin, Ohio, Virginia, and Kentucky, Texas, and Louisiana during the next several months. I would also secure interviews with researchers in Washington, Oregon, California, and Minnesota, enabling me to learn about newer areas and a larger variety of people. Still, that Harold invited me on his personal expedition meant a lot.

That's why I agreed to return to a place that freaked me out. Southern Illinois has more ticks than any place I had ever visited, something I had learned during a family trip the previous spring. A year earlier, an extraordinarily large tick, about the size of a fingernail, had attached itself to my thigh as I hiked through some tall prairie grass, not unlike that all around the bigfoot encampment. That was only the third tick I had encountered in about twenty years of hiking. By the next afternoon, I found another walking on my neck and one embedded inside my upper thigh. Six more ticks had burrowed into my wife, two daughters, and their best friend. We pulled countless others off. Needless to say, we cut our trip short, pulling up our stakes and departing after the second day. I had hoped that trip had been an aberration but dismissed that thought within my first five minutes of talking with Harold when a tiny, bloodthirsty arachnid walked across my shoe, smacking its tiny parasitic mandibles as it eyed my ankle. For some odd reason, I feel far less at ease around these bloodsuckers than I did hiking at night near eight-foot hairy beasts, coyotes, or snakes.

And, oh my, the Shawnee National Forest has its share of snakes. In fact, we would cross Snake Road, aptly named because more than a thousand snakes migrate across it each spring and autumn, moving between the two thousand–plus acres of swampland and the caves in the three-hundred-plus-feet-tall limestone bluffs where they hibernate. In autumn herpetologists flock to the area to watch thirty-five species slither through multicolored fallen leaves — essentially despoiling an otherwise gorgeous view from under the tightly packed hardwoods lined among rolling hills and sandstone bluffs. Old-timers recall when the roads looked like a slithering bowl of snake spaghetti during these biannual migrations. Cars, though, kill hundreds of snakes each year, and reptile collectors also snag a fair share. But that still left a fair share of copperheads, timber rattlers, and cottonmouths coiled in the woods we would explore that night.

Yet there I was at eight o'clock at night in late June, speaking with Rachel and her dad about their encounter six months earlier, trying not to think about the dangers or that it was still eighty-plus degrees. I sweat like a pro, soaking a second shirt that made me feel itchy as it scraped across my chest. (Or was that a tick crawling inside the tee?)

At 2:00 p.m., the temperature in the shade must have been ninety degrees, prompting Kristen to hide in my air-conditioned Mazda Tribute. Six hours later, the mugginess still made me feel clammy as I interviewed Rachel and her father about their encounter six months earlier.

It was January. The dusk offered just enough light for Rachel and her father to follow the trail up to Indian Point, an area that oversees part of the 280,000 acres in the Shawnee National Forest. They settled under some pines and started a fire, cooking bacon they brought along. Like other researchers, Rachel and Mark believed cooking meat was one way to draw in bigfoot.

"That was only our second time up there at night," she told me. "But we were pretty excited despite the cold weather."

They settled in, talked about their day, and waited. Mark used tree limbs to twice knock on a tree trunk. Two hours later they decided to walk back to their car, since both had to work at the restaurant in the morning.

By then it was pretty dark. Without their headlamps, they would have had problems following an unpaved path back. Halfway down, Mark paused to whoop a few times, a call intended to lure in bigfoot that sounds like a mix between a coyote and, at times, a chimpanzee. Nothing responded, although Rachel thought she heard the rising chorus of coyotes.

About eighty feet from the parking lot, Rachel was walking with her head down, her green headlamp illuminating the path. She hadn't noticed that her father had stopped a few paces back until he whispered, "Rachel, come back here."

When Rachel reached him, Mark softy said, "There he is."

To their left, Rachel saw two large, round eyes, shining whitish-green, about thirty feet away. The eyes appeared to reflect red from Mark's headlamp.

My god, Mark thought, *those eyes have to be as big as golf balls.* They also were farther apart than a human's, he noticed.

"Turn your light off," he whispered.

Before Rachel could, she saw the large creature turn its head. First it looked straight down the path, allowing them to see a large, rounded head silhouetted against the starry skies behind it. Then it briefly turned its head back to them, blinked, and turned its head sideways again, looking back down the path.

Its eyes bulged out farther from the front of its face than a human's.

"That's when it registered that I was looking at a sasquatch," Rachel told me.

They finally turned off the headlamps, which prompted the creature to take a few steps toward them.

Rachel took a step back as well. "Whoa!" she said, unable to control herself.

The creature started to retreat, taking six or seven steps back toward a ridge. Mark, though, wanted to lure him back.

"Should I whoop at him?"

Rachel responded quickly and emphatically: "No." She did not want to provoke it. Her heart was pounding. Her imagination was racing, so she decided to speak aloud to it. At that moment, she got hooked. She felt this creature was at ease with her, so she whistled to catch its attention, but it did not move any closer. Five minutes later they walked out to their car and drove off. Rachel was invigorated, knowing she had to learn more about this stealthy and intelligent animal. She joined four more BFRO expeditions during the following year, going as far as Florida, and also became an investigator for the organization.

"I couldn't believe how close we were to the parking lot," she told me. "It was so quiet, not making a sound. If my dad hadn't turned his head at just the right moment, we probably would not have known he was standing right there."

Kristen listened attentively to the story, absorbing it all. She is usually reserved around adults, refraining from telling jokes or making bad puns learned from her old man. Several other investigators related bigfoot tales from Alabama, Tennessee, and Utah. The sun dipped below the horizon, making it difficult to see everybody's faces in the growing darkness; however, I could see Kristen leaning in to listen a little more intently. I knew she was eager to head out.

By ten o'clock, we were sitting on a large flat rock atop the trail at Garden of the Gods. In daylight we would have had a spectacular view of the wilderness that sprawls east, south, and west. At 548 feet, this elevated observation area is about the best in the entire national forest. My wife and kids had hiked the short interpretive trail just last spring (in between dodging ticks). The girls climbed into crevices, ambled up overlooks, and crawled into shallow caves. We were awed by the spectacular scenery and by the stunning rock formations.

The sedimentary rock that forms these bluffs is more than 320 million years old and runs four miles deep. Over the years, the bedrock fractured, creating rock formations that look like camels, monkey faces, mushrooms, and anvils, which has resulted in eponymous names being assigned to these observation areas. Near Tourist Rock, tourists flock to view spectacular blazes of fall foliage, while at Buzzards Point, raptors and scavenger birds flock to look out over the valley for rodents, fish, snakes, and anything dead or dying.

Several of us sat near Indian Point, sticky and restless, after a half-mile hike along the interpretive trails. Pam Porter, who brought along a friend from Ohio, talked with Kristen about horses. I had not talked with Pam since the Oklahoma expedition, but we had shared a few emails. Pam owned several horses and used to ride competitively. Kristen owned a thirteen-year-old draft horse named Mooney, whom she groomed and cared for on her own. We were told to sit quietly and listen for unusual sounds while another group, which included Harold, would scout another area. We did not comply.

There's nothing like an old-fashioned ghost story when you're out hiking and camping at night. Ronnie Powell, a financial planner from Alabama, indulged us with a story about a recent encounter she had been told about in her home state, where a man started tracking a family of bigfoot back to its caves — even crawling through a tunnel into a cave where he found what appeared to be a very old, female bigfoot who seemed terrified. Said Ronnie, "The man thought this old woman must have been lovely when she was younger." The 'Bama man quickly crawled out and ran back to his home, all the while being tracked by a bigfoot, Ronnie said. A few days later the man saw his dog strung up on a tree, dangling and still alive. Believing this was a trap, he waited before going out to untie the dog, which survived (but was way too scared to go back outside.)

"I told him to stop being so aggressive," Ronnie said. "I started to get worried for him. I don't want him to get hurt."

She planned to investigate that area later that summer, after she returned home.

Colby, a college student, listened and said little. He said he had stumbled across bigfoot once by accident while tracking cougar here in southern Illinois. State officials, though, were just as likely to dismiss cougar as bigfoot living in this region. Officially, cougar have been wiped out from the region for more than one hundred years. But that's news to Colby and others who continue to report cougar all across the state. Wildlife officials usually call them escaped leopards or jaguarondi or say that they escaped from locals who illegally imported them from out west. A tawny cougar was recently hit by a train in Rudolph County, southwest of Murphysboro, and a wild cat reportedly had been spotted roaming along the Mississippi River. The Department of Natural Resources planned to test DNA from a six-foot cat apparently killed by an arrow. If the department refuses to accept that native cougar might still exist within its borders, how could it ever wrap its mind around a large creature that is more myth than historical?

Colby had unexpectedly found cougar evidence while hiking in southern Illinois. Footprints. Over time, he found scat and scrapes on trees. A large cat definitely roamed this wilderness area. Colby soon started bringing a video camera out on hikes.

Along the way, Colby believes he also stumbled across bigfoot farther south in the Bell Smith Springs National Natural Landmark. The only one camping at a remote location on a Wednesday night, he chopped wood for a fire. Around midnight, Colby heard wood knocks that he characterized as loud and aggressive in the nearby canyon. The knocks came five at a time. Then silence. Followed by another four or five. He eventually rolled over and fell back to sleep. Campers filled the site for the next three days. By Sunday he was alone again. Around 3:00 a.m., he awoke with an intense fear that something was approaching his campsite. When he left the tent, he heard footsteps about twenty yards away. He immediately packed and departed.

Investigators found fourteen-inch-long footprints along a creek near this camping area the following spring.

As always, one has to evaluate a source's story. Someone who regularly heads off alone into remote wilderness to camp is not likely to scare easily. You'd expect an experienced camper like this to dismiss sounds and feelings like the ones Cody described as, well, malarkey. Colby told me he was surprised by his reaction. Yet for some reason, fear overwhelmed him. That story sounded familiar.

Meanwhile, at Indian Point the sky put on a show. Away from artificial lights, we could see part of the Milky Way, which really did look like milk spilled across the Big and Little Dippers. Several meteors blazed across the night, trails imprinted across the sky for several seconds after they shot across. (I think we all made the same wish: to clearly see a bigfoot.) And the moon slowly turned red as it sat low over the horizon. Kristen and I leaned back, our arms folded behind our heads and watched it all. You can't beat nature for a good show.

But you can't beat the dark woods for a good mystery either. A large rock slammed against a tree about ten feet away.

"Could that have been a pinecone falling?" I asked.

"No, something hit that tree from an angle," Pam said. "And there's nothing above the tree."

Earlier Pam had unleashed a few whoops that echoed down the steep decline and across the valley below. No more rocks appeared, so we hiked down to another location and then looped back around to the parking lot. By around midnight, we stopped to decide whether to depart.

Rachel and Mark suggested we try walking on the trail where they had seen a bigfoot back in January. We went down to the first parking lot. Mark then walked us through the trees to the place where they had the encounter, a spot that, in person, looked even more remarkably close to the parking lot. Pine needles formed a soft bed under the many tall trees lining the trailhead. These needles absorbed our footfall, offering a faint rustle with each step, not the hard sound heard six months earlier.

Pam and Ronnie told the men to walk alone down the path. Once again, Pam agreed to become bigfoot bait. I paused. "Don't worry," Pam said, "if one bull-rushes us, I'll grab Kristen."

"I'll hang on to her as well," Ronnie said, laughing.

Kristen gave me a look. Even under the faint stars, I could tell what she was thinking as she looked at me, wide-eyed: "This is cool!"

Up the trail, the five of us heard nothing unusual. When the bullfrogs in a marsh stopped belching, someone suggested a bigfoot was nearby. But the frogs started croaking again when we left the area.

After about forty minutes, we returned. As we got closer to the trail, Ronnie called out to us to approach slowly. They had started to hear some footfalls not far from the trees where we had left them. In daylight we would have noticed that the area declines steeply into a ravine. On the other side, Mark said, were a few caverns that were partially hidden. He had checked the area after his earlier bigfoot encounter, but he did not go all the way across the ravine to check inside caves. That would have required expert climbing up nearly vertical rock faces on the opposite side. At night we could barely see farther than ten or twenty feet.

The women remained in place while we walked out to the parking lot. Ronnie heard slow, deliberate footfalls. "Not what you would normally hear from other animals," Ronnie said later. The footfalls were getting closer. And the strides, she estimated, were pretty wide.

In the parking lot, we were all frustrated.

I was annoyed because I could not really hear anything.

Colby was irritated because he could not see anything, once

again. He wanted to run out to the trees and tackle something. "I want a damn daylight encounter."

And Mark was disappointed that he could not see anything this time. He also wanted to head into the woods.

At these times, the protocol itself can be exasperating. Ronnie reminded us not to point, not to direct our flashlight where we heard sounds or to visibly level our night vision into noisy areas. Doing any of those things could scare off the bigfoot. In effect, we were limited to listening. This did not quench my curiosity. No photos, no visuals on night vision, nothing. In the end, all we could do was hypothesize, speculate, and wonder. Had we just heard a bigfoot circling us? Or had we imagined it all?

"Of course, we have no way to positively identify it as a squatch," Ronnie told me later, "but that would be my guess."

I might have disagreed had we not heard some unusual calls when we returned to camp around 3:00 a.m. Just as we disembarked from Harold's car, I heard three loud, shrill whoops, something that sounded like a mix between a coyote and a barn owl. But, at the same time, it sounded like neither one. I have heard my share of coyotes deep in the woods at night. This did not sound quite right.

"That was a call," Harold said a few minutes after the whoops dissipated. "I think they're letting the others know that we've returned to camp."

That night Kristen and I slept inside the car, more worried about humidity than a bigfoot approaching camp. I was too tired to set up camp anyway, so we turned on the air conditioner to cool inside the suv before we dozed off. I put a pillow over my head in case anything did peer through the windows, leaned back, and fell asleep.

Corn and soy fields lined State Road 13. It was 10:00 a.m. Besides Harrisburg and its ninety-six hundred people, little else existed here in southeastern Illinois except farms. For dozens of miles at a time, you won't find even a convenience store. So I looked to the sky. A few cirrus and nimbus clouds floated in from the west, a sign that rain might finally wash away this mugginess.

I've always loved imagining figures in clouds. Near the horizon, I saw a kid with spiked hair. There was also a goat that transformed into a genie. I also saw hybrids—a dog with a horn on its head, a submarine with a shark's dorsal fin, and something that looked like a Pokémon character. Kristen saw a horse. No shocker there. She read horse magazines, studied riding styles, and had memorized most equine breeds.

Like in life, we see what we want to envision in clouds. Eight years removed from Florida, my wife and I still saw gators where midwesterners saw logs. But that was reality in Florida. What appeared to be a floating log frequently revealed itself as a gator gliding on the surface.

As we drove past miles of plowed fields, I asked Kristen about the trip.

"So," I said, smirking. "You seemed pretty excited last night. Do you believe something was out there?"

Kristen smiled. "I think now I believe 49 percent 'yes,' and 51 percent 'no.'"

"Well, that's something," I said.

The clouds started to grow taller and thicker. Yes, I believed the rain would come sooner than I had thought. In the distance over a cornfield, I noticed something else emerge from the clouds—a creature with a pointed head and wide shoulders that peeked over another cloud. I half expected it to wink at me.

If only seeing the real thing were as easy. Or as possible.

I hoped bigfoot were not fictional like Pikachu or a chimera, but I found my thoughts about bigfoot starting to blend and form all kinds of hybrid ideas. Last night I had wished on that shooting star to see a bigfoot. I just hoped this was not as real as that dream gets.

4 GREEN SWAMP

FLORIDA

Even though they were the sons of preachers, neither John nor Dwayne expected to see the devil standing before them. But that's exactly what happened. The two teens had just finished jamming with their band in preparation for an upcoming performance when they decided to head back to John's home in Leesburg, a burgeoning city in central Florida's aptly named Lake County. Large lakes surrounded towns like Leesburg and Eustis. On that night in the spring of 1993, the young men were driving down a rural road on an isthmus surrounded by Lakes Eustis, Griffin, and Harris. Emeralda Marsh sat a few miles north, itself just a few miles south of the Ocala National Forest that sweeps across north central Florida. To the southwest lay the Green Swamp. Despite rapid construction, Leesburg remained bucolic.

Overhead, the stars sparkled. The night was cool. The young men were thinking of their pending gig. Or about young female groupies. Or record contracts. Or stardom. Up ahead, John saw something in the middle of the dirt road, but he didn't say anything, knowing the mind plays tricks at night — especially when fatigued after hours of strumming a guitar. When Dwayne slammed the breaks, he hoped he wasn't crazy. The car slid to a stop about ten feet from an eight-foot-tall creature fully covered in dark hair, which had glowing orange eyes and whose head swayed back and forth, sort of like a dog considering whether to bark or run. Dwayne flipped on the high beams.

"That's the devil!" Dwayne screamed. He repeated this about ten times while clutching the steering wheel. John could not disagree. For a few minutes the young men sat there watching it, wandering how they could get past the creature and make sure everybody in the house just up ahead was safe. John finally yelled, "Step on it!" As they accelerated, John wondered why the creature seemed to move off in slow motion. That was bizarre, he thought. A minute later, the two young men raced into John's house, terrified for themselves and their families.

Like most people, John did not share his bigfoot experience with anyone until a few years ago. Few people do, despite how it seems on TV and in the *Weekly World News*. John knew everybody in this small Florida community would think he was crazy. The cops would probably question whether these teens had been drinking or smoking something illegal—even though, as the son of a preacher, John probably had never tried either drug. John even feared using his real name in the report. But he kept having flashbacks, which is why he reported his experience on the Bigfoot Field Researchers Organization's website.

Outside the Pacific Northwest, Florida is among the most bustling areas for bigfoot, according to BFRO reports, getting as much activity as Ohio and Texas. In Florida, though, the creatures are called Skunk Apes, smaller, leaner, and far-stinkier cousins that have a strong, foul odor reminiscent of a dead skunk mixed with cow manure and rotten eggs. Growing up in Florida, I heard the stories. We all had. A bigfoot running alongside cars in Clewiston and Immokalee, throwing rocks at hunters in the swamps, or nabbing children in the sugar fields in south Florida. In Orlando, radio hosts like Jim Philips would ponder reports of creatures running along State Road 520 or near the Seminole Ranch Wildlife Management Area. Driving at night on rural roads, we'd roll up our windows quickly if we smelled that pungent scent and then hit the accelerator—not necessarily in that order. We were all mesmerized by the stories.

That we heard these stories is not surprising because bigfoot are no tourists to Florida. They've reportedly been living in the Sunshine State for as long as Florida natives can remember. The Seminoles called the creatures Esti Capcaki, which means "tall men," while the Cherokees who lived along the northern border referred to a hairy savage (Kecleh-Kudleh). The Choctaws had a more disconcerting name for the wild men, calling them both giant monster (*shampe*) and cannibal man (*kashehotapalo*). Indian legends refer to people called the sand people and the mangrove people. For good reason, native Floridians avoid large swamps like the one I'm in right now. Despite these stories, many researchers don't believe such creatures can exist outside the remote mountain regions of the Pacific Northwest and Rockies. Clearly these folks have never visited Florida, a state defined by its more than eleven million acres of isolated wetlands. People regularly get lost in the Everglades, Ocala National Forest, and the Green Swamp, areas that are hostile and sometimes impenetrable—a perfect place for large creatures to hide.

Of course, most tourists and residents steer clear of Florida's swamps, areas associated with muck and snakes and gators and bugs and slime and, sometimes, panthers and crocodiles. Tourists would rather stick to the interstates, the IHOPs, the beaches, and the theme parks. Residents know the swamps can be both beautiful and dangerous, that even experienced hunters who wander off the main trails can get lost. That's what happened to Jamey Mosch, a thirty-year-old New York transplant who was hunting with a friend in the Big Cypress National Preserve in the Everglades, not far from Naples. As his friends worked on their pickup truck, Mosch walked off to scout deer-hunting locations. A short while later, Mosch found himself lost in an area he later described as hellish. A panther stalked him. He fell into quicksand, saved from the mud pit only after he removed his pants, boots, and jacket. That left him exposed to the elements. As a result, mosquitoes and other bugs devoured him, leaving hundreds of red welts all over his body. Gators patrolled the area, snakes slithered nearby. At night, he shivered in the cool November air. By day, he wandered, ate raw catfish and bullfrogs, and, eventually, hallucinated before police found him four days later.

Florida's wetlands are unforgiving. People like seventy-six-year-old Charles Huff have disappeared in a southern portion of the Green Swamp, near Lakeland, never to be found again. An eleven-year-old girl bicycled into a local swamp in Winter Springs, not far from Orlando, to take nature photos only to get stuck for four terrifying days before a pastor found her. The swamps absorb both kids and adults, who die from exposure, starvation, drowning, or attacks by animals. There are those who suggest bigfoot are other culprits, a theory I've heard numerous times around several campfires. While investigators say bigfoot are not aggressive, they also speculate that bigfoot sometimes attack. I guess that's true of any species. Even golden retrievers sometimes bite people. But I find it hard to believe that creatures that are a few feet taller, several hundred pounds larger, and many, many times stronger than humans would be content to toss pinecones and scream in order to steer people from their home.

Bigfoot are much surlier in Florida—at least, if you believe the reports. Stories reveal confrontational creatures. In these accounts, bigfoot are a menace, chasing people into their trailers, racing cars down state roads, attacking family pets—and, in a few cases, allegedly killing people. In Apopka, for example, a bigfoot reportedly broke down a door to a building in an attack on a security guard, while in Belleview a bigfoot purportedly assaulted a hitchhiker on a rural road. Not far from the Green Swamp, a trucker claimed that a bigfoot grabbed him as he rested along Interstate 75, trying to pull him from the truck's cab. The two wrestled until the trucker blasted his truck's air horn, which startled the creature and sent it running into the woods. They also seem to snarl and growl a lot more in Florida. To be fair, Floridians can be equally cantankerous, perhaps thanks to tourists who clog highways, restaurants, and beaches, all the while complaining about how much better life is back home. A hunter, for example, fired six shots at an ape-like creature in the Ocala National Forest, while a Cape Coral man shot and hit a nine-footer in the chest before it grunted and ran off from the man's backyard. In Fort Lauderdale a man veered to avoid hitting what he thought was a black man lying on Hollywood Boulevard. But the creature jumped up, glared at the driver, and then outran a police car to reach woods that extend into the Everglades. One bigfoot invoked the wrath of a Baptist minister in nearby Marion County in 1977. The Reverend S. L. Whatley, cutting firewood in the Ocala National Forest with a chain saw, noticed that a large creature had been watching him from behind palmetto trees. At first he thought it was a deer, but then the sixty-seven-year-old saw a dark-chocolate-colored face that had no hair and a flat nose, so he grabbed an axe from his pickup truck. The creature departed, knowing not to mess with God's messengers, but the brimstone-fuming preacher headed into the woods, stalking it to no avail. "Me and that creature was going to mix it up," he said.

The most horrifying bigfoot story took place in 1829. At the time, stories circulated around north Florida about a race of giants that lived on an enchanted island in the middle of the Okefenokee Swamp, the 438,000-acre, dense wetlands that stretch across Florida and south Georgia. These creatures were allegedly superhuman, beautiful—and ferocious. So, of course, hunters from Florida decided to go spoil the one possibly bewitching, peaceful spot in this swamp, joining a few Georgians in their quest to capture one of these giants.

The Okefenokee was not much different nearly two hundred years ago. Large alligators patrolled the waterways, poisonous snakes slithered everywhere, thick swarms of mosquitoes drove people crazy, large panthers prowled for meals, and quicksand could swallow a person whole. Native Americans avoided the island for good reason. But not these nine men, armed with rifles, pistols, and swords, traversing the swamps for two weeks before their fateful encounter with a giant.

As the hunters set up camp one afternoon, a large creature covered with hair walked toward them, according to stories published in the *Milledgeville Statesman*. The men sent a volley of gunfire at it. The enormous creature responded in kind, ripping and wringing the heads off five hunters. The terrified hunters kept firing at the shrieking, roaring creature until it finally fell to the ground, still snarling and lashing out as its life drained away. After it died, the dazed hunters measured the creature to be thirteen feet long. Fearing the commotion might attract other giants, the hunters gathered their remaining weapons, left the creature lying on their headless comrades, and fled the swamp. When they returned with reinforcements, the creature's body was gone.

Still, bigfoot is not the first thing on my mind as I stand in the middle of the Green Swamp, a preserve that stretches across five central Florida counties, a labyrinth of cypress domes, wetlands, and flatwood. Not ten yards from the edge of the thick, swampy woods encircling our camp, I am far more worried about other things that could kill me. Despite what the tourist bureau claims, Florida is not the tame fantasy world promoted by Disney World, Busch Gardens, and Universal Orlando. Fairy dust won't turn six-foot rattlers into addle-brained foils like Kaa in the *Jungle Book* nor fire ants into kindhearted inventors like Flik in *A Bug's*

Life. Here in the Green Swamp, life is far more dangerous. I know that from experience, having moved here as a teen in 1977. I've been stung by wasps, attacked by fire ants, bit by ticks and spiders, devoured by mosquitoes, stung by jellyfish, attacked in a canoe by a gator, followed by a black bear, and chased by a water moccasin. I also know that I probably have swum within ten to twenty feet of sharks off Florida's coastlines. (A biologist at the Miami Seaquarium once told me that every shark in their tank displays had been caught within thirty yards of shore.) I know the real Florida, the one that is really a paradise for bugs and lizards and feral hogs and reptiles. When it comes to wildlife, no state is deadlier than Florida. Let me count the ways: fire ants, mosquitoes, alligators, eastern diamondback rattlers, black bears, panthers, coral snakes, bull sharks, jellyfish, black widow spiders, water moccasins, wasps, crocodiles, pygmy rattlers, brown recluse spiders, wild boar, copperheads, scorpions, Burmese pythons. And ticks. No state has more attacks from fire ants, sharks, or snakes. Let's not forget Mother Nature, who is equally aggressive. Florida is the lightning capital of the United States, attracting by far the most strikes to ground, injuries (more than two thousand since 1959) and fatalities (nearly five hundred since 1959). About seven people die each year from lightning in the Sunshine State, accounting for about 15 percent of the total number of U.S. fatalities each year.

Less than fifty yards away from our campsite, feral hogs have torn up a pasture, the two-hundred-plus pound beasts using their broad snouts to dig for bugs and roots. The ground appears as though it had been plowed, clods of dirt piled everywhere. Wild boar can be aggressive, especially when they are near their young. And their populations are growing so rapidly that they are moving closer to suburban areas like St. Petersburg, where a wild boar chased a woman up a tree, using its long, curved tusks to rip into her legs. In Cherokee City, Texas, a large hog used its tusks to push a sport-utility vehicle onto its side, crushing and paralyzing a young man. My flimsy nylon tent sits perched along the tree line, a micron of material separating me from nature. (Micron = fancy way of saying one-*millionth* of a meter.) In other words, if these boars return, they could impale my wimpy two-person tent on their eight-inch tusks as easily as they'd rip through wet toilet paper.

These aggressive hogs are part of Hernando de Soto's legacy in North America. Not only did the Spanish explorer kidnap families, steal food reserves from villages, instigate fights with local tribes, and pass along European diseases like smallpox, measles and chicken pox, starting epidemics that wiped out the population of entire regions, he also left wild hogs to harass campers like me at night. I'm not far from where de Soto and his merry band of conquistadors made it all happen by traveling up from Tampa in 1539 along the Withlacoochee River, whose slow-moving black water lolls past us a few hundred yards away.

This area has been part of several wondrous historic moments. I am camped on a swamp's western edge, not far from Bushnell, where native Floridians ambushed and killed two companies of American soldiers in 1835, starting the Second Seminole War, a seven-year campaign that ended when the Indians disappeared into swamps like this one, areas American soldiers could not navigate (nor did they want to enter.) That's pretty much the mind-set today. Few people purposefully enter these swamps. Before the Spaniards arrived in the early 1500s, wetlands covered more than half the state. Eleven million acres remain, an area large enough to cover New Jersey, Connecticut, Delaware, and Rhode Island combined. Florida has more wetlands than any state in the continental United States, several of which are exceptionally large. The Everglades stretches for more than four thousand square miles across the southern portion of the state between the Atlantic Ocean and the Gulf of Mexico, an area nearly as large as

Connecticut. The Ocala National Forest, which spreads across the north central part of the state, covers 607 square miles, or 388,000 acres, while the Green Swamp covers roughly 560,000 acres across central Florida and is the source for four major rivers—the Withlacoochee, Hillsborough, Peace, and Ocklawaha. At roughly 875 square miles, the Green Swamp is more than half the size of Rhode Island. Most of the reported bigfoot encounters in Florida have taken place in and around these swampy, or heavily wooded, areas.

Several other slightly smaller wetland and forest preserves ring the Green Swamp—the 157,000-acre Withlacoochee State Forest to the northwest, the 31,000-acre Chassahowitzka National Wildlife Refuge to the east, and the 11,000 acre Flying Eagle Ranch to the northeast. Several hundred lakes are scattered around the area, especially in the northeast, where the preacher boys saw their demon. This area remains as unyielding, dense, and inaccessible as it was for Major Francis L. Dade and his troops nearly two hundred years ago—and as baffling as when it misdirected and confused Hernando de Soto five hundred years ago in his quest to find China, not realizing he was way, way off the mark unlike the mosquitoes that are dive-bombing me or the female midge-like no-see-ums that are biting me, sucking my blood, and leaving terribly itchy marks.

At 9:00 p.m. I'm still sweating profusely while sitting on a bench talking with investigators from the Stocking Hominid Research Group. Fire ants have chewed on my shins, my clothes are soaked, and somehow it's getting hotter. I understand why, in Florida, bigfoot are frequently pissed off—chasing people into their trailers, smacking cars, killing family pets, and even twisting the heads off hunters. Out here, I'm already getting pushed to the edge after a few hours.

Despite the heat, humidity, and voracious insects, the real Florida is also beautiful. The wetlands are far more magical than

Cinderella's Castle or Universal's Wizarding World of Harry Potter. The sea of tall grass that extends across the Everglades is as lovely as any prairie, and rivers like the Hillsborough or St. Johns can reveal an untarnished landscape and glimpses of manatees, bald eagles, stingrays, large Spanish oak, largemouth bass, and of course, gators. Actually, gators are far less aggressive than their cousins, crocodiles, a species that resides primarily in the Everglades — although do not test this theory by sidling up next to one along, say, a river deep in the Ocala National Forest (and far, far from paramedics who can sew an arm or leg back on), as one German couple did. Along Juniper Springs, my wife and I saw these Teutonic tourists canoe up to a twelve-plus footer sunning itself along the edge of the water, its body wider than the canoe. I told my wife to stop paddling and to enjoy the show, expecting the gator to thrash its tail and knock the boat over before taking them into a death roll below the surface. Instead, the gator did nothing. So the man patted it on its back with his paddle. Floridians loathe tourists. You can see why. Perhaps God had his thumb on the gator's back. Perhaps the gator had recently eaten a small deer and could not move. Either way, the gator just sat there. So the German tourists departed, prepared to perform some other moronic move down the river — say, kissing a water moccasin on the mouth or hand-feeding a black bear. Either way, Betsy and I felt cheated at first. Later, though, we saw a doe sip from the river, watched an eagle soar across skies so blue we had to squint, and felt a warm spring breeze in a savannah. Nobody is ever gypped when canoeing along Florida's waterways.

In Florida's wetlands, beauty and danger are everywhere. You can still find rookeries where thousands of snowy egrets, blue herons, and white ibis swirl through the air like glitter, performing mating dances during the spring and winter. The types of birds vary through the year, but the view is always splendid. Deep in the swamps, you can also gape at cypress that rise one hundred feet and grow several feet in diameter, roots rising out of the water like little knees. Careful where you step, though, because water moccasins also like these areas—as do large banana spiders, more creepy than dangerous. Unlike other species, mocs will chase you. Still, you may want to sit and imagine what this area looked like hundreds, or thousands, of years earlier, when that cypress was a sapling. The Senator, which sits in a swamp not far from Orlando, is thirty-five hundred years old, dating back to the height of the Egyptian Empire. Away from the cookie-cutter neighborhoods, you can find majestic scenes like this, both grand and tiny—anything from large slash pine forests that extend as far as the eye can see to a five-lined skink, a lizard that pretty much looks like a pygmy snake with legs, a creature that would have driven my mom to jump onto a dining room chair and scream. Brilliant yellow lines a chocolate body with a tail that might be a radiant blue. During mating season the heads and cheeks can turn a jaunty orange, detracting from narrow snake-like eyes. In Florida one must be able to see past the creepy to appreciate the beauty.

But I did not see the grandeur in wetlands in 1977 when I moved from New Jersey to Coral Springs, a city built on land essentially drained from an eastern edge of the Everglades. As an early teen, I remained in the car when we drove through the Everglades National Park and remained on the paved paths at the Monkey Jungle. At the Miami Serpentarium, the glass partition did not offer nearly enough protection, causing me to leap back when Bill Haast picked up venomous snakes, one after another. I was content to ride my bike to the levees near the edge of town and look out over the Everglades, enjoying the view even if I'd never dream of sloshing through the tall grass. At the time, only those dirt levees separated the Everglades from Coral Springs. I was captivated by the long stretches of nothingness—even on roads like Wiles, then a two-laner that few people used at the city's western edge. Occasionally I'd stop and walk along the wide canals, watching exceptionally large largemouth bass languishing in schools, flipping their gills every so often. Gar, which look like two-foot-long spears, would swim slowly through the grasses and plants, their long, narrow bodies tapering into an even thinner nose. The world's largest gar, weighing twenty-one pounds, would be caught a few miles from this area in 1981. Dragonflies would skim the surface. Gators lurked below the greenish water, sometimes floating to the top and looking more like logs wedged into tall weeds. Gators would also sun along the edge of the canals, frequently blending into the tall grass. That danger was part of the allure to a fourteen-year-old kid roaming the edge of nowhere. And that's exactly what it felt like in 1977. To the west, swamp extended to the horizon (and for more than one hundred miles across the state toward Naples). North, across the canals, tangled, dense woods seemed impenetrable, but it eventually opened into large pastures for cattle. Beyond this, though, sat the Loxahatchee National Wildlife Refuge, which covered more than two hundred square miles. Today, those levees and much of the wetlands have surrendered to housing subdivisions, golf courses, a commerce park, and a high school that literally sits along the edge of the Glades. A six-lane expressway runs through it all. For a city kid in 1977, though, this area seemed like it was in the middle of nowhere, almost like my private getaway. But I knew I'd never venture any deeper into this wetlands than standing along the canals and levees.

Or so I thought.

Because that's precisely what I am planning to do this weekend in 2009 — walk through swampy areas up to my waist, march through trees and growth that could stop a pickup truck, and — please, please, please — avoid large gators, poisonous snakes, aggressive wild boar and banana spiders.

Population growth is not yet a problem here in north central Florida, about an hour northeast of Tampa on the Green Swamp's west central edge. The closest expressway is Interstate 75, more than ten miles to the west. There is very little development. The closest town is Dade City, several miles from our camping area. With just over six thousand residents, Dade City is Pasco County's seat—and, by far, the largest town in the region. This area has not grown much since the 1940s, when the United States chose it to stow away German POWs captured from Rommel's Afrika Korps, hardened soldiers accustomed to harsh conditions. American leaders probably decided that not even battle-tested veterans would want to escape into the Green Swamp—or into scrub areas that are home to thousands of eastern diamondback rattlers. This area has hosted a rattlesnake roundup for six decades, where snakes are collected in large, filled tubs. Just the type of place you'd want to bring grandma and the kids—or dump anybody from Wall Street.

Donna Cohrs is eating Chunky soup from a can, scooping out vegetables with a plastic fork. There's no pretense about dinner out in the woods. She stands as she eats, her right foot on the bench of a concrete table comically out of place amid this wildness. This is definitely not your typical picnic scene. To the east sits a cattle pasture that stretches for acres. To the west the Green Swamp stretches for about thirty miles. The swamp partially envelopes our camping site on the north and south sides as well, leaving a tiny peninsula of sand, scrub, and anthills—hardly a place to head out for a relaxing weekend escape.

After the two-hour drive from DeLand, Donna is loath to sit any longer. More than anything, she is tired from pulling quadruple duty as a teacher's aide, a full-time student, a mom to her teenage son, and co-founder of the Stocking Hominid Research Group. Donna has deep-set green eyes that evince sadness. Or maybe that's me imaging her struggles the past several years, having endured an abusive husband, a subsequent divorce, and financial struggles. Working as a teacher's aide pays very little but she loves helping young children learn. So she takes classes at night and on weekends. After she completes her degree, she eventually hopes to teach elementary school. She also loves searching for bigfoot, clearly an escape from her troubles. About every four to five weeks, she says, she flees to the woods, searching, camping, relaxing.

Donna, though, belies her weary appearance. She smiles frequently, laughs heartily, and talks easily. And she also inserts herself into the middle of her humor, saying her curly red hair is as long and stringy as a bigfoot's. She is fairly thin. She clearly needs the meal, even if it is a small can of soup.

Donna and her twin sister, Diane Stocking, research in relative media obscurity—unlike controversial characters like Dave Shealy, who lives amid the Everglades in Ochopee. Among most bigfoot researchers, he is considered a scam artist who allegedly fakes photos, videos, and reports so tourists will come to his camping area to purchase t-shirts, copies of his "documentary," and other souvenirs. The media, though, love him because he is accessible and always willing to offer an interesting quote or story. For example, Shealy recently said a bigfoot, sprouting a rather prominent erection, walked toward two women tourists who were photographing wildflowers near his camp. Not sure if the women were terrified or intrigued, but they escaped, probably when the creature's brain got fuzzy from losing so much blood at once. One can only imagine the money bigfoot could make in the porn industry. "It was what I believe was the mating season," Dave told the local media, further cementing the idea that bigfoot researchers are batshit crazy. Like P. T. Barnum, Shealy apparently does not care what you say about him, so long as you spell the name of his tourist business correctly. But this infuriates researchers like Donna.

Reports like that have prompted Diane Stocking to become more skeptical. A year earlier she had moved to Washington, where she frequently worked to disprove reports in the prolific

Northwest. Donna admits she has far more faith in bigfoot than her sister does. Donna says she has felt the creature's presence several times. "I've had those feelings of fear and anxiety," she says, "but it's just letting you know it's not feeling comfortable." Donna says a bigfoot once followed her along a river near Cape Canaveral and that another bigfoot once threw rocks at her. "One large rock hit a pine tree right above my head. If he wanted to hurt me, he would have. They have no interest to harm us. Absolutely none." In addition, Donna claims to have viewed a young bigfoot so clearly she could see its muscle definition. Plus, Donna says, she has been zapped, although she hates that word. "Zapped is just the feeling associated with the fear and the weird feelings. My Aunt Pearl used to say, 'If you have a bad feeling about something, don't do it. It means something.'" Donna says she also watched a bigfoot for three and a half hours through a thermal in Alabama, partly from a tree she climbed to get a better look. "The creature stood up, hunched down, crouched, moved side to side. It got on all fours. I saw its long arms and short legs. It kept moving. Two others eventually came near him." Like many other researchers, Donna tries hard to retain some skepticism, but she is just too eager. She admits that. "If I hear something and I can't identify it, I'm more inclined to believe it was a bigfoot. My sister, though, would have to see the words coming straight out of one's mouth. To me, it's all so logical that they exist. It's so plausible with the footprints and other evidence."

Among her other beliefs: bigfoot's genus is *Homo* and not an ape . . . bigfoot are not migratory, as suggested by many other researchers; instead, they have a home range that can encompass hundreds of square miles. . . . bigfoot have no desire to hurt humans. . . . they live throughout the state, mostly along waterways and near large lakes. . . . and for every reported sighting, at least fifteen go unreported. That means about a thousand people have seen a Skunk Ape during the past forty years.

Donna spends far more time on the east coast of Florida, particularly along the St. Johns, the state's longest river, which stretches from near Vero Beach to Jacksonville, a rare waterway that lolls north for some reason — although Floridians will tell you it's because Georgia sucks. She has only recently started researching the Green Swamp. The Chunky soup can emptied, Donna tells a story about the time the Space Shuttle scared several bigfoot. At first I think she is telling a joke. Sitting in her nylon camping chair, Donna describes the encounter she had near Cape Canaveral, where several bigfoot growled at her, scaring her out of the woods. The sun has now fled, inviting mosquitoes to feast on us. At 8:00 p.m., I can barely see her face, but I can hear the words and the tone. Donna is not kidding.

The incident, Donna says, happened the previous winter in one of her favorite areas. As she walked near a heavily wooded part of the St. John's River, she and another researcher kept hearing heavy footsteps (or *bipedal* footsteps, in bigfoot research jargon). Not far from a creek, Donna saw a footprint in the mud that measured about thirteen inches by six inches, which would equate to an animal measuring seven feet tall. However, she could not see the prints as clearly as she would have liked. The moon, a waning crescent, did not illuminate much. In the woods, it was pitch-black. Her partner, Darren, had just walked ahead to leave half a cantaloupe on a tree stump in an attempt to lure a bigfoot closer. Fifteen minutes later they heard several heavy, loud bipedal footsteps that stopped about twenty yards away. Cool, Donna thought. "They had no problem letting us know they were there," she says. They also heard a soft step into the creek, a tributary of the St. Johns. Periodically they'd hear soft whoops and calls that sounded like owls. "Big, hairy ones," Donna says.

A little before nine o'clock, Donna watched a bright light shoot across the horizon to the north — a Delta IV rocket that had lifted off from Cape Canaveral Air Station carrying a new generation of military communications satellite to help battlefield troops. The four solid-fueled boosters lit up the night. Not eight miles away, the rocket looked as though it were riding a column of fire. Donna and Darren watched it disappear into the atmosphere. As far away as Orlando, people can hear the distinctive double sonic booms from rockets and shuttles. Just a few miles away, though, you can feel them roll across your body like a supercharged bass amp at a Guns N' Roses concert. Under Donna's feet, the ground vibrated for several seconds and the air thundered twice. That's when all hell broke loose. Donna and Darren heard a deep, rumbling growl. Then came a second growl from another direction. "At that point," Donna says, "we decided that was it. We were leaving." As they gathered their items, they heard a third growl emanating directly ahead, along the exit route. They each took a deep breath. And then they started walking out. A minute later they heard two more growls to their left, not ten feet away. Donna said the growls sounded as though they came from close to the ground. "I think they may have been on all fours," Donna says. She did not think a bigfoot followed them to the truck, though, because she never felt anxious, as she had on other expeditions. This time she felt relatively calm, considering the situation—that a large, hulking creature was pissed at her and ready to break her in half or, at best, that an angry back bear or Florida panther was ready to pounce. "I think they associated the sonic boom and the vibrations to us," she says. "I'm pretty sure that's why the first one started growling." That's one heck of a spatial odyssey.

Pat Rance has just finished using his Ford F-150 to back in his trailer, a storage unit converted into a high-tech camper filled with expensive electronic gadgets, a comfortable bed, and food supplies. He looks like a businessman, sounds like a good old boy, and acts like a southern gentleman. Pat could also easily pass for an army officer. His brown hair is cropped around his ears, his moustache trimmed. He looks like a conditioned soldier (and more than a little like the NFL coach Jeff Fisher). Pat also has a deep voice, akin to actor Sam Elliott's. Pat is six feet tall, with broad shoulders, strong forearms, and thick legs. He looks great, even though he had a mild heart attack a few months earlier. Pat speaks clearly and intelligently, his humor more laconic than backslapping. In reality, Pat is an engineer for a firm just north of Orlando, in Longwood, which happens to border my former home in Altamonte Springs. He's also a father, having raised his teen daughter since a divorce more than ten years earlier. Before the marital breakup, Pat would spend most weekends hunting and fishing in the Ocala National Forest and other wildlife areas across central Florida. After the estrangement, he sold his guns, boat, and fishing gear and stayed home with his two-year-old daughter. As his daughter got older, Pat started looking for a new hobby. He missed the outdoors. At the same time, he started reading about bigfoot, creatures that allegedly roamed through Florida. As a hunter, Pat had occasionally seen an odd footprint, but he always had a reasonable explanation, if he thought about it at all. The more he read about Florida's Skunk Ape, the more Pat wondered. So he started to explore the woods to find out for himself.

Pat loves to hike, taking all-day trips through remote areas. Sometimes he'd spend the night. Pat started seeing more of the odd footprints, including fresh ones early in the morning. Who would walk out here in the middle of the night faking prints, he wondered, in the off chance that someone might find them on a trail that was rarely used? At other times, Pat would hike into an area for a day's visit. On the way out four to six hours later, he'd find tracks unlike anything he'd seen as a hunter. The prints revealed swirls and ridges on the feet, dermal ridges found only in primates. The tracks were also wider than a human's and not as round as a bear's. Why, Pat tried to understand, would someone create false footprints in the middle of nowhere? It's very quiet in the Florida wild. "You can hear cars," Pat said. "You know if anybody's out there." Once Pat found a place where something leaped more than twenty feet over a road. You can't fake that, Pat thought. He knew he'd have to investigate further.

Not long afterward, Pat had his first encounter, not far from where we're now sitting. The experience lasted fewer than ten seconds. But it was enough. Pat had pitched an empty tent along a smaller trail, frustrated that he could not catch anything on his thermal camera at night or visually by day even though he would find numerous footprints around his campsite each morning. By the empty tent, Pat placed open peanut butter jars, apples, and pancakes—a far healthier meal than most bigfoot researchers usually eat. Inside the tent, Pat placed a camcorder on a tripod and aimed it out of the opening. On the third day, something visited the faux campsite, eating the pancakes and apples and taking the peanut butter jar. Only the jar's lid and two of the ten apples, inexplicably smashed, remained near the tent. But he did not get any video, so Pat packed the tent and started carting it back to his main camping area. On the way back, Pat said he saw something standing on the trail about twenty-five feet ahead. "I think that guy was trailing us," Pat said. Caught off guard, it leaped into a stand of palmetto and thick brush along the edge of the trail, where it remained, watching Pat. At midnight enough light remained that Pat could see an outline—shoulders about eighteen inches wider than Pat's own on an immensely large body covered with brown, shaggy hair. When Pat raised his night-vision goggles, the creature bolted, breathing heavy and sounding like "choo, choo, choo" as it departed. Later he measured its size by comparing it to some trees nearby, determining it was around seven feet, six inches tall. Everything happened so quickly, Pat did not have a chance to get scared. Afterward Pat was impressed by its size, saying the creature was as "imposing as hell" and certainly large enough to kill him rather easily. From that moment Pat lost any fear of being attacked, knowing this impressive creature had run away when it had an opportunity to strike.

"I smelled him. I saw him. I heard him thump away." Pat paused, considering the moment for probably the thousandth time. "That made it real for me. It was like, 'Holy shit, they are real for sure.' It was only about ten seconds, but it was enough to know."

As he walked past the spot where it had stood behind the palmetto, Pat smelled the maple syrup from the pancakes, a pungent scent in the middle of the woods. "He must have had it all over his ass, his hands and face. It was pretty cool."

Now Pat spends many weekends looking for more evidence in Florida, Alabama, Texas, Oklahoma, and Mississippi. He's been interviewed on countless paranormal radio and Blog Talk Radio shows, where he talks about his other adventures, including one that seems too bizarre to believe.

Carolanne Solomon knows this swamp better than anybody, sometimes walking through the roughest parts of this area alone in the same manner some people stroll around a city park, unworried that a gator or python or panther could strike in an area where nobody would likely find her for weeks or months. Did I mention that Carolanne is crazy? That's what I told her. Even my wife agrees, chuckling when I tell her that Carolanne, who is only five feet seven and 120 pounds, walks alone, creating trails through heavy woods. Betsy used to be an environmental biologist for the St. Johns River Water Management District, collecting alligator eggs from nests and wading through water up to her armpits past moccasins coiled on lily pads to check on grasses planted in a lake. So Betsy knows crazy.

Some would say that Carolanne is bonkers for another reason. She says bigfoot visited her regularly as a child, peering in the window of her bedroom in Citrus Park, a small town on the northern edge of Tampa that was far more remote in the 1970s, when it was surrounded by woods, swamps, cattle ranches, dairy farms, and orange groves—the type of backwoods, off-the-beaten-path, secluded area where bigfoot are typically sighted. That, of course, is what happened, she says. Cattle mysteriously died, their little bovine eyes bulging and their internal organs ripped out, something that confounded ranchers and county deputies alike. Milo Thomas, who owned the largest ranch in the area on what is now West Chase, used to talk about a creature that could kill a full-grown bull. More frequently, he would find calves and deer with snapped necks and broken legs, missing their hearts, livers, and tongues, which had been yanked out. Today more than eleven thousand people reside in this area just north of Tampa. Back then this area was mostly tangled brush, trees, swamps, and grasslands. A few miles away from Thomas's ranch, Carolanne tried to sleep in her grandmother's trailer, each night worried that her own organs would be torn away—or worse, if that's possible. Carolanne took shallower breaths when The Thing, or It, came to her bedroom window. In a white trailer set under a canopy of magnolia oaks, nine-year-old Carolanne slept fitfully most nights, deathly scared of the monster that stood outside the opened double slats, taking deep, raspy, guttural breaths as it peered in on her. She wished dearly for air-conditioning and closed windows. On her worst nights, Carolanne would see its ape-like head partially wedged through the window slats, trying to get a closer look at her. On those nights she'd scream so loudly that her grandma would sprint down the hallway. But Grandma Bessie, a tough Cherokee woman, never believed Carolanne, convinced her granddaughter's outbursts had been cultivated by an overactive imagination. Carolanne told a few kids about The Thing outside her window, but, of course, they made fun of her. So she learned to keep her mouth shut and endure these frequent nightly visits. At times, though, Carolanne could not help noticing that The Thing's eyes had a gentleness to them and that its face looked human. Or maybe that is the adult trying to temper childish nightmares.

"Looking back and reliving it," Carolanne said, "I don't see or feel that it was trying to hurt me. And I'm not sure about it trying to communicate, but maybe just trying to get a better look at me or maybe being overly curious."

By age twelve, Carolanne had finally moved into a bedroom at the front of the trailer where her window was blocked by a storage shed. She slept much easier. That did not stop the dogs from barking wildly at times or her grandmother from grabbing her gun and firing it to protect her dogs, finally realizing something odd lurked around their home.

Eventually these moments faded. Carolanne went to school, graduated, took a job as a secretary at the Police Benevolent Association, and then stayed home to raise her three boys. She was never afraid to wander outside. When her longtime companion, Charles, would fish for bass in a local state park, Carolanne would instead walk through the back of the remote park, occasionally sitting and enjoying the woods. But she never saw anything unusual.

She stumbled across information about bigfoot a few years later when she bought her first computer. Searching for ghost stories to read, she located a website that featured paranormal stories. There she read a great deal about other people's bigfoot encounters. Maybe, she thought, The Thing was a bigfoot, too. From that point, she was hooked, reading as much as she could online, contacting researchers, and speaking with law enforcement officers she had met when she worked for the Police Benevolent Association. Two years later, a park ranger shared a bigfoot report with her, prompting her to start walking the woods in search of information.

Unlike many others, including me, Carolanne does not need proof that bigfoot exist. Instead, she wants to get information that can help others who have encountered a bigfoot through what she calls "mind- and life-altering experiences." "Last," Carolanne said, "and I mean last, would be proving their existence. With that said, if I am out in the field and I come up on the opportunity to get a clear, indisputable camera shot, video, or dead body, then yes, I will do it."

Carolanne wears a black tank top, camouflage pants that extend just beyond the knee, sort of like capris, and cowboy boots. During the day, she wears black wraparound sunglasses. Charles, her partner, wears a t-shirt. It's going to be ninety-plus degrees today, but we're all wearing jeans, knowing we'll be walking through tree branches, tall grasses, and vines that scrape and cut, as well as among innumerable spiders, ticks, and other bugs. Pat and Donna wear boots, protecting them from potential snake attacks. I'm wearing beat-up Asics.

We've just driven for more than an hour over nearly impassable dirt paths whose ruts make it feel as though we are hitting interminable speed bumps and potholes that have filled with more than a foot of water. Pat's truck got caught in one, its tires depressed so deeply into mud that we had to use Charles's truck to tow it out, no small feat when the truck doors opened directly into palmetto leaves that lacerated exposed skin and deep, thick mud that caught our feet. Water drains poorly from this flat terrain. A raised layer of porous limestone that sits just under the surface, at a higher level than anywhere else in the area, creates a water tank of sorts, so water remains close to the surface at all times. The Green Swamp's ability to store surface water, slowing the flow of floodwaters, has enabled it to sustain several of the state's larger rivers—the Hillsborough, Withlacoochee, Little Withlacoochee, Ocklawaha, and Peace—nearly four hundred miles of waterways and a major source of water for residents along the state's west coast.

A half mile back, we had parked the trucks near a gate,

something that seems as necessary as a gas station out here. Not sure why we need fences or gates deep in the woods. The land is further divided with barbed wire that separates federal from state preserves, slicing through the woods, rusting and blending into the roots and branches around it — a perfect scenario for getting gashed and developing tetanus. Backpacks on, we stand near power lines that cross through the woods, roll over a slight hill, and disappear from sight. That's where Pat believes we ought to look, on higher ground away from the flooded gullies, ditches, and pathways. More than ten inches had fallen on Tampa during July, about three inches above normal. The night before some other researchers had set up camp nearby, having heard about our expedition. Carolanne does not want them finding her primary research area. So to avoid them we walk into the woods on our right, trying to follow a firebreak that leads to larger wetlands. We crunch through dry fennels and tall grasses, slosh in shin-deep water, duck under low-lying branches, and hope like hell we do not step on an eastern diamondback, stumble across a gator, or walk into one of the numerous banana spiderwebs. It's noon, sun's blazing. In jeans, I am sweating profusely, which doesn't take much effort on cooler days.

Carolanne spots some tracks in the mud.

"Looks like a cat," Pat says.

"Like a bobcat following a deer," Carolanne says.

Carolanne hears a whistle, but nobody else does.

We do not hear or see much, besides a large banana spider hanging from a tree near Carolanne's head. It is typical for a female golden silk orb weaver to sit looking straight down from a web that stretches several feet across branches or between trees. I leap back. Carolanne laughs, but she hates them as well, even though these arachnids are more creepy than dangerous. A bite from *Nephila clavipes* will typically cause redness, maybe blisters, and some local pain, less than from a bee sting. But they look sinister, especially females, which can grow to three inches in diameter, most of it long, brown-and-orange spiny legs extending from a slender, cylindrical abdomen. Males, meanwhile, grow to about one-half inch.

While banana spiders are most visible, spiders live everywhere in the Green Swamp, but their webs are usually too small to see. An estimated one million spiders reside in each acre of this swamp, says Dr. G. B. Edwards, a taxonomic entomologist and curator for the Florida State Collection of Arthropods. That's far more spiders than reside in the country's southwestern deserts, where one-tenth this total live; however, this is about half as many as live in a British meadow that was recently studied by scientists. Edwards, sometimes called Your Friendly Neighborhood Spiderman, says spiders outweigh humans in England. That is certainly the case here in the swamp, where about 560 billion spiders reside, compared to a few roving lunatics.

We can never escape spiders, Edwards says. My backyard in Illinois, he told me, probably has more than one hundred thousand per acre. "I'm still amazed at the number of spiders in a small area," he said way too eagerly. "It's amazing what we fail to see in even our own backyards."

We haven't discerned any evidence of bigfoot out here, though. We're wandering, talking about bigfoot, cracking jokes, and sweating profusely until Carolanne decides to head back for some snacks. Like me, she is starved, but we are more than forty minutes into the trail. She says she'll grab some crackers and catch up to us down the firebreak.

Pat volunteers to head back with her, which aggravates Carolanne.

"I did this for, what, umpteen years until heading out with others," she says indignantly. "This is no big deal."

"I just don't want anybody going back by themselves," Pat says.

Irritated, Carolanne says, "You don't think I'm capable?"

"No, no, no, no."

"I caught that. No, I caught that."

Donna laughs.

"I caught that," Carolanne says. "He's saying the poor little woman is going back alone. . . . So what do you want to do?"

"You're not leaving us out here," Pat says, smiling. "We're not capable. We're following you."

Carolanne softens at this humorous reversal. "I'm more man . . . than you think I am."

This has given Pat an excuse to head back. Neither he nor Donna believes they will discern evidence or glimpse anything in this location. Besides, they're pretty tired from a hectic week.

Back at the truck, Pat asks, "So, did you have a good time?"

"I always like adventures."

"Me, too," Pat says. "We'll see what happens tonight."

Pat Rance says this story is completely true—even if he sounds psychotic. Pat makes no apologies for the story, telling it as easily as one about a family picnic. But, brother, it sounds delusional. Pat and another researcher in Oklahoma called Old Crow were sitting by their campsite late at night, preferring to draw something in than to traipse through the woods. At first, he and Old Crow saw eye shine. Then they saw something emerge into the clearing—an eight-foot-tall creature standing about twenty feet away. They tried to make contact, waving and talking, saying they did not want to do the bigfoot any harm, that they wanted to be friends, perhaps even visit with it, but Pat and Old Crow did not get a reaction from the creature. Several minutes later, four other bigfoot appeared behind the larger one, the smallest one being about three and a half feet tall with eyes that shone both white and mint-green. The biggest one's eyes shone bright red. "He came, at first, to determine, I guess, if it was cool," Pat said. "Or safe. Or if we meant any harm. Then the rest came in behind and around him. And we saw the others moving around; it's not like they stood like statues. They were checking us out and we were checking them out."

At times Pat and Old Crow turned and spoke to one another, thinking this would put them at ease. This all lasted for about an hour. Said Pat, "The longest danged time." Then Pat and Old Crow suddenly felt uncomfortable, as if a light switch of emotions had been flipped.

Said Old Crow, "Did you feel that?"

"Yeah."

"I think they're telling us it's time to go."

With that, Old Crow slowly walked over to her truck, grabbed two blankets, and got in. Pat then stood up, waved to them, turned, and walked to the truck, which he also entered before they drove toward a barn and fell asleep.

"I think they wanted to scrounge for food," Pat said, "and we were in their way."

As I have stated, Pat appears as sensible as most anyone I have met. I'm not sure what scared me the most—that Pat really saw several exceptionally large creatures that reside in woods like the ones around us or that I was spending the weekend with a madman who carried a gun. Not sure how well I would sleep either way.

State wildlife officers are driving down the dirt roads, seeking poachers who shoot deer at night. Hunters say the deer population has dropped significantly, blaming poachers more than hunters. In season, hunters seem as thick as spiders. Carolanne says most of the deer probably move through the barbed wire to the national tract to avoid hunters during the season. We can see headlights reflecting through the trees in the distance and hear a truck's engine rumble, but they never come down our side road. Apparently the rangers had been parked along the only road into this area on the northwest side of the park, but we had snuck down the road before dark, before they posted themselves. Charles heard the news from the other researchers. We parked behind a strand of trees, about thirty yards from the Withlacoochee, sometimes called the Crooked River because it flows in several directions—west, then north, then northwest, and finally west before it empties into the Gulf of Mexico south of Cedar Key, in Yankeetown. Cypress and live oak line the river, which is about thirty yards wide at this juncture, a bend that scoops close to our shore and then flows languidly west under branches that line the shore, forming a canopy across its edges. Spanish moss hangs like a beard from the oak's thick, Medusa-like branches that sprout very low from the trunk and create a natural jungle gym.

Gators grow large in this area. At night, gators like to wander along shore, looking for food. The sign at the entrance said, "BEWARE LARGE ALLIGATORS IN THE AREA!" (In a bizarre twist, the signage then asks that campers report anyone seen harassing these behemoths.) We are not heeding that silly advice. Instead, we have placed chairs about twenty-five yards from the Withlacoochee's edge, next to a thermal camera and a large electronic ear. In addition, most everybody in our group has night vision. Soon we are sitting in the dark, staring at the dim outline of the river, vaguely illuminated under a crescent moon.

This is much more comfortable than the excursion earlier in the day. I'm sitting in a chair, relaxing between Pat and Donna. Carolanne and Charles are off to the left, a few feet away, looking into thermal cameras.

"So," I ask Donna, "this is one of the best ways to research?"

"We just let them come to us," she says.

"We go to different areas and maybe hang out awhile and do a few calls and see if they can get interested," Pat says. "I've had the best luck hanging out at a campsite, where I do a couple of calls, sit back and pretend like we're doing camping."

So, I ask, why do people even head out into the woods? What's the advantage?

"There isn't one," Donna says.

There isn't one?

Donna: "Nope."

"I don't think so," Pat says.

"They know you're here," Donna says.

"If they're around, they already know you're here," Pat says. "You're not going to track them down. You're not going to outrun them. You're not going to out-hide them. If one's hiding, you're never going to see it or smell it or know it's there unless it screws up or wants you to know it's there. It just seems it's a whole lot easier to make yourself available. Let 'em creep in close and take a look. They're curious. Let their curiosity work. Give 'em something interesting to look at."

"You don't need to go crashing off in the woods," says Donna.

"Because then you become a hunter," Pat says.

"Yeah," Donna says, "and then they're gonna avoid you."

"Now you're being aggressive," Pat says. "You're in stealth mode because you're trying to creep around. And you're not going to out-stealth them. No way in heck."

"I've been out with people in Pennsylvania," Donna says, "and we were up one night when something threw something at us. And these guys go hauling ass into the woods, flashing lights and everything else."

"That's what Dave and John do," Pat says. "They run around all night in four-wheelers just tearing up the woods."

"You're not going to see anything that way."

"You're not even going to see a coyote," Pat says. "You know, you won't even see a deer. Animals hear you coming."

"They not going to let you see them," Donna says, "Unless they *want* to let you see them. They're not going to come close."

"Anytime I've had interactions or had activity, it's been because we were hanging at the campsite. Made a few calls. Let 'em know we were there."

"Just sitting there," Donna says.

Says Pat, "Every time."

That's how he saw that bigfoot the first time, by just walking quietly at night between the fake campsite with the camera and his own in the dark. He walked to the second site, replaced a tape cartridge, and turned back to his primary camp within thirty seconds, surprising it. "We almost ran into him. He was going toward us. I was going toward him. I think we both, all of a sudden, said 'Oh, shit.'"

Carolanne keeps hearing something with the electronic ear that sounds like bipedal footsteps rustling in the woods off to our left, but none of us can confirm these sounds. She speaks softly: "The feeling I'm getting is we're not alone. But I don't know what it is yet." As always, I don't hear, or feel, anything. "Something keeps telling me—over there, in that direction." We look furtively, trying not to turn our heads.

Pat believes he saw eyes shine about seven or eight feet off the ground across the river. Donna says she saw what looked like another pair along a different part of the river.

Be yourselves, Pat reminds us. If we hear anything, tone down the conversations but do not react—as hard as that may be. Try to ignore them. If they believe they're sneaking up, Carolanne says, they might try things, which does not give me comfort. Patience is the key, Carolanne repeats, and doing the same thing every time you research an area. Create a routine. In time, she says, they may start to recognize you—your smells, your actions, your voice, your tracks. "I think they can tell. I usually talk to them, saying, 'Hey, it's safe. Come on in.'" Carolanne is excited to learn anything during an encounter—hearing a tree knock or a vocalization, noticing how close they get, or seeing a footprint—that could lead to further understanding. "When you get them in a closed environment, anything you get is golden. It's like when Pat saw one swaying back and forth. Well, who would have thought?'

But nothing gets closer so we lapse into more storytelling. They talk about other researchers—"Like the Loren Colemans," Carolanne says. "I don't take too much stock in them because, it's like—"

"—he never leaves his house," Pat finishes.

"Right," Carolanne continues. "What are they doing to get out here and to do this research on their own? They're not. They're taking everybody else's—and look at how famous they are. That's not fair. And everybody looks at him like he's a god."

Donna talks about the Honey Island incident, where a hunter allegedly shot a bigfoot in the Louisiana bayou but could not carry it out for fear other local bigfoot would attack. The bigfoot screamed loudly after getting shot through the stomach, loud enough to attract others, but the hunter found it first, curled up in a ball near a tree, so he shot it through the back of the head. That's when three more came running toward him from several directions, having heard the piercing screams. The hunter, terrified, ran off. Of course, the next day the body was gone and DNA evidence revealed human tissue, so the hunter did not go to the authorities, fearing reprisals for a murder. Later, tribal elders counseled this Native American not to speak about bigfoot, a topic that is taboo among most tribes. So all that's left, as usual, are stories like this that sound more like myth than truth.

Still, Carolanne says the rangers here know there's something out here that could potentially be dangerous. Apparently the rangers inadvertently took a picture of one during a research project where they had used game cameras to calculate the number of feral hogs in the area. If the hog population grows too large, the rangers start killing some, or they create a lottery for an abbreviated hunting season. A few days after collecting the cameras, the rangers popped the pictures onto the computer, briefly looking through them. As they flipped through the photos, a ranger described one image as a black bear and moved on. The second ranger asked, "How big is it?" So they rewound and looked more closely. "That bear can't be that big," the second ranger said, estimating it to be seven feet tall. And the eye shine looked different, they both realized, not the red refraction from bears. After a while, they understood what they were viewing.

At a party months later, a ranger whom Carolanne knew confided in her. He used to look at her at social gatherings and shake his head, smirking at her exploits. At this event, though, he looked at her differently. Carolanne tried cutting him off: "Yeah, I know. You think we're crazy because of the bigfoot thing."

He took Carolanne aside. "Stop it," he said quietly. "You're not crazy." He then recounted how they found one on their game cameras. "We've got one here."

Carolanne said, matter-of-factly, "I know you've got one here. That's why I'm here on the stupid trip, because I've wanted to get in the back of Cole Creek for a long time."

Like other rangers, this one refused to say anything on the record. The National Park Service had always discouraged rangers from talking about bigfoot publicly. "I hate to do this, but if you ever call me on this in front of other people I will deny it. I want my pension when I retire."

Just two months earlier, though, the U.S. Fish and Wildlife Service had invited the nationally known wildlife educator Larry Battson to speak to its rangers about bigfoot at the U.S. Fish and Wildlife National Conservation Training Center in Shepherdstown, West Virginia. The next day the session, entitled "Cryptozoology: Bigfoot — Myth or Reality?," was broadcast on all Department of the Interior and U.S. Fish and Wildlife Service television feeds, reaching tens of thousands of people around the country. But this did not seem to change policy or philosophy because the rangers still refuse to talk about such things publicly. And tonight they have already turned back the other bigfoot group, telling them, "I know you're out here bigfooting. Tell the others to get back in their trucks and return." That's why they just called Charles, relaying this warning. But the rangers were more concerned with poachers so we never saw them.

Pat says another ranger disclosed that he had heard some monkey chatter more than twenty years ago. But that did not prevent this ranger from denying Pat an unlimited permit to search a closed-off area. "They do not want people converging on this area, spoiling it, and killing protected animals," Pat says. People already poach deer, tortoise, bear, and eagles. "Imagine," he says, "if the wildlife service admitted bigfoot also resided here? They'd try to poach them as well, forcing the bigfoot to go farther into the swamp or to depart for another part of the state." He adds, "These guys are smart enough and mobile enough and fast enough to pick up and leave. You can't tell me that bigfoot didn't once live where Disney is now."

By 10:30 p.m., Carolanne has lost that feeling and eyes are no longer shining at us from across the river. So we head back to camp.

Before she left for the night, Carolanne decided to make a few calls into the woods around our campsite. I'd heard several other researchers vocalize like this during past expeditions, but, at best, we'd hear a faint owl-like call in return. I did not anticipate what happened next. Nor did I expect to make the same mistake hundreds of others have made, leaving my recording equipment turned off back by my tent, about fifty yards away.

We were on the east side of our camp, on flat, cleared area. In daylight we would have been facing live oak, slash pine, saw palmetto, sand pine, and snags of dead trees packed tightly together. Spanish moss, hanging thick off branches, further obscured our sight, while tangly, prickly brier vines and tall grasses filled in the background, making it difficult to see far into the woods.

On a map, though, you'd find that there's nothing but woods and swamps for the next twenty miles. This is part of the area where we searched earlier that day.

At night the area was dense and dark. Translation: don't step into the darkness. As I said, I've watched enough horror movies like *Halloween*, along with most of the series *I Shouldn't Be Alive*, where people suffer from attacks by crocodiles, alligators, bears, and hippos. I was not about to become a protagonist on a future episode, so I remained about ten yards from the tree line, right next to Carolanne, who had just unleashed her first squatch call. It sounded, at first, like a languorous note from a flute, fluttering at times and rising before changing into a mix of chattering and caws. The call conjured goose bumps on my sweaty arms. In the distance we heard what sounded like a barred owl. A few minutes later Carolanne unleashed another call while Charles, Pat, Donna, and I listened.

After a few minutes the owlish calls increased both in volume and in number, as if several owls were talking to one another. Then we started hearing chattering, as if a monkey had chimed in. Within minutes the calls seemed angrier, as if several monkeys or owls, or both, were yelling at each other, all while they were moving closer toward us. Then the calls increased in volume as if the full army on *Planet of the Apes* were charging toward us. Within a few more minutes the calls seemed even more aggressive in tone, much higher in pitch, and growlier, until they seemed to emanate from a few feet inside the tree line, where they reached a fever pitch for several minutes. I did not know what to do, so I backed up a few paces, peered harder into the darkness (as if that would make a difference), and listened. Then it all ended as quickly as it had started.

What. The. Fuck. Carolanne chuckled. But that's all I could say. I could not explain this chattering, nor was I certain something was not staring directly at me from the briers and trees before us.

I was both terrified and mesmerized, both wanting the sounds to stop and wanting something to walk out of the woods and look at us with blazing orange eyes. Adrenaline coursed through me. I was addicted. I wanted more. But nothing else spoke or uttered or chattered or hooted or even broke a twig for several more minutes. Eventually we retreated slowly to our campsite and tried to make sense of what had happened. Carolanne said she believed the owls were definitely of the four- to eight-hundred pound variety. She later spoke with some wildlife officers who had studied owls, and they said these calls did not sound like any owls. I was angry that I had not used my recorder to tape them, authenticating them myself. Did I believe I had finally faced bigfoot? Later that night my bladder seemed filled beyond capacity, but I held it until daylight. I might feel safe with a few others beside me, even with something right in front of me, but I still hated the idea of being spooked by, say, something bent over and looking into the tent when I unzipped it or the feeling of a hairy paw on my shoulder as I urinated into the woods. There are some things far worse than an overly stretched organ.

Did we hear bigfoot that night? As always, I question what I've encountered. A year later, Carolanne tells me she feels the same way:

"Over the years I have questioned myself on whether I actually saw what I saw, through analyzing and reanalyzing those nights, and how even as a kid I seemed to be very level-headed when it came to stuff. I do believe that I did see one. I don't know if I would call it faith or what, but if I hadn't seen it then I do think my mind would still be open to the possibility of them existing. But I would be skeptical. I know some people who have so much faith in their religion that they are not scared to die. I know some who they have so much faith in a person that if that person said they had just seen a pig fly, they would believe them — no questions asked. My grandmother, aunt, and mother have, and had, such a peaceful feeling when it came to dying, but I don't have that feeling and I can't understand how they did and do. I guess it's their faith. I was taught that God and Jesus exist, and I pray, but I do, at times, wonder if it's true or is it all just something that was made up eons ago."

I'm learning, the search for bigfoot requires a skeptical mind, one that is sharpened by reflection, inquiry, and interrogation. While one may be a doubter, agnosticism dulls the intellect. While one may have faith, ideologies limit vision. To learn the truth, neither extreme is helpful. And the best we can ask for, in the end, is to think more deeply than we did before, to have faith that something exists beyond ourselves. That is the ultimate mystery that keeps us searching for the truth.

5 NORTHERN WISCONSIN

Looking out over the bog, I wonder, Would I have pulled the trigger if I had a bigfoot in the crosshairs of a high-powered rifle? We're standing by the spot where Don Young says he faced that exact dilemma here in northern Wisconsin. This is the same Don Young who had been scared out of the woods a few years earlier after bigfoot had allegedly eaten some family cats, had nearly broken the back of his dog, and had chased Don up a tree. It's late morning on Labor Day 2009. The sky is blue, the temperature is cool enough to require jeans. Leaves on trees have already started to turn vibrant red and gold, about a month ahead of central Illinois. A few weeks later, this area would endure a hard frost. We're about an hour from Lake Superior, farther north than I have ever traveled. We're also about an hour from a sizable city. Wausau, eight-five miles away, is the largest city in northern Wisconsin with about thirty-eight thousand residents. Eau Claire, with sixty-two thousand residents, is 114 miles away to the west. Just north of Wassau, U.S. 51 just sort of ends, dropping from six lanes to two and looking more like a rural county road than the northern tip of a 1,286-mile road that started in New Orleans. This region is filled with tiny towns like Phillips, whose population is about 1,700, Lac du Flambeau (3,004), Butternut (407), Prentice (509), and Catawba (149). You'll find far more wildlife than people in northern Wisconsin and far, far more hardwood forests and wetlands than driveways and drive-thrus. To the north, the Chequamegon-Nicolet National Forest covers 1.5 million acres inhabited by hundreds of black beer and tens of thousands of deer—or about twenty-four deer per square mile. The Northern Highland American Legion State Forest and Ottawa National Forest cover about another five hundred thousand acres in the north and east. Several other state parks and recreation areas add more than one hundred thousand acres of protected woods. Outside the parks, a great deal of the area remains unspoiled and wild.

One can get easily get lost in northern Wisconsin. That's why it was a favorite refuge for gangsters in the 1920s and '30s. Al Capone hid away near Couderay, about an hour's drive west, while John Dillinger and Baby Face Nelson holed up in Manitowish Waters, an hour's drive northeast. If you want to get lost, come to northern Wisconsin. Clearly, bigfoot got the message. Unlike Capone and Baby Face, bigfoot are not as well known in the area. An ecologist for the state's Department of Natural Resources dismissed Don's bigfoot sighting, telling me he had never heard of any reports. "Interesting," he said. "Being the heart of northern Wisconsin, though, I'm guessing the observer saw Paul Bunyan, and not a bigfoot."

Several years earlier, that was Don Young's perspective—that it was far more likely someone would see the folkloric lumberjack than a mythical beast. That was before Don wandered across bigfoot twice in a year. That was before he reported these sightings to the Bigfoot Field Researchers Organization. That was before people started snickering when he walked by. That was before he lost clients for his field guide service. And that was before people started calling his wife Mrs. Sasquatch. That was before. Some might say that was also before Donnie lost his freaking mind. That's why Don's pupils dilated when he saw the animal through his rifle's scope that morning in this sedge meadow. Don had a chance to reveal that he was not a lunatic, that he had not eaten one too many acorns. Yes, Don imagined, he would shoot a hole through the friggin' animal if he had the chance. About 150 yards away, it stood up in the marsh, its back a large target. An expert marksman, Don had few worries he could hit the animal. At first Don had believed the silhouette to be a black bear standing on its legs in order to look across the waist-high muskeg and tag alder packed densely in the sedge meadow. Like most sedge meadows, this wetland graded into a bog area filled with sphagnum moss that absorbs fifty to twenty times its own weight. Anything that walked into the meadow sunk its feet down into that spongy soil. Don would have sunk at least to his knees, submerging him from view at the fence. Deer would also not be discernible. At best, Don might be able to view the humped back of a large black bear if it were walking on all four legs. Yet Don could see below the waist of the creature standing out in the meadow. So he knew this animal had to be at least eight feet tall.

Don leaned against a wood fence, one rail now collapsed, and looked through a scope that magnified the animal by a factor of nine, allowing him to visually close in to about fifteen to twenty yards. The sun was bright. The meadow was clear. Nothing impeded Don's view of the animal. Don tells me he clearly saw a lengthy black stripe that ran down its back, under long, bristly hair. The animal's entire body had a brindle pattern, sort of like a tiger's. On its back, darker streaks flowed across lighter-brown hair, although the markings were more muted than those on a tiger. Don could discern neither ears nor a pointed head, unlike the bigfoot in the Patterson film. Through the scope, he also noticed hair was absent under the arms, on the inside of the legs, and in the stomach area. Don breathed deeply, fascinated by what he saw. The creature kept looking away, east toward some balsam fir whose thick branches looked like church steeples. That gave Don the opportunity he had considered for a while. From the neck down, Don was secluded behind the fence. Several bushes and a stand of balsam fir and black spruce surrounded him, providing additional cover. Don lay there watching and wondering. He knew he could hit the creature wherever he wanted. But what if the bullet did not hit the proper organs? Or what if another bigfoot lay out there? Deer regularly used the area for shelter. Don could probably flush out at least half a dozen deer at that moment, if he desired. Or what if this were another hoaxer, like the one he had caught in a military ghillie suit a few months earlier? At the time, Don had nearly shot that foolish man traipsing through the woods during deer-hunting season. Don certainly did not want to be arrested for murder. Many researchers say shooting a bigfoot is murder, but that was not a concern of Don's at the time. Unlike those other bleeding-heart bigfoot investigators, Don wanted a body—the only thing, he knew, that could prove that he is not crazy. Shooting a bigfoot is not a crime anywhere, except in Skamania County, Washington, where they have been protected since 1969. The ordinance passed by the county board set a $10,000 fine and five years' imprisonment as penalty for shooting a bigfoot, something bigfoot enthusiasts cite as evidence that the animal exists. But these same folks fail to cite the irony of Ordinance 69-01 having passed on April 1.

> Whereas, there is evidence to indicate the possible existence in Skamania County of a nocturnal primate mammal variously described as an ape-like creature or a sub-species of Homo Sapian [sic]; and
> Whereas, both legend and purported recent sightings and spoor support this possibility, and

Whereas, this creature is generally and commonly known as a "Sasquatch", "Yeti", "Bigfoot", or "Giant Hairy Ape", and

Whereas publicity attendant upon such real or imagined sightings has resulted in an influx of scientific investigators as well as casual hunters, many armed with lethal weapons, and

Whereas, the absence of specific laws covering the taking of specimens encourages laxity in the use of firearms and other deadly devices and poses a clear and present threat to the safety and well-being of persons living or traveling within the boundaries of Skamania County as well as to the creatures themselves,

Therefore be it resolved that any premeditated, wilful and wanton slaying of such creature shall be deemed a felony punishable by a fine not to exceed Ten Thousand Dollars ($10,000) and/or imprisonment in the county jail for a period not to exceed Five (5) years.

Be it further resolved that the situation existing constitutes an emergency and as such this ordinance is effective immediately.

Skamania County's board amended this ordinance in 1984, making the crime of shooting bigfoot a gross misdemeanor, punishable by a year in county jail and/or a $1,000 fine. In reality, anyone can shoot a bigfoot . . . or a leprechaun—or a troll for that matter. This animal, according to the U.S. Fish and Wildlife Service, does not exist so it cannot be protected under the Endangered Species Act. Most bigfoot investigators publicly say that shooting a bigfoot is murder. People who claim to have seen one are even more emphatic about this. Privately, though, more than a few confided to me that they would not mind obtaining a body at any expense.

Don was not worried about being vilified either way. Losing his life was more than enough motivation for shooting a bigfoot. At least, that's how he thought before that afternoon. Over the course of a few seconds, Don felt anger, fear, and concern while he looked through the scope and kept his finger on the trigger. Why did he hesitate? I have difficulty understanding. Granted, I have never hunted an animal, nor have I shot at one. (I once punched Peter Wright in the stomach when he stepped on a daddy long-legs during the third grade. And I *loathe* spiders. Plus, I always root for the Thomson gazelle in nature documentaries when it sprints futilely away from cheetahs, lions, leopards, or a pack of hyenas. I do not like seeing the Tommie during its final moments, squealing or spasmodically moving its legs. So I cannot imagine firing away at a creature that, if it exists, is rare and human-like.) Don, meanwhile, has regularly shot pretty much anything that has wandered through northern Wisconsin.

Don used to be a skeptic before all hell broke loose in his life. Raised in the woods of northern Wisconsin, he had spent days, nights, and weekends in remote areas all around Philips, hunt-ing, fishing, and hiking through the thick forests and swamps. His father taught him to survive in the woods at age five, when he had spent a night alone there. In all that time, Don had never noticed anything resembling a bigfoot, although his mom and grandmother did offer tales of a monster that lived in the woods, stories Don dismissed as a warning to kids not to wander deep into the woods and get lost or eaten by a bear, wolf, or coyote. Don had also heard the popular story about the Hodag in nearby Rhinelander, a mythical creature that allegedly had the head of a frog, the grinning face of an elephant, the back of a dinosaur, huge claws, and a long tail with spears at the end. That hoax had garnered national attention in 1893. Don might have also heard about werewolves attacking folks in southeastern Wisconsin, spec-tral nuns haunting an abandoned female seminary, or the vampire that cruised a cemetery in Mineral Point. Wisconsin has a rich history of tales about the bizarre and the paranormal. But Don had barely thought about bigfoot, despite several reported sightings in the region. It was unfathomable that an animal roughly twice the size of a black bear could exist in his woods, where he had made his living as a hunting and fishing guide for nearly twenty years.

At age thirty-nine, that all changed. Don had two fateful encounters that left him questioning everything he knew about the woods. His public reports to the Bigfoot Field Researchers Organization on the incidents left local folks questioning Don's sanity.

In the first incident, Don says he spotted something odd along a dirt access road in fall 2002 while he scouted deer for potential clients—a large, reddish-brown creature that walked on two legs, hunched over as if it had been punched in the stomach, and moved exceptionally fast. When Don raised his gun to get a better view through his scope, the animal leaped into the alder swamp and disappeared faster than any animal Don had encountered to that point. Don ran over to the swamp, looked for tracks, and peered into the trees, hoping to get another glimpse. He had a strange feeling that something was now watching him. Creepy. Uncertain what he had seen, he headed to the Internet, which in turn led him to the Bigfoot Field Researchers Organization, where he filed a report (No. 5507). Don wrote, "I seen what I seen." With his credentials, that should have been enough. But, of course, it wasn't. People in town started to talk, many wondering whether good ol' Don was creating his own hoax . . . until Don posted his second report.

The second encounter was considerably longer and more terrifying, Don says. In fall 2003 he headed out to scout another potential hunting location one afternoon, not far from where we now stand at the sedge meadow—and about three miles from the first sighting. Don noticed something had started following him deep in the woods, but he did not react when he saw the large animal. Instead he slowed his pace, kneeling down every fifty yards to ostensibly pick something off the ground. Each time Don would keep his head down, moving his eyes so he could look sideways, back toward the trail. The animal stayed in the shadows behind bushes and trees, off the path Don walked, which would be enough to hide from most hikers. Sometimes, Don noticed, the animal moved within thirty yards, close enough that he could see eyes that were completely dark, like a whitetail deer's. White sclera did not surround an iris like in humans. Like the animal in the first sighting, this one walked hunched over like an ape, had dark brown hair, and did not have a scent. After about an hour of this cat-and-mouse game, Don became anxious when the creature appeared seventy-five yards to his right, as if it were flanking him, cutting off his escape route from the woods. Coyotes hunted wounded deer in this manner. After another thirty minutes, Don emerged at an area that had been clear-cut by loggers; it was not far from his vehicle, so he sat there for thirty minutes, but the creature never reappeared. In his report Don wrote, "I am convinced that this is a creature that with some time I can get close to again. No one can tell me that this freak of nature does not exist. It showed itself to me twice."

Prior to filing these reports, Don had a solid reputation as an outdoorsman in the area, serving as a guide to hunters and fishermen who sought anything from black bear to fox to musky to walleye. He also published a book, *Beginner's Guide to Whitetail Deer Hunting*, and sold fishing lures like the Tailspin Bucktail through his company, Razors Edge Pro Lures & Guide. Don earned anywhere from $20,000 to $30,000 a year from his guide service, more than enough for an intrepid, self-sufficient woodsman to survive in Philips. After his encounters, though, other guides started spreading rumors that Don had gone crazy, sabotaging his reputation and whispering to potential clients, *Do you really want to go into a remote area with a man who believes in bigfoot and who carries a loaded gun?* Don knew guides were a jealous bunch, but he never expected his guide service to eventually shut down. By the time he spoke with me in fall 2009, he said he made about a hundred bucks a year, receiving about one or two calls a year. Clearly, Don had a reason to pull the trigger that morning here at the swamp. He could take the ribbing and comments because, he says, he saw what he saw. But then people started calling his wife Mrs. Sasquatch. That's when Don decided to prove he was not crazy.

"What keeps me going on this is that I have something to prove," he told me. "Once I prove it, then I'll get the guides back. Right now, I've lost the guides because they think, 'I'm not going to go out with him in the woods. He's nuts.' So if I can prove that these things are real, I can get my life back."

Yet there the animal stood, its back to Don, looking out into the spruce, fir, and balsam silhouettes that looked like church steeples. Don had the creature in the crosshairs of a high-powered rifle, finger on the trigger, ready to fire. At 150 yards, Don knew he could hit most anything, and usually in the best spot. For instance, he knows to shoot a coyote in the head if he plans to skin it, so the bullet will not spoil the hide. Plus, a chest shot will allow blood to pour out of the chest and nose during the skinning process, further spoiling the hide. The shoulder area, roughly the size of a dinner plate, is the best spot to shoot a deer because the bullet penetrates the heart and lungs. Hit only the lungs and the deer can still run far enough to hide. Hit the heart and you'll also usually hit the lungs, meaning the deer won't get far. Hit the shoulder bones and you'll also probably hit some vital organs and drop the deer on the spot. Lung shots are best for killing a black bear. To find these organs, trace the back of the front leg up about one-third of the way into the chest. A bear's lungs are positioned a little more forward than a deer's. Some hunters prefer a shot in the heart instead, but Don knows that can be dangerous. His father had warned him against taking such risks. That's the worst place to shoot a bear, Don tells me, because a bear would still have enough oxygen to keep going for another five minutes—and a hurt bear is frequently lethal. Aim for the spine or side of the head and the bullet can ricochet, further aggravating a four- to five-hundred-pound *Ursus americanus*. Shoot a bear in the wrong spot and it's gonna get you. Don's father had instilled that concern at a young age.

But damned if Don knew where to shoot this animal. Don had grown up in these woods, learning them as well as any naturalist. He knew what black bear ate, where white-tailed deer traveled, and how whippoorwill sang. But he knew nothing about the animal standing before him. Is a bigfoot's anatomy roughly the same as a human's, where a heart beats in the upper-right chest area and where lungs hang down along the rib cage? Like a bear, did its physiology allow oxygen to flow even after a shot to the heart—and would it have twice as much oxygen since it was roughly double the size of most black bear? Further, would a bullet penetrate the hide? Would its skull rebuff a bullet? Did it have a femoral artery, where it would bleed out? And how fast could the animal reach him, even while walking across sphagnum moss and sinking deep into the bog? In this bog, most humans would sink a great deal into the spongy, wet soil, probably up to their knees, meaning you'd probably see just see the top of someone's head out in the swamp, unless the person were significantly taller than six feet. You might see Shaquille O'Neal's shoulders or Peyton Manning's chin above the shrubs. Don clearly saw the animal's wide chest and waist above the tag alder and muskeg, shrubs that grow about four feet high, meaning this bigfoot could be eight feet tall. That could also mean this animal could drive its powerful thighs through the swamp quickly enough to catch Don were he not to puncture the correct kill spot.

Don Young never pulled the trigger that afternoon, obviously; otherwise we'd be recounting the moment when the world was formally introduced to bigfoot, which might now be classified as *Gigantopithecus*, no longer considered an extinct genus of ape previously thought to have lived one million to three hundred thousand years ago. Perhaps, though, the body would have revealed a closer relationship to *Homo erectus*, prompting a scientific name in honor of Don, such as *Homo youngus erectus*. Or maybe we'd be remembering the time a crazy hunter shot a dressed-up man in the northern Wisconsin woods. Sentenced to a few years in jail for accidental homicide, we'd remember. Crazy sonofabitch. Or possibly we'd never have heard anything because the bullet would have pierced the lungs of a rather large *Ursus americana*, just another dead black bear during hunting season.

So Don lowered his rifle. The animal disappeared into the meadow. And Don walked out of the deep woods a little uneasily, but safely.

It would be easy to discount Don's story as crazy. Frankly, it's easy to make fun of anyone associated with bigfoot, an assignment topic that causes TV and print reporters to froth rabidly, knowing they'll have an easy, humorous assignment — not caring that they would break at least a half dozen of the Society of Professional Journalists' ethical codes. As journalists, we are obligated to minimize harm and seek truth. These codes distinguish us as respectable news gatherers. Yet journalists who write about bigfoot constantly shred these codes. In their stories about bigfoot, journalists impose their own values on others, stereotyping, suppressing the open exchange of views, and trampling on the code's requirements that we show compassion for people, not act arrogantly, and show good taste. Bigfoot is like catnip to journalists. They are suddenly drunk with freedom, gamboling over fairness and batting aside professionalism. Fuck fairness. Let me at the crazy idiots looking for a monster in the woods. With bigfoot, readers expect fruitcakes and New Age loonies. So journalists deliver.

Like Don, though, my reputation as a journalist means a great deal to me. Out in the woods, my faith in the people around me is strong. Back home, it wavers. When people find out that I'm writing a book about bigfoot, they always cut to the chase—So, have you seen one? I'm not always certain if they are seeking information about the big, hairy guy or if they are trying to confirm whether I'm crazy. Sort of like when someone says they hear voices or that God is speaking to them. He is? Really? Is he talking to you right now? What's he saying? To admit to have seen bigfoot is to confirm that I'm a few bricks short of a load, mad as a hatter, lost my marbles. I emphasize that the book is not about bigfoot; rather, I'm reporting on those who search for bigfoot. Whether bigfoot exist does not matter. I'm just curious as to what drives those who search for bigfoot. Those are lies, of course. I'm helplessly mesmerized when people start talking about bigfoot or when a TV show focuses on bigfoot. I feel I have been tantalizingly close to a visual encounter several times, but I cannot offer tangible evidence that anything exists outside of my spry imagination.

Ultimately, the stories are the most compelling evidence. Did Pat Rance actually encounter several bigfoot for nearly an hour in Alabama? Did a creature look in Carolanne Solomon's bedroom as a kid? Did bigfoot grab the Virginia researcher Bill Willard's knee through a tent in eastern Texas? Did Don have bigfoot in his rifle scope in this meadow? Like Ernest Hemingway, I have a fairly good bullshit detector, honed by years working as a journalist and a teacher. I test people with lies all the time. I suspect these folks saw something that might have been a bigfoot. Without evidence, they are just stories taken on faith. And that's something that I've lacked for most of my life. It would be easy to poke fun at these folks for telling these stories. As a writer, in fact, I would find it effortless. But is believing in bigfoot any crazier than believing in the Bible? How do we know the information in the New Testament is authentic, that Jesus healed the leper and the blind man and fed thousands after giving the Sermon on the Mount? That was Don's response to a man in the hardware store a few weeks earlier.

"Are you the bigfoot man from Lugerville?" the man said, grinning smugly. Don was ready when the man fired away. "Can you prove that bigfoot is real beyond a shadow of a doubt?" the man asked, adding that he thought even the notion was a giant pile of shit. The man said he believed only what he could see. Don asked, "Do you believe in God?" Of course, the man responded. "Okay," Don said, "if you can prove to me beyond a shadow of a doubt that God is real, then I will go to church, because I only believe in what I can see." The man huffed and walked out of the store.

Challenging religion, though, is sacrilege. None of the apostles recorded anything about their time with Jesus, at least as far as anybody knows. Instead, we rely on testimonies from Matthew, Mark, Luke, and John, who recorded their accounts anywhere from twenty to sixty years after Jesus was crucified. Who knows how many times the information was passed along or translated before being recorded, and taken, literally, as gospel? Yet we refuse to accept stories from neighbors, coworkers, or friends who say they have seen something in the woods—not a fleeting glimpse of a leg that could have been a bear's or deer's but a full and extended view of something. Think about it—what sounds more bizarre: that a bigfoot researcher has glimpsed an undiscovered primate living in the woods or that a man was killed and came back to life and his body and blood are contained in the wine and bread in the Eucharist offered from the altar? Even Catholics like me can see the dubious nature of these suppositions. But we believe, mostly because we want to believe or because we sense that the stories are true, that a rainbow can be a message from God or that someone's recovery can be attributed to a saint or angel. Yet we do not have faith in the people around us, especially when the stories turn bizarre. No doubt that scam artists, hoaxers, and pranksters lurk. But the people who say they have clearly seen a bigfoot can't all be liars, can they? If so, why do they all want to spread lies about bigfoot, especially when, like Don Young, they can lose their livelihoods and their reputations? It just doesn't make any sense, at least to me, that so many people would put themselves in a situation where others could exploit and humiliate them unless something really happened. Few people want attention that badly, right? There can't be that many lonely people in the world. To me, the stories are the strongest suggestion that something exists out in the woods.

Yet I fight to believe in both bigfoot and God. I want to imagine that the world has some meaning, that a creator loves us, as did his son Jesus. Most of all, I'd love to believe in angels, heaven, and life after death. I truly hope they exist. In many ways, that's how I feel about Don's story. I want to believe him. I could hear the fear in his voice when he spoke about it—even more so later that afternoon when we walked through the woods near his home, where we showed me where he saw bigfoot and told me stories about other encounters far more frightening than any I'd heard so far.

We're attaching game cameras to trees along a game path near Lugerville, not far from a logging area—and along part of the trail where Don says he was tracked during his second encounter. It's midmorning. The sky remains blue and clear. It's still cool enough that Don's wearing jeans and a t-shirt that features a leopard across the front. Over that he wears an unbuttoned, untucked olive shirt. He dons a camouflage baseball cap that hides thick, black hair that is graying at the temples. A jvc tape recorder dangles from a strap on his neck. Silver, wire-rimmed spectacles complement the gray in his beard. He sometimes seems as though he's listening to something other than me. That's understandable, given his recent experiences.

At the moment, Don is bending tree limbs on a white pine in order to attach a ScoutGuard SG550—a small, compact camera—to the trunk. The camera is roughly 5¼ inches tall, 3¼ inches wide, and 2⅛ inches thick and has a single lens on the upper portion of a body covered by shades of green, brown, and black, giving it the appearance of a miniature, camouflaged R2D2, the devoted droid in *Star Wars*. Don likes this camera because it takes quality photos and video quickly during both the day and night. Cameras like the ScoutGuard emit infrared beams to detect motion or heat changes in an area that can cover a five-degree span closest to the camera and about a seventy-degree swath about thirty or forty feet from the lens. The coverage area, in some ways, emulates a baseball field. Think of the camera as home plate and the peripheral range where it can shoot photos like a field's foul lines extending down the first- and third-base lines. The farther the distance from the camera, the more likely the lens will capture an image down the foul lines. The range to capture an image is considerably narrower closer to the lens. Don folds branches back into place around the camera. The trick, Don says, is not to change too much, otherwise the bigfoot will notice. And then they are going to change their route. "If someone on our street painted their house and trimmed down a tree, we'd notice," Don says. It's the same for bigfoot. "This is their living room. If anything is out of place here, they're going to notice it." The white pine is on a slight ridge, so Don stuffs a stick behind the camera so it looks down across the trail. He snaps a few short, thin branches so nothing blocks the lens. Don stands back, eyeballs it, and then looks down the ridge where the path opens into a wider opening, about ten feet across and filled with knee-high plants and grasses. Balsam and pine surround this area. One night this camera captured an eerie video here.

Don suspected he might find something on his camera when he heard coyotes howl, a key indicator that bigfoot have made a kill, he believes. Bigfoot make several distinctive calls, Don says, that sound either like a long, continuous sound from the diaphragm that is slightly higher pitched than a moan or like short, repeat grunts or screams. "They're very vocal and they imitate."

Coyotes, Don says, have learned these calls. After a longer howl, he'll sometimes hear coyotes "just go nuts," quickly going from the first low-pitched howls to the rapid-fire yip-yip-yip. "That means the squatch has basically told the other squatches, 'I've got dinner.' He wasn't calling the coyotes but they have learned these calls. So they come right over."

Don heard some coyotes go bonkers near here one night. So he returned to this ridge the following morning, downloaded the video, and noticed two glowing, unblinking eyes watching a deer that wandered in front of the camera. The eyes were set too wide apart to be a bear's or another deer's and were at least six feet off the ground. I can't imagine what stood there that night. The closest road is more than a mile away and homes are farther away than that. No person would have a reason to walk out there—and, if they did, their eyes would not glow. The glowing, unblinking eyes have never appeared on another video. Grass had been flattened near the tree. On the path, Don also noticed tracks where the deer had apparently bolted, leaving deep hoof marks in the ground as it jumped away—perhaps only a few seconds after the camera had stopped rolling. On the video, Don says, he can see a dark body part near the bottom of the trunk, although, he acknowledges, that image could be a shadow. On the YouTube video, I cannot discern anything. But to be fair, most anything could sneak up on me in the dark woods—probably even people on a BFRO expedition.

About a quarter mile down the path, Don stops near a patch of dirt along the grass trail. He bends over an indentation. "That could be a handprint," he says.

"Why a hand?"

"They sometimes walk on all fours," Don says. "Could be that he was grabbing dirt for a bath." Animals frequently use dust baths to cleanse themselves of parasitic insects like ticks, mites, and lice. I'd seen buffalo go down for lengthy scrubbings in Yellowstone.

But this spot looked like an old anthill. "The anthill is gone," Don says. "It probably started up in here, but the dirt is more fine over here." Don digs his hand into the ground to his wrist, pulling up dirt and several black ants that crawl over his palm. He slowly lets dirt and bugs slip through his fingers to the ground. This dirt patch has grown during the past several months. At this spot, a small opening enables sun to sneak through the trees. This would be an ideal place to bathe, warm up, and relax, he says. Bigfoot would lie down in the dirt, roll around, throw dirt on themselves, and just lie there.

Don checks these trails about twice a week, pulling video card readers that he downloads back home, adding new cameras, and moving others. Overall, he says he has hundreds of cameras, whose prices range from $100 to $650, meaning he keeps at least $10,000 worth of equipment across several research areas, including a few right outside his home. He walks these trails frequently.

It's clear he knows them well. He points to a small area past the dirt patch. "Buck bed," he says. About another quarter mile ahead the grass path yields to dirt, which reveals tracks of all kinds going in all directions. Don looks at the imprints, calling them out: "Rabbit. Raccoon. Squirrel. Coyote. Deer." Deer tracks, especially, are everywhere, hooved indentations cutting into one another. "That's why he [bigfoot] uses deer trails," Don says. "If it weren't for the deer, you'd see their tracks. But look at how many deer have come across and destroyed everything." About a half mile ahead, a large rock about the size of a Nerf football lies alone in the grass, far from any other rocks or pebbles. "That's a weapon," Don says. "Totally out of place. A bear wouldn't have carried it from the ant mound. There are instances of squatches throwing rocks at people. I've also come to the conclusion that they don't use sticks. Rocks are easier to use and more reliable. Grab a stick. Whoosh. It breaks."

More than a mile down the trail we reach the place where Don was stalked, an area that could be an oasis for animals during all seasons. A canopy of trees hides an open, oblong area about fifty yards in circumference. It feels much cooler than elsewhere on the trail. In winter, Don says, the tall trees block out the frigid winds, the canopy helping retain warmth and keeping snow from the ground. The ferns, which grow thick here, offer sustenance. "When they're just coming up and having that little curl, they taste just like asparagus," he says. (I don't want to ask what sort of internal animal organ or bug would be used for the hollandaise sauce.) The ferns can be eaten raw, of course, but Don sometimes cooks them. The peat, or sphagnum moss, that grows thick under our feet offers food, healing, and comfort. "It won't be the best-tasting tea, but it'll have a lot of nutrients." The peat also sucks out poisons and toxins—sometimes immobilizing bacterial cells—along with enzymes and antibodies secreted by invasive pathogens. Peat is also four times more absorbent than cotton, a reason it was used to stem bleeding and to disinfect wounds from the Bronze Age through the Russian Revolution. The moss is beautiful, looking like a batch of mini palm trees. Don says bigfoot will peel the moss in chunks to create a thick, spongy bedding. Don says the peat gets so thick in some areas that if you fall too far down into it you'd be buried. Poof.

This is also a terrific ambush point, Don says. "I could just sit up there in the trees with my bow, the fallen branches hiding me—"

He stops midsentence.

"I thought I heard something."

He pauses. "I did."

We listen for a few seconds. "There's something crawling around."

I look nervously around. As usual, I can't hear a thing.

"They used to check me out more frequently," Don says. But these bigfoot are not as curious anymore. "Now they pretty much know me. So unless I have someone along—*like you*—with new scents, they don't come out." Don's not smiling. I can't tell if he's trying to get a reaction out of me, but I'm game for an encounter. I think.

Don surveys the area. "People wonder how bigfoot can feed itself out in these woods. You know, I could feed a large group of people out here. They might not want to eat what I find them." Don finally smiles. "But they'd survive."

As we trek back, Don tells me a story about another encounter, one that's both wacky and terrifying. For decades, hunters have used pheromone chips to lure and shoot deer. A pheromone is a chemical secreted, or excreted, by animals that triggers a social reaction from animals of the same species. Essentially, pheromones tell male deer, "Hey, big boy, want a good time?" This is not much different from a woman wearing a Victoria's Secret no-show V-string and a lace garter skirt and splashing on some Noir Patchouli — or, really, any woman showing absolutely any interest in most any guy anywhere. Men are always easy pickings. Hunters love these chips, realizing it is far easier to sit in an enclosed platform in a tree than to traipse around in the woods to find a deer. So they place them near their enclosed blinds, waiting for the proper-sized deer to appear, at which point the hunter, hopefully awake and sober, grabs his gun and blasts away at a poor buck trying to find a mate. (Not much different, actually, than when a teen boy shows up at a girl's house for a date.)

Don took this idea to another level, deciding to use both a pheromone chip *and* a used tampon to lure in a bigfoot on a local trail near a large bog. With two teen girls, I have grown accustomed, sadly, to finding used tampons all over the house, in all hallways, garbage cans, near toilets, under a desk. The girls toss them aside like gum wrappers. And our dogs love to snack on them. So, I thought as he spoke, maybe this was a pretty smart idea.

At the bog, Don first scouted the area by walking a trail that circles a waterfowl refuge before heading down some animal trails toward the creek, where he noticed cattails had been pulled out and flattened on the opposite shore. He took some photos before walking along several other trails and the road to his camp, completing the three-mile trek in about two hours. While snacking on some Pop-Tarts and a Snickers bar, Don set up some game cameras aimed toward both the woods and the tent. He planned to use the tampon and pheromones to lure a bigfoot back to camp. Once there, perhaps the bigfoot would pause to eat part of the dyspeptic feast Don had laid out near several cameras—sliced beef liver, apples, and black licorice covered in honey. Inside the tent he placed a recorder that would play sounds of his snoring, making it seem as though he were in there rather than in his truck.

Then Don created his irresistible lure. He tied the used tampon and pheromone chip onto a ten-foot string and coiled the other end onto his belt loop. Don had used this same technique with deer tarsal glands to create a scent trail that would go past a location where he would have the best shot at a deer. Don would emulate this approach, using the items to lure bigfoot back to what he thought would be a trap. How wrong he would be.

At 6:30 p.m., the sun was setting. Don sat on the back of his truck and finished a bowl of soup before he set off on the trails around the water refuge. As he departed, he wore a knife, carried a canteen, and pulled a string. The tampon and chip bounced and skidded behind him.

Along the way, Don would pour water from the canteen on the tampon and chip, stepping on them to drive the scent into the ground. It was growing darker so Don diverted from the path. Instead of going around on the trails, he stopped at a walking bridge by an area where loggers had cut down a wide swath of trees. He sat there for about an hour, listening to the sounds of the still night. Crows screeched in the distance, near the creek, and jolted Don from his reverie. So he headed back toward the regular trail.

By the time he reached the animal trails, the sun had completely set and the moon offered barely enough light to see in front of him. As Don pulled out his canteen to pour water over the tampon and chip, a branch snapped down the trail, perhaps two hundred yards away but audible in the windless night. That's when Don heard moans coming up the trail that sounded like MOOOOWAAAA. That was enough for Don, who pulled his knife, cut the string, and threw it down the trail before running like hell along the trail as best he could in the darkness. The moans got closer. So Don climbed a small balsam tree, its trunk only about eight inches in diameter. When he reached as high a point as possible, Don wrapped his arms around the trunk and remained silent. The moans moved closer. He could also hear footsteps and heavy breathing, which moved right under the tree, but Don could not see a thing in the dark. The animal stopped below the tree, it seemed, where it moaned even louder, snorted, and started shaking the tree. Don clung to the trunk for dear life.

The animal then started climbing toward him. Several times, Don heard branches snap, sending whatever-it-was slipping down to the tree's base. Finally, the animal managed to hang on more tightly to the tree, moving almost directly below Don's feet — sort of like a nightmare where you're flying above some monster on the ground but only a few inches above the creature's grasp. But Don could not awaken from this terror. *Get the fuck out of here*, Don thought. *Ahhh, fuck!* He could not climb any higher, so he drew his knife, prepared to slash at whatever breathed on his shoes. He was nearly crying. The creature slipped again before Don could swing his knife. At that point Don heard a high-pitched whine from down the trail that sounded like WEEEEEAAAAA — like a bull elk's bugling. But no elk lived in this area.

"That was total fright," Don tells me. "You see something. You can't explain it. It's scary. It's no different than swimming in the ocean when something bumps you. You can dive under the water and hope it's a flounder and not a mako or great white shark. If you can't see it, you will be more scared."

Everything went silent. Don remained motionless for nearly an hour, terrified that something was peering into the tree. Finally Don pulled off his pistol belt, wrapped it around the balsam's trunk, and inserted his arm into it, using it like a safety harness. No way in hell did he want to be on that ground. Anything that could disappear that quietly could reappear just as quickly. His arm soon lost some feeling, tied tightly to the harness; his left leg ached from the odd angle at which it was bent. At dawn Don climbed down, which proved difficult because most of the branches had been snapped off the trunk. He had to drop at least ten feet from the tree. At the time, he did not notice the reason for this because he ran directly to his truck and sped home, leaving his tent and cameras in the woods. The tree did not have any scratch or claw marks, as one would expect for a bear. Don knew more than most about bear, having raised two from cubs. But damned if he could find a single claw mark. Nor could he find tracks or hair. A cherry tree next to the balsam was nearly crushed, though, and the area smelled like a wet dog.

Yet Don did not really need evidence. He knew what had tried climbing up to him.

"Not sure but I think that was a youth, a teenaged squatch at the tree," Don says. "And the call was the mother saying, 'Get away from that.'"

Why would a bigfoot climb after him? Perhaps because Don had blood, estrous discharge, and maybe even some ovary follicles on his shoes from regularly stepping on the used tampon. How could anyone resist, much less a hormonally challenged teenage great ape? Even monsters have feelings, you know. In retrospect, Don says he should have tossed his shoes away before he climbed the tree. Better yet, he should not have dragged a bloody tampon behind him through the woods. Nothing good can happen if you do that. Nothing.

Don suspected a coyote or bobcat had been killing, and eating, his cats here at his cabin. So he placed a ScoutGuard sg550 on an old animal trail in his backyard, not far from the stacks of cut wood that lined a fenced area and continued like a maze toward a small workshop where he created his fishing lures and stuffed and mounted animals for clients. The wood, stacked as high as my stomach, could heat the cabin for two to three years, yet he keeps cutting and stacking it. This is where the cats lie for parts of the day, in the shade of the trees and as rulers of the world. Typical cats. As Don and I spoke, a calico walked atop the wood toward some sucker who was certain to pet it for a while. Which I did. These cats really were easy pickings.

Don's cabin stood about thirty yards from the camera. A light attached to a pole shone just enough light to reveal silhouettes.

A month later, Don noticed a blinking light on the game camera that denoted its battery had nearly drained. Don replaced the battery, took out the video card, and dumped twelve pictures onto his computer that, on first glance, appeared all black thanks to the weak battery and dead flashbulb. Don deleted all of the photos except one that revealed a shard of light, probably a reflection from the light pole in the front yard. He said he could kick himself for deleting the others so quickly. Later Don played with the photo, lightening some areas with photographic software to reveal a shocking image—a silhouette of an animal standing on two legs, arms at its side, and looking directly into his house. The animal's shoulders are massive, spreading very wide before rising into a stout, thick neck, while its arms extend out before hanging down, sort of like a bodybuilder's. The head is large and slightly cone shaped. Backlit by the pole's light, this animal is barely outlined, allowing the imagination to run wild.

The image would have been perfect for a 1950s horror flick. The picture looks absolutely fake, but Don is adamant it is real. It looks so fake, in fact, that it starts to look real. Why create a photo as unconvincing as this? Frankly, the picture gives me the creeps and kick-starts goosebumps, like so many of Don's stories and photos in the woods. Don has captured more than ten thousand images of wildlife, everything from deer wandering past to bear pausing to look directly at the camera lens to roaming bobcats and coyotes. He also has his share of creepy and bizarre photos like this. He's captured images he claims are orbs or will-o'-the-wisps, photos of eyes reflected in his cabin window, and hairy close-ups that he claims are bigfoot arms and legs. None creeps me out more than this one that looks like The Thing or a greatly oversized werewolf. This creature, easily eight feet tall, could weigh at least six hundred to eight hundred pounds. Hell, who knows really? I do know that this creature-thing would make Michael Oher, the six-foot-four, three-hundred-pound lineman featured in *The Blind Side* look like a chump, shoving him aside as easily as Shaquille O'Neal would bounce me off an NBA court with a soft hip check. When I look at the photo, I'm not sure whether to laugh or shudder. If Don Young viewed something like this a few times, why is he anywhere near a tree or a dirt road? Why doesn't he live in Milwaukee or Chicago—anywhere but here?

Big Phil is not the only bigfoot to have visited this cabin, Don says. On another occasion, Don and his wife saw yet another large animal skulking around their cabin. As his wife backed the pickup truck into the yard, they saw two large, red eyes about ten feet away. They kept the truck's lights on the animal for a few seconds as it stood and blinked away before turning and bolting into the woods. "Funny," Don says, "how they can be stealthy at times where you can't hear a peep and then can sound like a herd of elephants." Don's dogs started howling and barking; the oldest one, ironically, frantically dug under the fence to get out. It was this oldest dog, not the mastiff, that had faced off with a bigfoot several months earlier, leaving it crippled. Don believes a bigfoot either tossed her onto a large rock nearby or cracked her in its hands. Either way, the *muscle* that holds the dog's vertebrae in place sheared off, meaning a vertebra essentially floats. As a result, she walks around the fenced area as though she has to go to the bathroom, her back end hunched up. Sometimes she shifts to one side and falls. It is painful to watch her move. When a large animal wanders into the yard, though, she's the first to bark and the one who tries like hell to get out once again, Don says. The youngest also gets excited. "She's always been gung-ho," Don says. "The other one, well, she's just stupid." Two others, including one that's half coyote, try to hide in the doghouse.

The dogs were barking wildly the night Don Young says he captured a baby bigfoot on a FLIR thermal camera several months earlier, shooting amid the thick trees that surround his cabin. In the video, shot not one hundred yards from his cabin, a small animal appears near a tree. It stands near the base of a fairly large tree for about eleven seconds before it looks left and then very quickly climbs up the tree and out of sight. Don panned left and right, not realizing that it had gone up. Don did not know at first what he saw. At the time, he was scanning for a larger bigfoot, like Big Phil or Blinky. When the video is slowed down, the animal does look like a small ape, but it also looks like a bear and an alien. Thermal images won't ever prove the existence of bigfoot because they can be faked rather easily and because details are blurred, like in an ultrasound. Ultimately, people see what they want to see in thermal videos. And people extrapolate a great deal, especially from videos and photos. For example, Jack Barnes analyzes video on his Facebook page "FindBigfoot." Typically he'll critique videos that have been posted online or that have been sent to him. Jack slows video speeds, sometimes stopping at key moments in order to magnify blurry images and lighten dark backgrounds. Jack does a fine job reciting the key elements of a video, usually by reading the details as they scroll down. For Don's "Baby Bigfoot" video, for instance, Jack cites the following: that the video was shot from fifteen to twenty feet away, that the animal in the thermals appears to be about four feet tall, that the video is one hundred feet from where Don shot another video, of Blinky, and that the animal has a human-shaped head, long arms, and huge forward eye sockets. Details like this are discernible, for the most part. But then Jack starts to concoct theories, stating them as if they were scientific facts. When the animal peeks from behind a smaller tree, Jack says matter-of-factly, "Remember, bigfoot perceive the world a lot faster than we do. They may have eight perceptions a second as opposed to our one every three or four seconds." People like Jack make researchers look like bumpkins. Comments like these drive science from bigfoot research. Psychologists and physicians have tested human perception for more than one hundred years, debating how the brain makes sense of images. The answers are still unclear. Yet Jack can assess a bigfoot's perceptive abilities based upon watching a few hundred videos—and with enough accuracy to say they have *precisely eight perceptions* each second. Even if bigfoot exist, we do not have any way to test this. This is all kinds of crazy.

In another video, Jack diagnoses two bigfoot with either hemiplegia, partial paralysis, or cerebral palsy after watching them walk across a ridge in Utah. In the video, two alleged bigfoot watch a family sledding before walking off. They are barely discernible in the upper-right portion of the screen, yet Jack can discern that they have spastic hemiplegia, a problem that—depending on the severity—can make someone walk like Dr. Frankenstein's Igor, dragging a leg after taking a step with a good leg. Even with the video enlarged and in slow motion, this diagnosis is a stretch.

But Jack makes even more irrational, unfounded statements in his conclusion, stating:

- Two of three alleged bigfoot in the Utah video are twins. Cerebral palsy is twenty times more likely among identical twins. Both of these animals appear to have a limp. Therefore, these creatures are twins.
- Sasquatch parents will stay with their disabled children. (That's pretty cool, he adds.)
- The family group resides within two thousand meters of the hilltop.
- Congenital maladies that affect human children are visible in bigfoot youth.
- Humans descended from bigfoot by moving from the mountains to the plains.

Don Young hates armchair warriors, although he did not mind Jack's analysis. He says he does not mind conjecture as much as ignorance and incompetence. He has dismissed many notions held by bigfoot investigators. For instance, he does not believe bigfoot zap people with infrasound. He's never felt anything in his encounters. Plus, how can an animal narrowly focus infrasound? Hippos send infrasound over a large area when trying to stun fish in a river. Lions and whales and dolphins also send infrasound across a wide path. He doesn't believe people when they say they have been zapped by infrasound. "I'm skeptical when the person next to you gets nailed and the other doesn't. It's a sound. It broadcasts. Both people should get knocked down. So one person must be lying. It's like playing a stereo. You can't direct it; the sound goes to everybody."

Don scoffs at the notion that everything one sees out in the woods is a stick structure. Most can be explained, he says, sometimes by weather. "Trees snap in winter and during harsh conditions." We stop by some trees that are bent over one another.

"There are those who think every structure is a squatch. Do you realize an elephant couldn't snap that thing?" If anything, he believes bigfoot play with sticks, just like primates in the wild. "They don't mean anything at all." Bigfoot cannot speak, he says, but they are very vocal, perhaps able to imitate human speech.

The government knows about bigfoot, Don says, but refrains from addressing them because they would lose a fortune when people stopped going to state and national parks. "They're not going to go camping. They're not going to buy a hunting license." He laughs. "They're going to lose a lot of revenue if people know there's a primate out there watching from the shadows. Plus, you'd have to fork out a whole lot more money to protect them."

A year after we talked, Don caught another video, allegedly of a bigfoot peeking out from behind some bushes, which earned him more national recognition. By this time Don had stopped answering my emails, responding on Facebook, or returning my phone calls. He had seemed guarded during our phone conversations, uncertain whether he should share details about his experiences. But once I arrived, having driven more than nine hours to get there, Don had been kind, generous, and at times, eager to show me his evidence and to walk me through woods where he encountered bigfoot. Maybe he's been heading to the north woods, leaving out bowls of food and communicating with these animals? Or he might be writing his autobiography, as he had suggested in an early phone call; thus the hesitancy to tell me anything. Or perhaps he no longer wants to answer questions from a hack like me. Regardless of the reason, Don's stories were powerful enough that they reinvigorated my passion for this book and for finding bigfoot.

6 EASTERN KENTUCKY

It's Friday night in northeastern Kentucky, not far from Ashland and closer still to the West Virginia border. We're in the foothills of the Appalachians, a twelve-hundred-mile range that stretches from Belle Island, Canada, to northeastern Alabama and that includes some of the poorest regions in the United States. Here some residents neglect their health as they try to scrape a living. Kentuckians smoke, chew tobacco, and use meth like almost nowhere else. Their teeth don't have a chance, not even those rooted in younger kids like the fourteen-year-old girl who refused to lift her head for a visiting dentist, too embarrassed to show him the rot in her nearly toothless mouth. The elderly pull their own infected teeth with pliers, while everybody guzzles cheap, sugary sodas and drinks well water absent decay-fighting fluoride.[1] As a result, Kentucky has more residents under age sixty-five without teeth than any other state. Blame, in part, the coal industry's decline following World War II, when about a half million Americans mined, primarily in the Appalachian region. By 1998, the United Mine Workers had about half as many members.[2] Nowhere is this poverty more evident than in eastern Kentucky, where Martin,

Clay, and Owsley are among the poorest counties in the nation. Life can be grim in these and nearby counties. More than 40 percent of residents live in poverty conditions, often unable to afford running water for their trailers or food on about $22,000 a year for a family of four, which is the median household income for Owsley County. No region is more destitute than this, although a section of Mississippi along the great river comes close. So it's no surprise that I'm standing next to an older, worn trailer — one of many that dot this rural landscape — and watching rusted-out trucks drive past. At the convenience store near the interstate, an overweight woman with a lazy drawl worked the counter. A thousand potential Kentucky-bigfoot jokes percolated, but I'm not going to pile on, making jokes about inbreeding, low intelligence, toothbrushes, and poor hygiene, because the reality is far too sobering.

For mid-October, the weather is unseasonably cold, the air just warm enough to keep the mist from crystallizing into snow but cold enough to make me shiver almost uncontrollably. Inside the trailer, at least the mist and wind are blocked out. I seriously consider driving an hour to the nearest hotel, ordering pizza, and camping under the covers to watch anything, even infomercials, on television. For the past twenty-four hours I have been stuck camping in someone's backyard, not exactly how I envisioned this expedition with the American Bigfoot Society.

I'm here because a man named Doug claims that bigfoot regularly walk through his yard, a point strenuously confirmed by those who regularly watch a live video feed each night emanating from four infrared cameras perched in trees and on a small trailer home sitting in the middle of a three-quarter-acre lot, part of a rural fourteen-hundred-acre property where unexplained events keep happening, Doug says. That's why he created the Kentucky Live Research Project (KLRP). He wants to capture video evidence of a creature he's heard and seen countless times. The KLRP has relied on donations from bigfoot enthusiasts and organizations to keep the live video streaming. In addition, Doug has tried raising money by designing t-shirts and mugs. Eventually the video stream caught on in bigfoot forums, on websites and Blog Talk Radio shows, and during conversations at conferences. "I'm not sure what I do is research," Doug says. "All I know is that I keep these cameras and I keep an eye out."

Doug claims to have had several encounters with bigfoot in this area while growing up in Grayson, about twenty miles west of this location. At age eleven, he says, a creature with Tommyknocker green eyes the size of silver dollars growled and threatened Doug, his brother, and their friends as they explored the woods behind his house one night. Terrified, he dived and rolled down a hill, eventually scrambling to his feet and running into the house. His father smiled slyly and asked, "You ran into that thing, didn't you?" Several years later a bigfoot chased him and his sister from the woods and into his home after Doug pointed at the large creature, not three hundred yards away. Doug also felt the presence of a bigfoot in the woods several other times. His father's friend claimed she found a dead juvenile in the woods, but of course, that corpse was never found.

In Grayson, his mother once saw what might have been a bigfoot. As she cleaned dishes in the kitchen, she saw what looked like an Indian woman through the window, standing by the woods and staring at her, so she called the police. "The state police said unless the woman was eight feet tall," Doug said, "she wasn't standing where she claimed it had appeared." Two days later something threw rocks at Doug's mother from the tree line in the backyard.

"I've always had an interest," Doug says. "It just never occurred to me that here were other people who felt the same way. I've never even considered going out camping to look for it because I know it's out there—and I don't want to be in the middle of the woods camping. When I do go camping, it'll be in an area that I'm familiar with. I don't want to go camping out in these hills. There is no possible way I'd go out in these hills and camp overnight. No way."

People on the Internet bought in, believing they could find a bigfoot if only they watched the live stream long and hard, scrutinizing every sound and image. By the time I arrived, the site had more than four million views. People like Carl and Kelly, who are American Bigfoot Society members, say they've sometimes watched for twelve hours in a day. Like everything else in bigfoot research, the evidence viewed online is circumstantial. Doug tells me that he has felt something large banging on the side of his house, heard bigfoot walking on strewn Pepsi cans late at night, found a few footprints, and seen something large run from backyard when a friend dropped him off after work at a Bob Evans Restaurant. That friend, Doug says, refuses to drive back to this property.

The website is mostly a place where bigfoot enthusiasts meet, not unlike forums where fans of antique cars, vintage World War II airplanes, or the Chicago Blackhawks debate, reminisce, and compare notes. Mostly the people on the site forge relationships, happy to be communicating with others with the same interests. As they view the KLRP feeds, bigfoot fans record what they see and hear, such as "strange" screeches, "weird" howls, large shadows moving through the yard, faint whistles, high-pitched whistles, growling, eye shine emanating from a field where cows graze, "unusual" animals (probably with antlers) by a salt lick, agitated horses, something "large" sniffing a mic, and a four-legged creature loping down the road. This backyard would be an exciting spot to camp for any of these viewers; for someone accustomed to hiking tall peaks along the Smokies, Appalachians, and Rockies, this backyard adventure is insipid. But the viewers love it. They kibitz about bigfoot and connect with others with similar beliefs, and some try to more fully understand a sighting or inexplicable interaction they've had in the woods. Viewers take large logical leaps and offer imaginative conclusions, such as when some felt bigfoot was stalking a dog on the hill across the backyard creek. Here's an excerpt:

> *green_eyesn*: "Dogs worked up, heard fence noise, many footsteps, nothing on cam."
> *maxsdad*: "Gunshot, dog barking, rustling in the woods." [Twenty-four-second pause] "Barking dogs screaming out in pain."
> *tam1952*: "One dog yelping as though hurt, then no sound."
> *ghsthntr*: "Sounded like dog was snatched and dragged away."
> *watcher88*: "Beagle probably killed by something."

The next night viewers reported hearing another attack on a neighborhood dog chained in a backyard.

> *katbos*: "biped walking several mins. Dogs getting attacked."
> *watcher88*: "Heavy walking heard and then a rush to the dog in same instant. Neighbors out seem agitated, another dog in distress. Something grayish in background."

Later Doug says he confirmed that a beagle had been killed and that its large doghouse was found deep in the woods. "You could hear whatever it was literally creeping up on that dog. Could hear the leaves on the ground, sticks breaking. You could hear the dog going from barking wildly to literally getting scared."

Says Kelly, "It was sick."

Wildlife officers say wolves can develop a taste for dogs, selecting them over typical fare such as deer or moose.[3] But wolves no longer roam Kentucky. Foxes, which are skittish, usually run from noises and are poor opponents for all but the smallest of dogs. Even if victorious, they'll typically leave a dog where it falls. Opportunistic coyotes, which prefer rabbits, rodents, and carrion, will stalk and eat smaller dogs, charging into backyards for an easy meal. A coyote killed Ozzy Osbourne's Pomeranian in his backyard several months after this expedition, perhaps beating Oz to the punch. Ozzy once bit the head off a bat during a concert, chomped the head off a dove to get the attention of music executives, and regularly shot his family's pets during drug binges, at one point plugging all of the family's seventeen cats.[4] No word whether music's Prince of Darkness recently lurked around eastern Kentucky.

That leaves bigfoot as the culprit, right? That's what many bigfoot investigators say, including Ron Coffey, author of *Kentucky Cryptids: The Search for Kentucky's Hidden Animals* — published by a press he and his wife, Lori, own. In an article for the online newspaper Examiner.com, Ron wrote that bigfoot is no fan of dogs: "In reality, they do not actively seek out dogs to cause them harm, but they probably view dogs as a threat to their secrecy thus a threat to their safety. A Bigfoot's existence is dependent on its ability to escape detection; it is impossible to do this with a dog yelping at its heels."[5] Matt Moneymaker told me that he could track bigfoot's path in the Uwharries by listening to dogs — the closer the canine howls, the closer bigfoot to our location. Each night we'd quietly listen to howls rolling up that mountain in North Carolina. Some of these opinions sound reasonable; however, conjecture like this can lose integrity when you read that the author is also a "foremost" expert on werewolves and is a "certified" ghost hunter.

As we converge on Doug's place, the website's audience is growing. People tune in even during daylight, when nothing's on the website video except for color bars across a screen. I was among eleven people online at 10:13 a.m. CST a few days before the trip. But the evidence is flimsy — a fourteen-inch footprint, blurry video of a large biped (or man) walking along the road, grainy footage of movement of something (perhaps) between cars in the front yard, the shadow of something large walking past a window, and some eye shine. All in all, nothing conclusive to show for Doug's efforts—and for spending hundreds of dollars on cameras and hundreds more on electricity bills that have doubled since he placed the cameras outside. Doug says he's tried to lure a bigfoot by hanging large hams near the cameras, but the only thing that happened was that a two-by-four wood board was thrown at the cameras, an attempt to knock them out, he says.

Most everything is based upon Doug's claims. Like many others before him, he could be creating a scam to make some money, but that does not appear to be working for him. He rents a small trailer home that is no Taj Mahal. If he's really a trickster, asking the American Bigfoot Society to visit would offer some credibility.

Melissa Hovey, president of the American Bigfoot Society, tells me that she does not believe the evidence is as strong as many believe. But she respects Doug for being brave enough to create this project. "People can call him a liar, but he's not making a thousand bucks a day off this thing," she says. "He's not making money. He's not writing books. He's not going on television shows. He's just asking for help."

Doug says few neighbors and friends trust his conclusions about bigfoot, nor do they agree that a large hominid lives in this area. "People who know what I do think I'm nuts," Doug says. "At work they try to be supportive, but they don't mean it." That's a little surprising, considering Appalachia's rich folkloric history and its residents' unyielding faith and willingness to suspend belief for the sake of a good story. Few places in the world were as isolated, dangerous, and rugged as the Appalachians during the colonial period. Settlers worried constantly. That Native Americans, such as the Cherokees, would attack. That rocky, uneven terrain would not yield enough food to endure a long, stark winter. That they were too isolated to receive assistance if something horrible were to happen. These early settlers were stubborn, relentless, and self-reliant; however, the isolation of this region also made them wary—and, frankly, scared. As a result, these pioneers interpreted the woods differently than a modern weekend camper would, spinning tales filled with paranormal creatures that revealed their vulnerabilities. After all, who knew what lurked in the woods? Frequently these tales had a moral that was revealed after a human came in contact with a supernatural being (not unlike the early tales told by Puritans in New England and later purloined by writers such as Nathaniel Hawthorne). The mostly Scots-Irish pioneers eventually embroidered these tales with even more paranormal elements, further revealing the fearful, bleak thoughts of those who lived in desolate wilderness. Those stories reverberate today. Numerous books have been written about ghosts in eastern Kentucky and along the southern Appalachian range. Around Ashland the undead are far more prevalent than the walking dead. For example, Kentuckians claim to see a partially decomposed human body watching television in a local home at midnight, a young girl in a bloody wedding dress walks around Ashland's Central Park, and a man with a machete embedded in his skull appears at Kirby Flats. Plus, people claim to see a woman with a demon head changing shirts in an apartment, a sniveling man with half his head cut away near the entrance to Carter Caves State Park, and a lady who has worms crawling out of her nostrils floating like a balloon. So why wouldn't locals believe that an uncharted hominid lives in the woods?

In addition, many people living along the Appalachians are willing to suspend logic by faithfully embracing New Testament verses from Mark and Luke that instruct them, they believe, to handle eastern diamondback rattlers during services. The Pentecostals in this region believe literally in the following verse from Mark 16:17–18: "And these signs shall follow them that believe; In my name shall they cast out devils; they shall speak with new tongues; They shall take up serpents; and if they drink any deadly thing, it shall not hurt them; they shall lay hands on the sick, and they shall recover." Luke writes this more concisely, of course, in Luke 10:19: "Behold, I give unto you power to tread on serpents and scorpions, and over all the power of the enemy: and nothing shall by any means hurt you." In this holiness movement, snake handling is evidence of salvation and not of stupidity—even though nearly one hundred pastors have died from handling snakes during services since the movement's inception during the early 1700s, including one in nearby West Virginia a few years after my visit.

Did I mention that people in this region have embraced Mothman, a creature described as having large wings and glowing red eyes that appeared countless times in Point Pleasant, West Virginia, in the summer of 1966, inspiring an Associated Press national story, regional hysteria, and a book and movie entitled *The Mothman Prophecies*? Now the town, about an hour up the Ohio River from Ashland, holds a festival to honor a creature that, some say, appeared to warn of a bridge disaster. It would be crass to say the town created the festival just to make money and not to honor those who died on the Silver Bridge, which crossed the Ohio River to Gallipolis, Ohio. Or that the Miss Mothman pageant is anything except a way to attract tourists to the tiny town. By the way, cover all tattoos with Band-Aids if you plan to compete.

Kentuckians, ironically, might have been the first non–Native Americans to embrace bigfoot. In 1782 Daniel Boone claimed he killed a ten-foot, hairy giant near the Montgomery and Powell County border, which is about eighty miles southeast of Ashland. Boone called the creature a yahoo, a term he likely lifted from one of his favorite books, Jonathan Swift's satiric *Gulliver's Travels*. In the book, Yahoos were hairy, filthy, ignorant, man-like beings who fought over materialistic goods. Boone and his companions frequently poached terms from Swift's book, such as by calling Shawnees "brobdingnags," rational giants as large as church steeples who resided in a peninsula as large as a continent. The folklore scholar Hugh H. Trotti believes that Boone's yahoo stories fueled the bigfoot legend in North America. Few men were more respected than the legendary Boone, who plotted and cut out the two-hundred-mile Wilderness Road through the Appalachians and into Kentucky. Lord Byron and other writers glorified "the rippin'est, roarin'est, fightin'est man the frontier ever knew."[6] So if Daniel Boone says he killed a yahoo, or bigfoot, then it must be true. Other frontiersmen probably shared Boone's stories across the region, Trotti postulated in a column in 1994.[7] But that is too neat an explanation. First, several Native American tribes told stories about a large bigfoot-like creature for centuries. The Cherokees refer to Tsul 'Kalu, a "sloping giant" who was invoked during hunting rituals, and the Shawnees have Misignwa, a spirit that punished hunters who disrespected the woods. Native Americans also carved two large, four-toed, human-like feet into cliffs along the Red River Gorge at least several hundred years ago. The feet in these petroglyphs resemble plaster casts made of potential bigfoot prints across the globe. Myth and truth, though, often blend together in Native American fables.

Kentucky had 86 reported bigfoot incidents at the time of this visit according to the BFRO's database, or 220 according to the Kentucky Bigfoot Research Organization, making this one of the more active states. Bigfoot have been reported in more than half the state's 120 counties. Bigfoot is no stranger elsewhere in the Appalachian region. West Virginia has eighty-one BFRO reports, while Tennessee has eighty-five, North Carolina has seventy-eight and Georgia has one hundred. Many of the incidents reported occurred along the Appalachian range. Unlike Florida, bigfoot in this area are far less aggressive, according to reports, although one bigfoot apparently overturned an RV at night. Bigfoot have rarely been called yahoos, despite Boone's influence. In the 1800s reports referred instead to a wild man. In 1894, for example, a wild man kept stealing chickens, young pigs, lambs, and eggs in Dover, about ninety-five miles west of Ashland. Long, white hair grew on the wild man's face, hair as coarse as a horse's covered his legs, and fiery light came from his eyes, a newspaper reported.[8] Eventually, Eph Boston and his sons chased the wild man from their barn, tracking him to a cave filled with bones and feathers. From deep inside the cave they heard an "unearthly yell," which kept the three men from going inside. After this incident the wild man was never seen again—although a few months later a wild man appeared in Sailor, Indiana, where he raced on all fours after he was shot, and another wild man attacked a boy in Stout, Ohio, while a gorilla-like creature was seen in Rome, Ohio.

There are countless reports, coincidentally, in Kentucky's Daniel Boone National Forest, which is less than an hour from here—although only the witnesses might be referred to as yahoos. In one incident a BFRO investigator says she clearly saw a bigfoot's eerie eyes and gentle, intelligent face. A couple riding on an ATV said a bigfoot chased them, running twenty-two miles per hour to keep up in another part of the forest. Most reports emanate from the northeastern part of the forest. Farther east, toward us, a white-haired, ten-foot bigfoot nicknamed Big John reportedly wandered in the Carter Caves State Park area, several miles from Doug's boyhood home. For some reason, residents cite a high number of white-haired creatures.

Furthermore, bigfoot have been reported by locals not far from Doug's house. Josh Sparks, for example, reported that he and his five-year-old boy had seen a bigfoot two years earlier on a walk through the woods. The boy suddenly recognized bigfoot, a seven-foot, four-hundred-pound behemoth glaring down at them from atop a ridge not fifty yards away. When they both pointed at him, the creature broke a small tree in half, slammed it into a large tree trunk, and started grunting, scary enough actions to make most folks defecate a body organ. But Josh and his son were unfazed. "Every time I see a bigfoot," he told the Kentucky Bigfoot Research Organization, "I just freeze up and can't help but to admire their enormous size and yet see the gentleness they portray." Finally, the creature walked toward them and unleashed a loud, grousing scream, probably a gentle reminder that he was going to rip them in two if they kept staring. That prompted Josh and his son to amble away as leisurely as if they had just witnessed some elephants in a zoo, unconcerned that a massive, angry animal followed them, prompting me to question everything in the report. At age five, my girls were terrified if you simply turned off the lights in a room at night. Had they viewed a hulking, screaming, tree-smashing creature, my daughters' spirits would have departed their bodies, cartoonishly strumming a harp as their souls floated to the heavens. I'd be more apt to react as Dawn and her boyfriend had several years earlier, when they hit the accelerator in their car after an eight-foot creature peered at them while walking across a two-lane road not far from our current camping area.

A far scarier incident was reported in 1991 at a location equally close to where I now stand. A *sixteen*-foot creature growled and screamed at a deafening level while it ran on all four legs before stopping fifteen feet away from two youngsters out exploring a haunted bridge in an isolated hilly area. Somehow these kids did not let loose some body organs. Instead they ran to the car, according to the Kentucky Bigfoot Research Organization report, until an approaching car scared the creature away. Nobody has ever described bigfoot as being nearly that tall. On the other hand, one's imagination can play amazing tricks under dire stress. I'm also certain a large, fast creature like this could have easily outrun the two people to the car. But many researchers believe bigfoot's intent is merely to scare, not to attack. Either way, one wonders why so many people question Doug in an area that boasts a trove of paranormal stories and bigfoot reports. The truth is, though, that most people don't want to admit to believing—whether it's in bigfoot, love, or God. Actually, this problem run particularly deep in the United States, where many Americans dismiss ideas and facts that run counter to their entrenched beliefs—even if that means leaning toward partisan advocates in order to rationalize lies, deceptions, and misappropriated comments made by political figures. If bigfoot were to exist, the minds and souls of these people would convulse as they staved off revolutionary thoughts and anarchistic spirits. If bigfoot exists, would evolution make more sense? If bigfoot exists, would the national government need to spend more money protecting another imperiled species? If bigfoot exists, would we need to fear the woods as our ancestors had? Is it scarier to know the boogeyman really lives in our closets? That's not to say that many people aren't fascinated by bigfoot. That's been my experience, especially when they hear what I'm doing. But few are willing to admit publicly that bigfoot might exist, preferring instead to remain anonymous or to make easy jokes.

Some people in the South, though, think it's crazy *not* to believe in bigfoot, says Billy Willard, founder of Sasquatch Watch of Virginia. Billy grew up in northeastern Tennessee, lives in Virginia, and researches in West Virginia. "Some people in the South look at bigfoot as a normal animal. I come across people who don't even know why I'm fascinated by it. They'll say, are you talking about—and they'll offer a different name for it. Like 'booger' or 'bush ape.' You start talking to people about bigfoot and they start looking at you funny because you're fascinated with it. But it's normal for them to see."

It's Friday afternoon. We're all assembling tents in Doug's backyard. More and more, this expedition feels like a backyard slumber party and I have been wondering why I drove six hours and missed my daughter's soccer game for this. Melissa Hovey is inside her tent, straightening the base, as her fiancé, Wayne, attaches nylon strips to thin, graphite poles. Wayne's been fighting a cold all week. When he's not coughing, Wayne sounds like CNN commentator

John Cafferty, who also has a rich, baritone voice. At about five feet ten, Wayne, wearing a denim jacket, is angular and muscular—perhaps sinewy is the proper term, although covered up as he is in this weather it is difficult to prove. He wears his dark-brown hair long enough that it rolls out from under his hat, and a goatee covers his chin.

Melissa's scream jolts us all. By the time we look toward her, Melissa is halfway out the tent entrance, a flap draped over her back. Wayne races from the back of the tent. Melissa exclaims, "A spider!" Kelly Fain-Cockrill, a researcher from Texas and one of Melissa's closest friends, walks over, looks down at Melissa, and put her hands on her hips, shaking her head in disbelief. "You can go through the woods and the muck," Kelly says acerbically, "and now you're afraid of a spider?"

Wayne bends down, preparing to enter the tent and gather the arachnid. He chuckles. "I bet it's only this big," he says, holding his thumb and forefinger apart to about the size of a nickel.

Billy Willard and I both laugh at the absurdity of it all—that the president of the American Bigfoot Society, someone who treks through wilderness in order to find a hulking four-hundred-pound creature would spring back and shrill when she sees a bug the size of bigfoot's toenail.

Melissa leans out of the tent and flips us off. "You can all kiss my ass," she says loudly, before heading back into her tent. I can glimpse a smile.

That's typical Melissa Hovey, never too shy to say what's on her mind and usually self-aware enough to make light of a situation—not that she fears confrontation. That's clear to anyone who has ever read her blog *Searching for Bigfoot*, listened to her blog radio talk shows *Let's Talk Bigfoot*, *The Sasquatch Experience*, and *The Grey Area*, or followed her comments on several bigfoot forums. Melissa's going to say what she believes, regardless of whether her stance is popular. Frequently others do not appreciate her perspectives, in part because she's resolute but also because she's a rare female bigfoot researcher.

Her advice to women: do not hesitate to offer your opinion, do not take "any crap," go out and suck it up and play like one of the guys, and you'll do well. Plus keep an open mind, and don't be disgusted if others do not accept your ideas. After all, nobody is an expert in this field. That said, it's not like she doesn't have detractors who call her airheaded, lecherously comment on her appearance, or say she's making shit up. To be fair, the bigfoot community can be a jealous, spiteful, backbiting group.

"There are guys who will make it known in no uncertain terms that you shouldn't be out here," Melissa says. "The second a woman starts to openly say her opinion, you might as well forget about it. If you're a female and you don't have a spine, you're not going to last in this field." One researcher suggested she spend more time looking for handbags than for bigfoot. "I thought, 'So you're a jerk *and* a sexist. That's great.' That's the mentality I've dealt with. What we're doing is something seen as what guys should be doing, going in the woods and being stealthy. Yada, yada, yada."

Besides Melissa, few other women are interested in finding bigfoot. There's Carolanne Solomon, who regularly slogs through central Florida's swamps by herself. There's Donna and Dianne Stocking, who research the Pacific Northwest and Florida. There's also the ubiquitous Autumn Williams, who started the popular Oregon Bigfoot website, served as host of *Mysterious Encounters* on the Outdoor Life Network, and guided the *Sci Fi Investigates* crew into the Oregon woods for a segment on bigfoot before writing the controversial book *Enoch: A Bigfoot Story*, about a man who has befriended a squatch. There's also Bobbi Short, who has investigated bigfoot in California and elsewhere along the Pacific Rim and who created a research website, Bigfoot Encounters, that reports sightings, media coverage, and scientific research related to cryptozoology. But the number of women in the field is low.

This is reflected, in part, by lists compiled by those such as the "Find Bigfoot" Facebook page, which cited twelve women on its list of top one hundred bigfoot researchers. That should not be a surprise given the bias toward men in all such lists. ESPN, for example, cited nearly as many horses (three) as it did women (seven) on its list of the one hundred top athletes of the twentieth century. Of course all such lists are highly subjective, reflective of those who vote. On the Find Bigfoot Facebook list, many of the women cited do not actively research bigfoot. Autumn Williams, the highest-rated female, at number 15, has investigated in Oregon for decades, but the artist Sybilla Christine Irwin (29) does not research bigfoot, nor does the anthropologist Jane Goodall, whose speculation that such a creature exists lifted her to number 32. Bobbie Short (36), Kathy Strain (44), Carolanne Solomon (53), Melissa Hovey (60), and Diane Stocking (96) do research, but Marian T. Place (70), Montra Freitas (73), and Janet Bord (99) primarily investigate topics to track reports and to write books on unsolved mysteries, including bigfoot, while Sharon Lee (76) blogs about bigfoot conferences, alleged sightings, and updates by field researchers. Myra Shackley, at number 92, is an archaeologist who has written exhaustively on preserving historic sites. She has investigated whether the Almas, wild men who allegedly lived in Eurasia, could be descended either from Neanderthals or have a biological link to yetis. On the other hand, nobody on the list has found an actual body nor done anything more than speculate based upon vague evidence. As always, such lists are as moot as those citing the top alien investigators, ghost hunters, or unicorn researchers.

Melissa Hovey gained national prominence in the bigfoot community after she was featured in an episode during *MonsterQuest*'s first season that sent an all-female team into the Pacific Northwest woods, testing the hypothesis that bigfoot feel less threatened by females—an idea fostered by Goodall, who spent more than forty years studying chimpanzees in Tanzania. At one point chimps accepted Goodall into a chimpanzee society in Gombe National Park for twenty-two months. Goodall, incidentally, supports bigfoot research, having divulged to National Public Radio several years ago, "Well now you will be amazed when I tell you that I'm sure that they exist."[9] Unfortunately, the MonsterQuest producers sent a male camera crew to tape the segment, effectively spoiling the premise. The MonsterQuest team included archaeologist Kathy Strain, Texas Bigfoot Research Conservancy founder Monica Rawlins, botanist Kristine Walls, and BFRO member Tracy Herigstad. They found nothing besides a circumstantial footprint.

Melissa was not impressed by her sudden fame, dismissing the ridiculous notion that someone can be a bigfoot "expert" when the animal has not been found. "I did not think I had somehow gained all this secret knowledge or had something no one else had simply because I was on MonsterQuest," Melissa told me. "I did the show in the hope of encouraging other women to become involved in this field of research.

"I had someone once tell me, 'Melissa, your problem is that you're too opinionated.' Well, sorry, that's their problem. I said, 'Who died and left you as the king of the world?' My dad told me never to take a backseat to others. He said my gender is only an obstacle if I allow it."

Melissa, fortunately, has never really cared what people think about her. That perspective serves her well as president of the American Bigfoot Society. Unlike most other bigfoot groups, the American Bigfoot Society has a national scope. Most other organizations focus on local reports, usually because doing so is easier and less expensive. In particular, these groups typically concentrate within a state's boundaries, such as the Ohio Bigfoot Organization, Virginia Bigfoot Research Organization, Sasquatch Watch of Virginia, Texas Bigfoot Research Conservancy, Minnesota Bigfoot Research Team, Oregon Bigfoot, and the Pennsylvania

Bigfoot Society. Several groups aim more hyperlocal by focusing on a portion of a state, such as the East Tennessee Bigfoot organization, which investigates areas in the more mountainous regions north and east of Chattanooga to the state's borders with North Carolina, Georgia, and Kentucky, and the Southern Oregon Bigfoot Society, which is based out of Grants Pass in Josephine County. Several organizations investigate regions. The Gulf Coast Bigfoot Research Organization focuses on the South, ranging from traditional Dixie states like Georgia, Mississippi, and Tennessee to Texas and Oklahoma. The North East Sasquatch Researchers Association, meanwhile, cover sightings from New England to Pennsylvania, New Jersey, and Delaware. Few groups have the resources or ambition to journey across the country, besides the BFRO and North America Bigfoot Search.

Most bigfoot organizations grow quickly, peak early, and then fall into neglect when the originator of the group loses interest, time, faith, finances, or a combination of these factors. It takes a great deal of time to develop a website, but it takes even more time to feed it regular updates, commentary, and information based upon reported sightings in the region. In addition, someone needs to call and sometimes visit people who have had sightings in the area. It's all fun and games early on, especially when a local reporter finds the website and writes a story, propelling researchers to their proverbial fifteen minutes of fame. That's when the hard work begins and the phone calls start arriving, including those from quacks, crazies, zealots, trolls, and disbelievers. These calls grind down one's enthusiasm. After a while, this hobby yields to other interests or to growing family responsibilities. That was the case with the American Bigfoot Society (ABS). Sean Forker started the group in 2005 at age twenty after having been inspired by John Green's book *Sasquatch: The Apes among Us*. He loved the mystery of if it all, so he enthusiastically jumped in with both feet. Forker started a Blog Talk Radio show with Henry May, a southern researcher, entitled *The Sasquatch Experience*, and he later started producing another show with Eric Altman, founder of the Pennsylvania Bigfoot Society, entitled *Beyond the Edge Radio*. During the next several years, though, Forker started other business interests, got married, and started a family. One child had diabetes, which required extra care. Life was taking over Forker's free time. In the meantime, other researchers drifted off as well. So by May 2008 Forker decided to close ABS and posted the following announcement on several bigfoot forums: "Since its inception in mid 2005, the American Bigfoot Society has gone through a few periods of inactivity; and has undergone many 'corporate' restructures. While our focus on the cause has been true, we have faltered on our mission. Our approach has been just, but our activity is lax. Any resources we have shall be folded into a future research organization. It has been decided that the American Bigfoot Society shall cease operations as of this day." Forker continued to host his radio show until 2010 and to produce Eric's until 2011. But the ABS ceased to exist.

Later that year, Melissa, then a researcher for the Texas Bigfoot Research Conservancy, decided to resuscitate the American Bigfoot Society. She had just left Dallas, where she worked as a paralegal, for Ohio to be with Wayne. Earlier that year Melissa had joined Forker as cohost of *The Sasquatch Experience*. A year earlier she had appeared in the episode of *MonsterQuest*, which in the bigfoot community yields the same prestige that an anthropologist would get in the scientific community for having appeared on a National Geographic documentary. No doubt, Melissa was a rising star.

Melissa, though, disagrees with conventional wisdom on the best approach to investigating bigfoot. She does not want to sponsor large research expeditions; rather, she prefers to gather thinkers who will evaluate information and analyze reports. As a paralegal, she had learned truth is usually hidden within larger narratives cited in depositions and interviews. Besides, she told me, most sightings happened when people were not trying to find a bigfoot. Sitting by a campfire in the middle of the woods, she believes, is as effective as any other approach. "In a lot of these organizations headed by men, they have their game cameras, their scent cans, their tree stands — they hide in the middle of the night playing commando. But that's not what people are doing when they're having sightings."

Melissa realizes that this approach is antithetical to how others approach research, but her father, a sergeant in the army, had taught Melissa to stand her ground. In fact, Sergeant Hovey thought all excuses sounded like whining. "When I first saw the movie *Heartbreak Ridge*, I thought Clint Eastwood had followed my dad around before filming. He's also where I get my sarcasm. I don't like to fail because I have to face my dad."

Two resilient, compassionate women raised Sergeant Hovey during the Depression. His father died when he was sixteen years old. Besides working a farm in Iowa and feeding the family, his mother started working at a bar, serving drinks to men at a time when most women were not even allowed to be in a bar. His aunt Janice, meanwhile, worked a farm and helped feed neighbors struggling to survive during the 1930s. From her father, Melissa learned that women could do whatever men could. "I'm very lucky to have had these role models," Melissa said. "That's why I'm strong-willed today. Bigfoot research has been a boys' club for many years. For a woman to throw herself out there and have an opinion, you've got to be willing to throw the dice. And I've realized nobody has a better opinion than me."

Melissa has been through far more onerous challenges than justifying herself to bigfoot researchers. This task is a trifle compared to what she faced as a teenager battling the local police chief after her brother died.

They found Melissa's brother, asphyxiated, in the family garage, a half-smoked cigarette on the floor and an automobile running in the closed building. With a cursory look, the police determined her brother's death a suicide, believing the young man had purposefully inhaled the toxic fumes spewing from an idling car in an enclosed room. After all, about two thousand people kill themselves each year with carbon monoxide.[10] On the other hand, more than four hundred people die each year from accidental carbon monoxide emissions, which is not too surprising since the gas is nearly undetectable, without any taste, color, or odor to forewarn potential victims. This gas can escape from malfunctioning gas water heaters, propane heaters, gas stoves, and kerosene space heaters, making winter a dangerous time in colder climates. As many as fifty thousand people get treated for carbon monoxide poisoning each year in hospitals across the country, most near-victims believing they have the flu, with symptoms such as headaches, dizziness, nausea, and vomiting. At times they might also get chest pains. Ultimately, one gets confused, unable to think clearly or to act physically — even if one realizes what is happening — and then loses consciousness. At this point, death is imminent, primarily because less oxygen is being absorbed in the body, replaced by carbon dioxide that more efficiently binds with red blood cells. Eventually the body does not have enough oxygen for even basic functions.

Melissa persisted because she knew her brother had not intended to kill himself. Earlier that morning, Melissa had talked with him before heading off to classes at the university, joking about her algebra woes and discussing plans for that night. He bummed a cigarette, smoking it as he cleaned his car in the garage, whose doors were closed. Except for the hardiest Cheddarheads, you won't catch many Wisconsinites opening garage doors as they work on their cars. Adam, who had health issues that Melissa would not discuss, apparently suffered in cold weather more than most—his health issues, Melissa believes, made her brother more susceptible to the carbon monoxide.

The police chief refused to listen to Melissa, failing to follow up on the family's suggestions and insights. The police, Melissa said, felt they knew more about her brother than she did. So Melissa started digging, collecting, analyzing, and calling the chief with new evidence. When the police chief asked to review it, Melissa declined, saying the police would either discard or lose anything she submitted. Frankly, she told him, she did not trust him to do his job. At that point the chief threatened to arrest Melissa for refusing to submit evidence. After a two-year battle, the coroner in Beloit, Wisconsin, changed the cause of death to undetermined and the police changed their report to accidental death. Eventually the police chief lost his job for failing to diligently investigate other cases, Melissa said. "You think the police will do what's right," she added. "Now, we'll never know what happened. They never even did an autopsy, all because of a snap decision of a police chief."

Melissa returned to the University of Wisconsin for a while, but she could not stop thinking about other families who faced similar challenges with authorities. So she earned her paralegal degree and worked for the public defender's office, where she fought to help those unfairly accused of crimes. Several years later she became interested in bigfoot, not so much out of worry that a bipedal hominid might be walking the woods or for the joy of listening to stories for a scare. The woods did not appeal to her either. She preferred beds to tents, business attire to ghillie suits, and French manicures to dirty fingernails. Rather, it bothered Melissa that those without evidence immediately label those who report seeing bigfoot as liars. "Nobody was listening to these people," Melissa said. "Nobody. Nobody took the reports seriously. Nobody cared."

By 2005 Melissa had started investigating bigfoot witness reports for the Texas Bigfoot Research Center, in part because of her brother. She did not want people's stories so easily dismissed. She analyzed bigfoot witness reports in the same manner that she reviewed witness reports for legal proceedings. She believed this process would yield more insights than wandering through the woods. Little did she know she would soon be frequently thrust into the woods, especially by her fiancé, Wayne Larson, an avid outdoorsman.

A paved, two-lane road unwinds from some rolling hills in the east, moves within twenty yards of Doug's house, and stretches west past tall grass, horse fields, cow pastures, and miles of undulating hills that rise two to three hundred feet before disappearing into distant hollows. Cows sometimes wander onto this sleepy road used mostly by local residents. Car engines thrum in the distance, growing louder as they approach and sounding like giant bumblebees before blending into other ambient noise, forgotten before they're unheard.

To the east of the house, an open field stretches several hundred yards away toward a line of trees. Tall grass grows thick enough that it could hide a person's lower body after walking away thirty or so yards. A shallow creek, narrow enough that I could easily leap over it, runs through the back of Doug's yard, rolling along below a sharp hill that rises fifty yards and about a half mile past the western tree line. Several homes sit atop this hill. It is at the home right above us where several viewers of the KLRP live feed claim to have heard a bigfoot stalk and kill several dogs. A fallow field, separated by a wooden rail that's cracked and wire that's either bent or snapped, hems us in on the right; weeds and tall grass grow so thick we can't always notice when a cow is grazing twenty yards away.

The main investigation will take place by a pond in a hollow less than a mile away. But the American Bigfoot Society members plan to spend most of their time sitting in the middle of Doug's yard, which the Kentucky Live Research Project monitors through four cameras that are partially funded by bigfoot organizations and enthusiasts. It's late Friday morning and we're walking toward the pond. That anybody can function is a miracle. A few hours earlier Billy made a meal even Adam Richman wouldn't ingest on *Man v. Food*. Billy cooked at least a pound of bacon over an open fire but then left the grease in the large skillet after taking out the pig's meat. Then he cracked about a dozen eggs into this liquid lard. Billy says the grease gives the omelet more flavor. He's not alone in this belief. In Germany, flavored lard is a delicacy called "schmaltz" that yields 99.8 grams of fat per 3.5 ounces. Billy may have added some other items, such as sausage or green peppers, but I was repulsed, watching what looked like a recipe for arteriosclerosis. I slowly munched on two plain Strawberry Pop Tarts and drank some orange juice, sickened when everybody gobbled Billy's omelet down with several large pieces of bacon.

To get to the pond, we had to walk about a half mile down the two-lane road, past separate fields that enclose horses and steers. There was also a larger, newer home right across from the path where we turned off the two-lane road. This newer home did not have fences, nor roaming chickens, nor a large pickup truck, like a Ford F-150 or Chevy Silverado. It appeared to be owned by an older couple looking to escape the suburbs. We had to climb a large swinging gate and go through a pasture filled with large, black steers. The farm's owner had already granted permission to cross through his fields to reach a hollow that Doug suspected would yield some bigfoot activity. So we marched through tall grass, past a few annoyed steers, and along a creek on the east side. Hills rose steeply on the left, or west, side all the way to some thicker woods that hid a depression and the pond.

The area does not seem unusual in any manner. The pond is small enough that I can easily skip a thrown rock across. Trees line low-lying banks. On the west side, we have to nearly climb hand over foot to navigate through bramble, between branches, and up a steep incline to a path that offers a bird's-eye view of the hollow. On the opposite shore, Wayne and Melissa cut apples in order to enable the scent to waft and then place them on a log while Billy places infrared cameras in a nearby tree to record any movement. Billy, Wayne, and I walk around the pond to scout tracks. It all feels more like play, which, to me, has always been an attractive part of joining these expeditions. If you ever liked playing in the woods as a kid, you would enjoy bigfoot expeditions, even those less rigorous like this one. Overall, this all probably took no more than three hours, by far the most physical activity I'd have all weekend.

Soon enough, we all settle in around a smoldering fire back at the trailer. It's late afternoon. The skies are mostly clear, temperatures in the midfifties, and light has started to slant from the west. In October night creeps in much earlier. Like the early pioneers, people still love to tell ghost stories around the campfire—even if night is a few hours away. Billy has more ghost stories than anyone I've encountered. He has lived in several older homes, some built in the 1800s, where he felt spirits watching him. He has walked through woods where battles were waged in both the Civil and Revolutionary Wars, such as the Battle for King's Mountain. Friends and local hunters would see shadows of soldiers traipsing out of the woods. Strange lights emitted from an abandoned church in northern Virginia. Once inside, Billy says, lights would turn on and a piano would start playing. "I used to take people up there back when I was stupid," Billy says. "We would sit real close to the church. Last time I went up there, I took my wife. We pulled up right in front of the church. I told her, 'We're gonna park right here.'" They kept looking at the front doors, which were made of glass, until a shadow walked up to the door. Billy shined a flashlight at the door, revealing a figure that appeared to be pure white. "Have you ever seen an alien head? That's what it looked like." Billy put the car in reverse, hit the gas pedal, and sent rocks everywhere as he swung the car around and drove as fast as he could out of that area. "Scared me to death," Billy says.

Billy blames his ghost problems on the fact he is descended from witches on both sides of his family. He's related to John Willard, who was executed in August 1692 during the Salem witch trials along with four others at Gallows Hill—so named because eighteen people were hanged there during the supernatural hysteria that took place in several Massachusetts villages. Ironically, John Willard had been the constable who brought accused witches to Salem's court. Willard, though, grew to distrust the accusations, which prompted Ann Putnam to accuse him of witchcraft and led to his execution beside John Proctor, the protagonist in Arthur Miller's *The Crucible*. Billy says his great-grandmother used witchcraft to cure his grandmother of seizures by cooking something and then putting a spell on it before feeding it to Billy's grandmother, who never had another seizure. "I used to be fascinated by that stuff," Billy says, "until it started bothering me."

Ghosts still harass Billy, and his dog, in his home near Manassas, Virginia. He blames his grandfather, who died in the house. "He was particular in how he cooked," Billy says. "He hated leaving utensils in pots. Hated it. One night when we were cooking chili, we left a spoon in the pot. All of a sudden, we hear 'clang, chuck, chuck.' We turned around to see that the spoon had left the pot and landed on the floor. It was a deep pot, so it did not lean out and fall on its own. The spoon was deep inside the pot."

At times his dog will just stare at a spot before getting up and walking away. At other times the dog will jump up as if it were kicked and take off running. "There's something in that house," Billy says. "There really is."

Billy's more fearful of ghosts than bigfoot, at least, I suppose, until a bigfoot starts harassing him in his home. A ghost, though, never grabbed Billy's knee in the middle of the east Texas woods. That's a tale I'll share later.

It was foggy when we returned to the pond in the nearby hollow. It was also very dark, the hills blocking ambient light and the nearly new moon failing to offer illumination. Had we been able to see the sky, the moon would have appeared as a thinly lined crescent. I could not even see my hand, once extended. The winds pushed the water toward our shore, creating waves that lapped against the soft-packed ground. Limbs fell from trees; something splashed in the water. Suddenly this playful area seemed scarier. Melissa had ridiculed our trek up here when we had departed Doug's yard. "Remember while you're up there freezing your butts off that you asked for this." Melissa's goal with the American Bigfoot Society was to assemble a group of good thinkers, believing expeditions like this yield very little. After all, she had said, people usually encounter bigfoot when they are picking wild blueberries or bird hunting or looking for wildflowers. They're not finding anything on these expeditions. She'd rather analyze the data, like some bigfoot wonk. But she also recognizes that an investigative group needs to seek evidence, and perhaps she also realizes that boys (and girls) just want to have some fun out in the woods. So we pressed on, testosterone rising. Billy had turned to me halfway down the two-lane road. "Don't worry," he said. "I put a trail cam where she usually goes to the bathroom. We'll get her back."

Besides Billy and me, three others traveled to the hollow—Joedy Cook, a paranormal and bigfoot investigator from Ohio; his assistant, Scottie; and Wayne, who was coughing harshly, trying to fight off the flu. The plan: place Billy and me on opposite sides of the pond in order to confirm sounds and to place the two others along a ridge area that, in daylight, offered a clear view of the hollow from about one hundred feet above. The fog, eerily reminiscent of a scene from *Creature from the Black Lagoon*, ended that idea.

Earlier Billy had told me a story about an investigation where he heard a large splash in a nearby lake at night, something that had made him consider whether a bigfoot had belly flopped into the water to swim across toward him. "Just for the record," Billy said as we stood a few feet from the pond, "we will not be putting our backs to the water. I'm not having anything come up behind me."

No sooner had Billy placed his chair about ten yards away from the edge of the pond, facing toward it, than the clouds opened up. Joedy and Scottie came down from the ridge. It was time to go, they all said. No need to get soaked. Yet we did get very wet while marching back through the woods and down the two-lane road before getting into our tents, where I sulked for a little while, feeling as though my time had been wasted. Eventually I changed my clothes, walked to the car, turned on the heat, and opened my notebook to record some observations, displeased by the abbreviated investigation but realizing that even wild animals hunker down in the rain. There was nothing to do, which was tough to endure after days of essentially doing nothing.

Scottie had me mesmerized. Not so much by his stories about blue ghosts hovering in his bedroom as a kid. Or because he described a "beautiful" unidentified flying object stretched across the entire sky near Atlanta. Or because of his story that, as a teenager, he viewed an even bigger, more "beautiful" UFO in Cincinnati that blocked the sky in 1966. ("It was a mile wide, if not bigger. It scared the hell out of me. I tried to reason it away.") Or even his account of how another flying object chased him and his fellow band members on a remote two-lane highway in northern Nevada in 1977 (not that musicians in the seventies took hallucinatory drugs or anything). It was more that Scottie believed each of these stories, which worried me on many levels. We were standing under an overhang in Doug's driveway that protected us from the rain, which had now slowed to a drizzle. After the night's expedition I had changed clothes, but I needed another sweatshirt. As I returned from my car, Scottie was standing there drinking wine from a bottle. He offered some, but I declined, preferring his intoxicating stories instead. As far as I could tell, Scottie was in his mid- to late fifties, although he looked younger despite decades of playing in bands, tending bar, and, based upon his stories, having a pretty good time along the way. He had spent time in the Florida Keys, the Rockies, and New York. He currently lived in Ohio, where he helped Joedy Cook with his paranormal investigations.

I've read the *National Enquirer* and watched countless reenactment shows on television. I get it. People claim they've seen ghosts, unidentified flying objects, and bigfoot. In fact, I love it all. Some people claim interactions with aliens, the dead, and hairy hominids, which make for even better tales. The hair on my arms rose when Billy told me his ghost stories. With Scottie, I never fell into a trance, imagining what it felt to encounter something like a ghost with an alien's head in a secluded northern Virginian church. With Scottie, I kept trying to conceptualize why he told each story. As an artist, he must certainly be creative. Was it the songwriter in him that compelled Scottie to piece together these paranormal stories? Did Scottie learn as a kid that telling stories like this would prompt adults to stop and listen to him? Based on a single, thirty-minute conversation, there's no way to tell. It's fascinating to believe that aliens regularly visit our planet and egotistical to think we're worth studying. It's comforting to believe that our spirits exist even when our bodies perish. And it's liberating to believe that intelligent hominids can exist in the wild.

As a kid Scottie also frequently saw a blue image float in his bedroom. Somehow, he said, he thought little about it at the time, especially since turning on the lights extinguished the amorphous figure. As an adult Scottie started to read about ghosts, which further prompted him to research his home. Apparently a man had died of a massive heart attack in his bedroom before Scottie had moved in. Scottie also claimed to have seen a ghost in a North Carolina home where the director of *I Was a Teenage Werewolf* resided. Ghosts are more likely to appear in vortex areas, he said, which reveal interdimensional shifts. "I don't like to mess with it too much because I don't know what I'm getting myself into with stuff like that."

Don't get him started on shadow people, apparitions that appear as unclothed, black shadows. They might be time travelers or demons, or perhaps even astral projects from sleeping individuals—although that does not explain the terrifying red eyes. "I honestly believe shadow people are probably within our dimension," Scottie said. "I don't know who they are or what they are, but they live among us." That's when a shiver ran down my spine.

Scottie sidled closer to me and spoke more softly. "Have you ever seen a rod before?"

I eased back a little. "A rod?" I said, my voice rising.

"Yeah, they look like a long stick."

"Uh huh."

"They have wings on them, you know," he said.

I did not know this.

"And they fly so fast that you can't see 'em."

That's when I remembered a show about rods on either *In Search Of . . .* or *MonsterQuest*. "Oh, rods. Right."

"If you shoot a camera in high speed, you can catch them occasionally," Scottie said. "Especially in vortex areas, they come in and out. They actually hit people. There are several instances where this has been shown. They have one on film that hit Tiger Woods. He sort of shook it off like a cold chill. There have also been several football games where referees have been hit by one."

At that moment either a rod pierced my neck or I shuddered at the idea that someone truly believes this. As a journalist, I attempt to remain as neutral as possible, despite what media detractors say. At times during our conversation I was not sure whether to chuckle or sigh. Either way, there was no stopping Scottie when it came to rods.

"Do you know how a sea slug moves? The rods have long, cylinder shapes but they have wings that make it look like a sea slug—and they move around us all the time." At this point Scottie was talking so quickly I could barely keep up. His voice kept rising with each new profession. Thank God for the tape recorder in my right hand. "They're usually neat to watch. You can see examples if you type in 'rods' online. I think the shadow people are just a higher vibrational entity that exists within our same frame of dimensions. There are a million theories out there on this stuff. But that's my read on it."

Somehow, Scottie has never seen a bigfoot, has never felt one's presence, and has never found any physical evidence. He's here only because of Joedy. Scottie is fascinated by bigfoot, believing the evidence to be overwhelming, and he's certain the government has already captured one. Bigfoot, in all probability, are connected to UFOS, Scottie said. "They may have been put here for a reason. Why? I don't know. But we'll all figure it out later. I believe in our lifetime that we'll have the answers for everything."

The rain was now mostly vapor, cooler moisture clinging to my uncovered face. I wasn't sure how much longer I'd remain here at Doug's, especially if sleet or snow hit, as predicted, later that night. But I determined to bundle up and sit very close to the campfires, where, I knew, bigfoot investigators loved to talk. Before I left, Scottie started to weigh into another theory, on why bigfoot are rarely photographed even when people see one in the daylight. "I know damn well that the government has a belt for invisibility," he said, "just like in *The Philadelphia Experiment.*"

I told him I need to check something in my tent, but I really needed to check back into reality. As a poet, I believe anything is possible. As a journalist, I demand verified facts. I understand that the easiest person to deceive is ourselves, particularly when we passionately want to justify a belief. I do not know Scottie's life story, but something drives him to interpret what he saw. Have aliens visited Earth? There may be as many as ten thousand billion habitable planets in just the known universe.[11] But, like the esteemed astrophysicist Carl Sagan, I need evidence that aliens have toured our planet or abducted humans. Before he died in 1996, Sagan stated in an interview that we need to use the most rigorous, severe standards for all evidence:

> I personally have been captured by the notion of extraterrestrial life, and especially extraterrestrial intelligence, from childhood. It swept me up, and I've been involved in sending spacecraft to nearby planets to look for life and in the radio search for extraterrestrial intelligence. It would be an absolutely transforming event in human history. But, the stakes are so high on whether it's true or false that we must demand the more rigorous standards of evidence—precisely because it's so exciting. That's the circumstance in which our hopes may dominate our skeptical scrutiny of the data. So, we have to be very careful. There have been a few instances in the [past]. We thought we found something, and it always turned out to be explicable.[12]

That's how a bona fide scientist approaches research—by keeping his mind open to all possibilities but requiring that the most rigorous standards be used to evaluate evidence. Sagan thought alien encounters plausible, promoted extraterrestrial research, and outlined in his novel *Contact* a means for possibly communicating with those who might reside on planets so far away that we cannot even see them. Like Sagan, Scottie probably desires to connect with others, whether they are aliens in spaceships that blanket the skies over Cincinnati and Atlanta, shadow people who reside in other dimensions, or a fellow bigfoot researcher under an overhang in eastern Kentucky. It's easy to poke fun at someone like Scottie, whose risible theories prompt sniggers. But that doesn't mean he's lying or delusional. Later in Sagan's interview I found illumination, even if the astrophysicist's statement reads like a confusing haiku poem: "The fact that someone says something doesn't mean it's true. Doesn't mean they're lying, but it doesn't mean it's true."[13]

You can learn a lot about people by listening. Sadly, few people do this. Instead, we gab incessantly about our lives, our thoughts, our theories, and our feelings, in part because we have been empowered by Facebook and Twitter, where we can share even mundane details about our day—"Fred is now at Starbucks," "Trying out a new goatee," "It's snowing!" "Stupid friggin' snow," "Headed to the gym." To be fair, we do not need social media to talk about ourselves. Everybody's favorite topic = themselves. I'm no exception. I'll gush on about my daughters for as long as you can stand it. Conversing with others has always been a competitive sport, where we battle for supremacy in topic choices and offer personal reflections on another's topic. Most people listen only to find a way to reply. A casual conversation might go like this:

Boring friend: "Shark Week started tonight! Did you see it?"

You: "No, but in Florida I used to see sharks all the time. Once while I was fishing in water to my waist, I saw a shark's fin rise not twenty yards away. Fortunately, it was going away from me."

Boring friend: "I love Disney. Would love to get back to Space Mountain."

You: "Ever go hiking in the Smokey Mountains? Man, that place is beautiful. The temps can drop into the thirties at night in July, which causes the bumblebees to sleep on the flowers until they get enough energy in the morning."

Boring friend: "I cannot even function in the morning without coffee. Wish I could just use sunshine to get going."

As a kid I learned a great deal by quietly sitting by my parents, aunts, uncles, and grandparents around the dinner tables during holidays, hearing them revisit stories from their youth while sneaking sips of Chianti from the large jug on the dinner table. As a Stephen minister, I learned that listening is essential to helping others heal. While buying party favors for my daughter Sarah's first birthday party, for example, I had a brief conversation with the cashier at Wal-Mart. It was around 1:30 a.m., right after I had worked a shift as a copy editor at the *Orlando Sentinel*. The store was pretty empty except for the two of us. She appeared to be in her early sixties, probably working because her retirement funds did not cover expenses.

"Oh, you're having a birthday party?" She picked up the *101 Dalmatians* hats, napkins, and plates, scanning them slowly. I acknowledged a party was imminent, but she already knew this. That question was an excuse to talk about her own grandkids, whom she rarely got to see thanks to a daughter-in-law who was angry at her for an indiscretion she did not divulge. The woman's eyes widened, though, as she described her granddaughter, who was a few years older than Kristen. The woman left the scanned items on the conveyor belt while she talked for several minutes. I was fatigued from working late, but I let the cashier brag about her little darling. Eventually she bagged the items in plastic so I could head home. Everybody has an interesting story to tell, but some need to also confess their sins, even if they do it obliquely, as this woman had. So, I tell my girls, listen intently when people talk. You'll be amazed the insights you'll learn about life—and the good deeds you can do for those who need someone to hear them, even if just for a few minutes.

As a journalist, I have learned that if you discuss topics people feel passionately about, they will talk exhaustively. That has worked for me with athletes, administrators, city officials, and ordinary citizens. They're all eager to talk about their hobbies and personal lives, eyes widening, for example, when you ask about the most compelling aspect of quilting. Those lessons have served me well with bigfoot investigators, among the most passionate people on the planet. On the phone, I usually sit quietly and take notes. On expeditions like this, I essentially do the same thing by turning on my digital recorder, sitting back in a chair, and letting everybody energetically talk as we gather around a fire. Frequently these investigators just let loose, finally able to speak about their experiences, theories, and beliefs with others who share the same beliefs. At times I'll pose a question, but essentially I want to learn why they do what they do so fervently.

It's Saturday morning. The shivering is consuming me. The sky is overcast, the temperature is dropping, and we've heard it's snowing across the river in West Virginia. So I roll up my sleeping bags, empty and dissemble my tent, and place it all in the back of my Mazda Tribute. As I walk to my car, Joedy says, "You're not going to miss anything. With this weather, there won't be much to see or hear around here tonight." Plus, we never really tried the previous two days.

After saying good-bye, I head down the two-lane road, along a larger county road, and out to Interstate 64, where I can essentially cruise until I reach Indianapolis in about four hours. It's difficult not to appreciate the fall foliage along Interstate 64, the burnt oranges and browns and yellows exclaiming the beauty of the Daniel Boone National Forest, a land once traversed by the legendary pioneer and an area allegedly inhabited by bigfoot. But I'm not scanning the woods for bigfoot today, because I do not expect to see anything—not a glimpse of a hominid or a dark figure walking along a power-line trail or running along the tree line high atop a hill. I do not believe a cut, squat tree is a motionless bigfoot or that the deer running through a pasture are seeking to escape a squatch. In many ways, I have lost my faith in bigfoot.

Fortunately, I am headed toward a far warmer place for both

my body and my spirit—a hotel near Indianapolis where my wife and daughters had checked in the night before for a youth travel soccer tournament. On the four-hour trip there, I call my wife, telling her how exasperating the trip was, mostly sitting by a campfire. After this call, I turn the radio back on, listening to West Virginia and Marshall play in the Coal Bowl, an appellation used to define the competition between the state's only Division I football teams. Like bigfoot researchers, the two schools hate one another. And, like always, West Virginia ultimately defeats Marshall for the ninth consecutive time. But I am only half listening to the game, worried that I have nothing much to report from this expedition except for stories and theories. That Billy believes ghosts follow him. That Melissa feels that sitting around a campfire is a good way to attract bigfoot. That Scottie thinks rods impale us in some cosmic manner and that shadow people and ghosts flit through our universe. None of that matters right now. Instead, I listen to Dave Brubeck and company improvise on my iPod. Like this jazz impresario, I mentally also take five, riffing about my family, baseball, and bottles of Blue Moon that my wife has chilling back at the hotel—hopefully, with a slice of orange.

7 SALT FORK STATE PARK

OHIO

Late at night in the middle of the woods, Don Keating sometimes wonders what normal people are doing, people who, you know, do not spend hours following footprints in the snow in the middle of the woods on a frigid winter night or who do not get poison ivy (or sumac or oak) so frequently that their hands and legs welt, requiring steroids—and even become so allergic that merely thinking about these plants appears to cause skin problems—or who do not scrape money together in order to wander through thick brush and eat campfire food in Canada, Oregon, and Idaho or who do not receive prank calls from people reporting fake bigfoot sightings or who do not endure deprecating stares in at the grocery store or, for that matter, people who do not get mocked by radio hosts, TV anchors, and reporters for investigating bigfoot. But Don knows what (he thinks) he's seen and (mostly) trusts what he's heard in the woods and during interviews with normal midwestern folks like himself. How much time, he wonders, have I wasted in my life in pursuit of something that may not exist? But he keeps sitting and wondering and listening here at a picnic table in Salt Fork State Park, hoping there will be a payoff. But he's losing faith.

Don looks like a retired fullback. He has broad shoulders, thick legs, and large hands but a little extra weight around the middle. He typically wears jeans, a collared shirt, and sneakers, as he does today at this pavilion located in the northern part of a state park he has traveled extensively. He's spent way more than a thousand hours walking through dense brush, hiking along trails, and traipsing through marshy areas in all seasons and at all times of the day—without a single visible encounter. So, Don figured, it might be better to hang out in areas where others have reported activity. After researching for twenty years, he realizes he is just as likely to interact with a bigfoot while sitting at this picnic table as he would by traipsing through the woods—and probably catching poison ivy for the nth time. One does not find bigfoot; instead, they find you.

Bigfoot first located Don Keating in July 1984 in the Newcomerstown, Ohio, library in the form of John Green's *The Apes Among Us*, a 492-page book that documents historical and contemporary reports of bigfoot in North America. Like me, Green was once a journalist, serving as a reporter for a newspaper in British Columbia. By 1984, though, Green had established himself as bigfoot's primary historian, and this book, published six years earlier, was already considered the seminal work on the subject. Green had also viewed the infamous tracks found in Bluff Creek, California, in 1958 that gave bigfoot their name and also introduced this animal to modern American society. After reading *The Apes Among Us*, Don tracked down Green and spoke with him on the phone for more than an hour. Afterward, Don returned the book to the library and, he says, did not think another moment about the subject while working as a farmhand and driver for a local produce company—until he read a story in the *Newcomerstown News* the following month about three young men who "smelled something rotten" before rounding a bend on a path in the woods and seeing a large creature pulling and eating leaves from a tree.

The three young men immediately ran off in the opposite direction. Don, then twenty years of age, interviewed the young men, who appeared sincere. From that moment, Don actively pursued evidence of bigfoot by researching local reports and interviewing eyewitnesses.

A year later, Don says, he saw a large, upright creature that towered above the five-foot-high goldenrod weed as it walked toward him outside Newcomerstown in December 1985. It was there one minute, Don said, and gone the next. The creature had murky, hollow eyes, Don said, that emitted a bright, yellow glow.

Don eventually started the Tri-State Bigfoot Study Group, produced a monthly newsletter, and initiated the Ohio Bigfoot Conference in 1989, which remains the nation's oldest symposium on this topic.

Several years later, Don inadvertently videotaped what many consider the best evidence that bigfoot exists after the Patterson-Gimlin film. He did so in an area near New Moscow, Ohio, about forty miles west-northwest of Salt Fork State Park, where locals had reported finding exceptionally large footprints in June 1992. Don drove the twenty-five miles to the state wildlife wilderness area filled with ponds, lakes, and slurry ponds. He parked near a red gate on an old mining road that prevented anyone from driving down an access road used by workers to check wells. From there Don walked toward a large pond he planned to film. But Don decided he didn't like the view so he placed his video recorder, which was still taping, on his right shoulder and moved toward a better spot. That, of course, is when he captured a white figure many believe to be a bigfoot.

The video camera faced west at an open field about 262 feet away that was hemmed in by thick woods Don had just passed several minutes earlier while walking to this ridge, where he eventually taped the lake below. But he did not see anything, so he returned home and placed the tape on a shelf. It sat there for sixteen months, until December 21, 1993, when Don reviewed it in his living room.

Here's what Don watched more than one hundred times that December night: A very large, light-colored figure walks across a road and into the woods, covering twenty-eight feet in four steps and 1.55 seconds. This is not an impossible task for the world's fastest humans, though. After all, Olympic runners can run eleven yards per second, roughly 22.5 miles per hour. Usain Bolt covered about eight feet per stride when he won the 100 meters in 9.63 seconds at the Beijing Olympics in 2012. Bolt took 41 steps in the race; Justin Gatlin, who took the bronze medal, took 42.5 steps. At the time, though, both Bolt and Gatlin had to build momentum by powering out of the blocks and by powerfully raising their knees. At maximum velocity, Bolt reached an upright position like that of the figure walking across Don's video, but only after moving his legs cyclically, dorsiflexing his ankles, and reducing contact with the ground. Bolt, who is tall for a sprinter at six feet five, would have passed the figure walking across uneven, rocky ground. By Don's calculations, the white figure was at least eight feet tall, about twice as tall as the forty-nine-inch posts in the ground along the road.

A film engineer eventually analyzed the thirty-nine frames that held the figure, but the VHS tape became too pixilated to properly evaluate during an episode of *MonsterQuest*. To Don's credit, he immediately called the figure an "individual" even though the rest of the bigfoot community unabashedly tagged it a white sasquatch and bragged that this was further evidence bigfoot exist. "We don't know if it's a bigfoot or not," Don said on *MonsterQuest*. "But it's quite tall and quite fast. I just don't know what it is."[1]

Ohioans constantly see things they cannot identify: angry witches, trolls under bridges, hypnotic aliens. Buckeyes love their state so much they linger in large numbers after death, if one can believe the several dozen books chronicling ghosts in Ohio. Cities such as Akron, Cincinnati, Columbus, Hocking, Marietta, Parma, Toledo, and Zoar are brimming with ghosts, as are the shores of Lake Erie and the halls of a residence at Ohio Wesleyan. I had not realized that ghosts also have sexual preferences, which is outlined in *Queer Hauntings: True Tales of Gay and Lesbian Ghosts*. You can also read a series of five books entitled *Haunted Ohio*, along with *The Haunted History of the Ohio State Reformatory*, *Ghosthunting Ohio*, *Lost Ohio: More Trails into Haunted Ohio*, and *The Big Book of Ohio Ghost Stories*, to name just a few. Joedy Cook has published ten books himself on purported paranormal and cryptid activity in the Buckeye State, with topics ranging from the grassman to alien abduction to zombie survival—as if anybody besides Daryl Dixon or Rick Grimes could offer such advice.

No other state has a place like Salt Fork State Park—a sort of Disney World for bigfoot enthusiasts, where one's dream of finding squatchy evidence often comes true, if you believe the press clippings and TV reports. *USA Today*, for example, called Salt Fork State Park one of the top ten places to "walk in the shadow of bigfoot."[2] Newspapers in Ohio appear enamored with bigfoot, making it appear as if these creatures do indeed walk along Salt Fork's trails like Disney characters. The *Daily Jeffersonian*, published in nearby Cambridge, frequently writes about bigfoot reports, events, and conferences, usually offering details in a far more objective manner than most snickering media outlets. Stories also appear in the *Marietta Times*, *Columbus Dispatch*, and *Toledo City Paper* and on TV outlets such as WBNS-TV. Television shows like *Finding Bigfoot* and *MonsterQuest* have focused on Salt Fork as well. As a result, people like Dave Nowakowski pile into the park looking for bigfoot by walking the trails and setting up field cameras. Nowakowski told the *Marietta Times* he always experiences "some sort of strange activity."[3] These are the same people who fall prey to psychics and telemarketers. And these people are everywhere at Salt Fork thanks to the publicity, and much to the chagrin of Don Keating, who's worried that people will get hurt trying to be bigfoot superhero investigators. That nearly happened when researchers headed to Hosak's Cave in 2009 the day after a twenty-year-old girl died after she slipped and slid off a sandstone cliff that sits about sixty feet above the cave's floor. The cave, once a shelter for Confederate raider John Hunt Morgan's cavalry, is a major attraction. But water trickles onto the trail that leads up to it, which creates risky conditions during the day. At night the place is treacherous, so the cave area closes at dusk. Yet bigfoot researchers, who consider the area a potential hot spot, continue to head up there.

"I'm not so fool-hearted that I'm going to be crazy enough to break a law at Salt Fork State Park and go to a dangerous area that closes at night," Don Keating said. "We have a good working rapport out here. Why should I do something to jeopardize that relationship?"

Salt Fork State Park's directors, realizing the potential boon in having visitors, embrace the stories about a large creature walking in the park's woods — something you'd think would scare off potential visitors — by allowing park rangers to discuss the creatures and by renaming its primitive camping area "Bigfoot Ridge," a place where sadistic parents can terrify their kids for the night. Plus, the lodge hosts the nation's longest-running bigfoot conference, which Don started more than twenty-five years ago. At Salt Fork State Park, one can have a literal bigfoot jamboree.

Salt Fork sits in the southeastern corner of Ohio, far from the state's large manufacturing cities — Cleveland is about 120 miles north, Columbus is 90 miles to the west, and Youngstown is about 120 miles northeast — and in one of Ohio's many pockets of wilderness. Before Americans settled the area in the late 1700s, Salt Fork lay in the middle of a seemingly endless forest that stretched from the Appalachians to the Great Plains — the heart of the world's best hardwood forest in terms of tree size and variety. The region was filled with hickory, beech, oak, ashes, walnut, maples, and chestnuts, some trees as tall as 150 feet. Early settlers, more concerned with survival than ecology, slashed these towering trees in order to build homes, roads, wagons, and tools. By 1900 the area had been decimated, trees replaced by towns and farms. Today some of these trees have returned thanks to conservation efforts that have yielded thick, dense forests containing one hundred hardwood and twenty-five softwood tree species among more than three hundred woody species.[4]

Ohio retains 7.9 million acres of forests, mostly smaller parcels owned by private individuals and corporations and situated primarily in the eastern and southern parts of the state. But the state also contains large swaths of protected woodlands in eighty-three state parks, twenty state forests, twenty-eight state wildlife areas, nine state reserves, four state nature preserves, three national wildlife refuges, two national parks, a state natural area, and the Wayne National Forest, which includes 240,000 acres (and has had more than twenty reported bigfoot sightings through the years). Salt Fork State Park has more than 17,000 acres. "One of the misconceptions is that Ohio is nothing but large cities and farmland," Don tells me during a visit to the picnic pavilion. "It gets much more rugged as you head east." Bigfoot can survive much like bear in these regions, he believes—a point disputed by skeptical natural biologists, wildlife officers, and anthropologists like Kent State's Richard Meindl, who told the *Burr*, the university's student-run magazine, that there's no chance that a creature like bigfoot thrives anywhere, even in the Pacific Northwest. "For an animal that big to go undiscovered, there has to be a few of them in order to reproduce. It'd be like missing a herd of bison. This state is covered by people. We're everywhere. It's not like two hundred years ago when we were kind of sparse."[5]

But researchers strongly disagree, of course. And why not? Bigfoot have made celebrities of several investigators like Matt

Moneymaker, founder of the Bigfoot Field Researchers Organization, who is featured on Animal Planet's highly popular show *Finding Bigfoot*," along with Cliff Barackman, James "Bobo" Fay, and Ranae Holland. Bigfoot have enabled researchers like Joedy Cook—who, besides writing his books, has appeared on History Channel's *MonsterQuest*, SyFy's *Sightings and Encounters*, and the Learning Channel's *Top Ten Mysteries of the World*—to get star billing at events such as paranormal and cryptid conventions. At the American Bigfoot Society's expedition in Kentucky, Cook told me he could not believe that people would pay ten dollars for an autographed photo that cost him about a buck to produce. Don Keating has also received considerable media exposure, having appeared on *MonsterQuest* and NBC's *Today Show*, once hosted a radio show, been a guest on numerous other radio and TV shows, and been quoted in dozens of newspapers. Ultimately, these researchers have little incentive to truly challenge the existence of bigfoot. If they perpetuate the idea that bigfoot are stalking the park, the media will keep requesting their "expert" opinions.

Ohio is considered among the best places to encounter bigfoot outside the Pacific Northwest. Ohio is about even with Oregon, Illinois, and Florida. Maybe that's why Ohio has a burgeoning group of bigfoot researchers that includes the Tri-State Bigfoot Group, the Ohio Bigfoot Organization, Central Ohio Bigfoot Research, Southeastern Ohio Society for Bigfoot Investigation, Mad River Sasquatch Study Group, Ohio Bigfoot Hunters, and the Ohio Center for Bigfoot Studies, to name a few. Or maybe the reason is inverse, where the greater the number of organizations, the higher the number of reported sightings. After all, Illinois has had a marked increase in its total of reported sightings, vaulting from the lower echelons to the top tier, thanks to ambitious, hardworking BFRO investigators such as Harold Benny and Stan Courtney.

But one should not rely heavily on a BFRO database that is fairly unscientific, a premise the organization has refuted. When *Wikipedia* claimed that about three-quarters of all reported sightings in the BFRO database are fake, the BFRO lashed out in a post on its website that attacked *Wikipedia* and trumpeted its investigators as infallible. Here's an excerpt:

> neither Wikipedia, nor the unqualified people they cite, mention that much depends upon whether the reports in question have been investigated or not. A substantial percentage of the uninvestigated reports are indeed fake. (But not nearly 70–80% — that is poppycock.) Very few, if any, reports shown publicly on the BFRO site are fake, because any reports that seem very dubious are not shown on the site at all. And then if a report that doesn't get shown publicly later turns out to be fake (which happens at a rate of 2–3 per year — out of 500 or so reports every year) that report is immediately removed from the collection. Thus, it is very possible that 0% of the reports shown on the BFRO are fake, though a very uneducated and unqualified person (like Diane Stocking — cited as a source by Wikipedia) might not believe more than 20%–30% of what she reads.[6]

The BFRO further states that all contemporary reports are meticulously investigated using approaches similar to those used in law enforcement, journalism, and the legal system. Ultimately, the BFRO concludes that its anecdotal reports are essential to the advancement of science, even though evidence of that is dubious. For example:

Interviews are essential for gathering information in law enforcement and journalism. But eyewitness testimony can be unreliable. As a reporter, I have learned that few people have photographic memories and fewer still can remember basic details about an event or individual. In journalism classes I reemphasize this point by pacing students through the following exercise. A guest speaker walks into class for a few moments, and I walk out.

The guest speaker tells students their assignment: describe what I was wearing. Consider that I had been standing in front of class for anywhere from five to twenty minutes. Few, if any, students even recall the color of my pants and shirt. Inaccurate eyewitness testimony confounds police investigations, too. Misidentifications contributed to about 75 percent of the 320 convictions in the United States that have been overturned by DNA evidence, according to the Innocence Project.[7] So why should the BFRO expect a perfect record, even if it relied on degreed, experienced scientists instead of mostly volunteers? Such an expectation is absurd.

Nobody has any idea what percentage of reports are false, although clearly the figure could be as high as 100 percent. But fabricating statistics won't change anything, whether that's Diane Stocking's claim that 70 to 80 percent of reports are false or the comic Steven Wright's humorous assertion that "42.7 percent of all statistics are made up on the spot." Ad hominem attacks on Stocking, whom the BFRO deems "unqualified" and "uneducated," also can't inoculate the organization against false or poor reporting. The world, in many ways, is a giant Rorschach test. For the record, Stocking has a degree in forestry, which makes her relatively well qualified in a field that includes researchers with little to no scientific education.

One cannot authenticate a potential sighting decades after it is reported—such as number 4837, which allegedly took place in the winter of 1977 in Ashtabula County, located northeast of Salt Fork State Park along the Pennsylvania border—unless one can unearth lingering evidence. In August 2002 a rabbit hunter reported an alleged incident to the BFRO that had taken place twenty-six years earlier.

During rabbit season in 1976 myself and four other[s] went hunting just off Stanhope Kellogsville Road. It was one of the worst days to go hunting. It was snowing and unbelievably cold. We had been in the woods a couple of hours when I got separated from the rest of the hunting party. The next thing I remember is a very loud sound like a freight train coming threw [sic] the woods. All I got was a five-second look at what ever [sic] it was it was It was huge in size and running on two feet full steam ahead. There was no one else around. I do believe they were in front of me by a hundred yards. I told them about it when I caught up too them and they just laughed and said it was a deer. It was no deer and I have been hunting for 26 years. I have never been so scared in my life even though I stood there with a loaded shot gun [sic].[8]

Here's the follow-up report by an anonymous BFRO investigator: "The witness added that it must have weighed 800 pounds. . . . as big as a Moose. He told dad but he said it was probably just a big deer. The creature was Dark brown in color and was close to eight foot tall if not bigger. The word massive kept coming out of his mouth. He still hunts today but is very leery going into woods by himself." For all we know, this man remembers as well as he spells. The report, littered with adjectives and adverbs such as "huge" and "massive," offers few specific details beyond estimates that the creature was about eight feet tall and weighed eight hundred pounds. These anecdotal reports reveal where people are most likely to report bigfoot, but they are not evidential. Yet report number 4837 remains as a credible sighting. The BFRO needs to stop kidding itself that its approach is foolproof.

In the late 1700s Salt Fork State Park lay on the edge of civilization for pioneers who traveled over the Appalachian Mountains or along Zane's Trace from West Virginia to reach a wild region populated by Indians, dense woodlands, and myths. As these early settlers explored Ohio, they started reporting wild men covered in hair who walked among the tall grasses. The Delaware Indian tribe that lived in Ohio warned settlers they needed to leave food for these wild men in order to maintain peace. Eventually settlers started calling these creatures "grassman." Parents would warn their children not to leave the yard unless they wanted the grassman to get them. William Venable, a respected Ohio educator, wrote in *A Buckeye Boyhood* that the grassman was "particularly fond of the taste of cowardly blood" during the mid-1800s.[9] The grassman officially became recognized in 1869, when a gorilla-like man, which the *Hillsdale Standard* described as gigantic, naked, hairy, and with "burning and maniac eyes," reportedly leaped out of the woods near the Ohio River town of Gallipolis, pulled a man from his carriage, and attacked him like a wild animal, biting, hitting, and scratching him. The man's daughter watched as they rolled on the ground and wallowed in mud, her father nearly suffocating beneath the creature's bulk. The young woman eventually threw a rock that hit the wild man in the head, causing him to run off into the trees.

Like the bigfoot, sasquatch, yeti, and Skunk Ape, the grassman are described as large, hairy creatures—generally six to eight feet tall, weighing five hundred to eight hundred pounds (not that one's ever stepped on a scale), covered in a shaggy coat that's typically reddish-brown, and emitting a strong rotten-egg odor at times. Like the other creatures, grassman throw large rocks, knock on wood to communicate at night, break tree limbs, kill (and eat) dogs and deer, make stick structures, and overall, look like massive gorillas that can walk on two feet. The grassman are also identified by their languorous, moaning howls and by their affinity for traveling in groups.

Some researchers claim the grassman are aggressive, similar to reports about Florida's Skunk Ape. In 1897, for example, another "wild man" killed sheep and lambs and fought with a man who drove it off about eighty miles upriver near Rome, adjacent to the Shawnee State Forest. That same year a nude wild man was spotted in Hopewell Township, about fifty miles west of Salt Fork. The grassman are clearly not passive creatures even during contemporary times. An experienced hunter said he was stalked while fishing late at night in 2005 near a Salt Fork spillway, while three teens say a bigfoot chased them through the woods during summer 2006. Several years ago a man in Licking County purchased a 9mm handgun when something large kept striking his rural home late at night, daring him to come outside, the man said. Bigfoot have been blamed for the disappearance of three Kettering teens who camped at the far end of a field in the 1980s. Let's not forget Dallas Gilbert and Wayne Burton, who are featured in the 2008 award-winning indie film *Not Your Typical Bigfoot Movie*, which chronicled the Ohio Bigfoot researchers' dream of finding bigfoot. Nine years earlier, Dallas claimed he had already encountered bigfoot nine times, including one moment when a hairy creature picked him up and another when one almost scared Dallas to death. Wayne, meanwhile, says he was nearly attacked when a bigfoot charged within twenty feet of him. "I turned around and Bigfoot was gruntin', growlin', and carrying on," Burton told the *Daily Times* of Portsmouth, Ohio.[10] The intrepid reporter failed to ask either man for specific details, unfortunately. But one can only assume these guys are either crazy or bigfoot magnets.

During the 2010 Annual Bigfoot Conference/Expo at Salt Fork State Park, Roger Eddy told me another terrifying, but far more bizarre, tale about a bigfoot encounter. Roger was twelve years old and living in southwestern Ohio when he walked into the woods one evening. In the moonlight about fifty feet ahead, Roger saw a tall, golden-haired creature. At the time Roger did not know anything about bigfoot; however, he did recognize that whatever stood before him was amazingly large. To the creature's sides, Roger saw three slightly shorter versions, all with hair the color of ravens or crows. One of the smaller creatures pointed at Roger and then to the larger creature, which moved its head side to side, gesturing "no." In his own head, Roger believes he could hear the smaller creature's thoughts of asking to "have" Roger. That's when Roger reached for his penknife, as if the tiny blade could save him from a creature that was more than seven feet tall and weighed at least four hundred pounds. But the knife was not in his pocket. He couldn't outrun the creatures, nor out-climb them, so he decided he would just have to fight them. The small, black-haired creature turned to Roger at that moment, smiling (or so it seemed), and walked away with the others. That was the only time the fifty-one-year-old Roger viewed what he now believes were bigfoot. Since then, Roger says, he has viewed other bizarre things, such as aliens.

I grew to really like Roger during our conversation. He appeared to be a gentle, engaging man who was unafraid to share his innermost thoughts, even with strangers like myself. Roger said he constantly sees alien heads and partially hidden bigfoot in photos. So he takes random photos of wooded areas in order to scrutinize them later. Inevitably, he'll see what others cannot. Later that night at the bar, Roger slapped down a book of his photos that included circles where he saw alien faces and hairy bodies. Despite having consumed four Sam Adams ales, I saw only trees and leaves. When I looked more deeply, I envisioned faces, eyes, ears, pointed heads, and thick, muscular necks—in the same manner in which I discern dragons and whales when I contemplate cloud formations. After a while the faces emerged from behind the leafy tree branches and shrubs. In retrospect, perhaps I had really consumed six Sams. Frankly, I had lost count. Or perhaps I really wanted to mollify a friendly man who had nothing to gain, and everything to lose, by sharing his abilities. Several times Roger referred to himself as a simple man, which was stereotypically reinforced by his attire of denim bib overalls and a worn cap emblazoned with a farm-product logo. He was also missing several teeth. I wanted to see a far more perceptive man, one who initially defers to others before revealing illogic and brandishing his own superior conclusions, as Benjamin Franklin regularly did in works such as *Poor Richard's Almanack* and in numerous speeches. Ultimately, I could not suspend logic, despite the effects of the summer ale. Before departing, Roger said he would not attend the seminar sessions; instead, he planned to go squatching around the Salt Fork lodge in an area where he saw something walk in the woods by a bridge earlier that day. John Horrigan, a folklorist who researches potential paranormal events in New England, had also been listening to Roger's stories. "In some places, you'd be considered crazy," Horrigan told him. "But you're around people who understand here."

Bigfoot can also be neighborly in Ohio, say local residents. Take the Minerva Monster, an inappropriately named creature considered a gentle pet by families living in a trailer park about seventy-five miles southeast of Cleveland. The creature, said to be anywhere from six to seven feet tall and at least four hundred pounds, peeked in windows, walked along an abandoned strip-mine pit, and strode through the trailer park at night during the summer of 1978, attacking only the residents' olfactory senses with a fowl stench reminiscent of stagnant water. Eventually the "monster" settled into a routine, even munching on late-night snacks of fruit and vegetables left by Evelyn Cayton each evening. The creature is still spotted in the area from time to time.

Few stories are as scary as Roger Eddy's; however, Joe Etterling was just as terrified during his childhood encounter. Like most twelve-year-old boys, Joe loved walking through the woods and playing along the shore of a pond, never thinking that a monster could be watching his every move. That's why he blithely walked alone through the woods, he told me, and was inattentive to anything but the whims of a young boy enjoying a carefree day exploring. Eventually, he wandered farther toward the water, walking past a few scattered saplings and down a slight decline to the pond's shore, where he probably skipped stones and curiously watched small fish skitter along in the shore's shallow water. That's where Joe's world changed in two harrowing, intense minutes.

At first Joe did not believe what he saw. He knew darned well that dinosaurs no longer existed, or so he had been told. He had also heard stories about bigfoot walking through the Ohio woods, but he had dismissed those stories as well. After all, adults had told him that monsters don't exist. Yet a hulking eight-foot-tall, dark-haired creature stood up perhaps twenty yards away, turned, and started to walk toward him. Joe thought: Is this the day I'm going to die? His heart raced, but his feet did not, mostly because he was too petrified to move. Is this monster going to eat me? Beat me? Would it chase me if I ran? Joe did not move as the monster closed in. The creature had the smell of death, he thought, something like a cross between a dead animal and swamp muck. Joe kept looking, but he could not believe his very wide eyes. The monster moved closer, towering over Joe. Miraculously, Joe thought, the monster walked past him and into the woods, never pausing to look down. After the monster departed into the trees, Joe managed to exhale — perhaps it was more of a whimper — and then probably took off running home as fast as he could. For weeks afterward, Joe had nightmares that relived those few minutes alone with a creature that others said did not exist. But Joe knew otherwise. He felt the need to understand the creature so he headed to libraries and checked out every available book that addressed bigfoot. He checked for magazine and newspaper articles in order to learn where these creatures survived in the woods, what they ate, how they evaded humans. He wanted to know everything, anything, something. Eventually Joe overcame his fear and returned to the woods in order to look for bigfoot, believing they meant no harm and that, in fact, they were *not* the monsters he first imagined.

This desire to learn more about bigfoot never left Joe. As an adult, he searched for more details about the creature, eventually enlisting his brothers and some friends to create the Ohio Bigfoot Research Team, which investigates claims across the state. In the summer he spends hours in the forests, spending at least one day each week researching with his team, which is a challenge, with everybody's family and work responsibilities. He also spends hours interviewing witnesses, writing reports, and posting them on the organization's website. They spend far less time out in the woods in winter, when he pays more attention to witness reports and the website. "This all sounds impossible at times, but we manage to gather a lot of data," Joe told me in 2008. "We all have schedules we have to go by, but each member spends time doing research that adds up rather quickly. If I could be a full-time researcher and support my family by doing it, I would do so in a heartbeat. But that is not possible right now. Basically, if there is a spare minute that isn't taken up by my responsibilities I will devote it to research." At the time, the Ohio Bigfoot Research Team received five reports per month, Joe told me.

After our initial conversations and emails, Joe stopped responding. Concerned about privacy, Joe would never call me from home nor email me from his work computer. I tried to head out with his group, but Joe told me the members wanted to keep their investigations private. The group eventually planned a few tours, but I never got to tag along because that's around the time I lost contact with Joe. He stopped responding to emails and the group's website disappeared like a sasquatch into the woods, the previous URL redirecting viewers to a web search site.

Several years later I tried reconnecting with Joe, but I did not find anything except for a brief reference on Cryptomundo, a website dedicated to news about the paranormal, to someone who appeared to be Joe's son or nephew, a lance corporal who had died in a helicopter crash while serving as a marine in Iraq during January 2005. In the post, author Loren Coleman said the young soldier, Jonathan E. Etterling, was a member of the Ohio Bigfoot

Research Team, but he did not say how Jonathan was related to Joe. Until finding this reference, I had felt like this had all been part of some catfishing maneuver, where I was squatch-romanced by some duplicitous bigfoot hoaxer. But then I found a single report that apparently had originally run on the Ohio Bigfoot Research Team's website. Joe, along with Richard and Bill Etterling, report that they had stumbled upon a bloody, dissembled calf corpse in the Wayne National Forest in southeastern Ohio, in a dry creek bed that also contained body parts, hair strands, and stomach contents, clearly evidence of a bigfoot attack and not, as I feared after watching too many episodes of *The Walking Dead*, of a mass zombie onslaught. Had I been at that creek bed, you can bet I would have been boring holes into the surrounding woods with my eyes, prepared to dash at the first sign of a decaying, walking corpse. Joe and his family did believe they were being watched. Plus, they reported hearing rocks clanging at regular intervals and an owl-like call as they departed the woods.

Other than this report, little else remains of the group's investigations—at least online. Melissa Hovey, president of the American Bigfoot Society, told me she had never heard of Joe, while Don said he barely recalls Joe; however, he did not have contact information. If neither of these two people knew anything, then Joe probably had ceased investigating. That's not unusual, though. After the initial excitement, many researchers lose interest, and many groups disband when they realize how much time and effort are necessary to investigate reported sightings, interview potential witnesses, write and edit reports, correspond with fans, and post information on a website. Still, the number of investigators continues to grow. There's Doug Waller, Marc DeWerth, and Tim Stover, to name a few of the newer researchers. Don Keating says too many groups are territorial, more concerned with personal glory than with working together to determine trends and to track the busiest areas.

We're sitting in a remote pavilion where people come to enjoy the beautiful rolling hills, dense woods, and lovely flowers that abound in eastern Ohio. This area is a few miles from the lodge and sequestered at the end of a cul-de-sac off the two-lane road that meanders through the park. Nobody casually pulls into the area unless they have a picnic planned, not that many do so far from the main visitors areas. Yet this is where Don Keating now spends most of his time researching bigfoot—sitting on a bench under the pavilion's wooden roof. The woods appear to be closing in on the area. A narrow, barely discernible trail heads down toward the lake but ends before anyone could pick up enough speed to sprint. In the dark, I can't see anything except a few nearby tree trunks. Beyond about twenty yards, everything is pitch dark. A pavilion seems like an odd place to search for bigfoot, but no odder than camping in somebody's backyard in eastern Kentucky or crazier than sloshing through a swamp filled with poisonous snakes and sharp-toothed alligators in central Florida, really.

It's around 11:00 p.m. on a cool spring night. Above, clouds obscure stars that are usually bright, vivid and captivating in a location that is far from any large city. This area boasts primarily woods and rolling hills. In many ways, eastern Ohio and western Pennsylvania are an extension of one another. Eric Altman, the director of the Pennsylvania Bigfoot Society; Billy Willard, the founder of Sasquatch Watch of Virginia; and Abe Del Rio, founder of the Minnesota Bigfoot Research Team, are walking around as well after a meeting of the Tri-State Bigfoot organization. We're here with a few others to investigate Don's main area. A year earlier, Billy said, a very large branch was flung at them after he had discerned something large walking in the woods. Tonight, though, we're getting no action, so Don and I sit and talk. He appears to like the folks here, but several researchers claim that he's lazy for lounging by a picnic area and that he's hoaxed evidence in the past. He waves off such comments, saying his true friends know better and punctuating his sentences with phrases like "what in the Sam Hill"; however, it's clear these allegations bother him, even if he shows it by going on the offensive. He dislikes crazy talk that bigfoot's an interdimensional being, loathes bullshit, and has no patience for people who make wild, unsubstantiated claims, much like his friend Rene Dahinden, whom Don respectfully called a "son of a bitch." Dahinden who wrote the popular *Sasquatch*, tracked the original location of the Patterson-Gimlin film, and became the leading authority on bigfoot in the Pacific Northwest before his death in 2001. "If you'd never met him before," Don said, "you'd think he was a little prick." Like Don, Dahinden sometimes questioned his own passionate pursuit of bigfoot, once telling fellow researcher Chris Murphy, author of *Bigfoot in Ohio*, "You know, I've spent over forty years—and I didn't find it. I guess that's got to say something."[11] Unlike Dahinden, Don started shifting his passions elsewhere, eventually creating a weathercast website, handing over the bigfoot conference to a new host, and disbanding the Tri-State Bigfoot group after thirty years.

"I've got some criticism from other bigfooters who say, 'He just leaves his car and walks a few feet away and just sits there,'" Don says. "But, guess what, I live in the middle of the country where, within twenty minutes, I can be at a place where there's been many sightings. Where recordings have been made. Where footprints have been discovered. Why do I need to go several hundred yards into the wood line? At night. And risk my neck. To try and find something I have just as good as a chance to find here in Salt Fork crossing the road in front of me on the way home. Going into the woods won't increase the odds of an encounter. There is no set MO [modus operandi] to have a bigfoot sighting. I'm just as likely to have one in that gazebo or this picnic area. It makes no sense to me why people want to be Tarzan and do some crazy stuff. If someone gets hurt trying to be Superman up at Hosak's Cave at night, maybe I'll visit them in the hospital and say, 'Don't you wish you were back up there right now so you can try it again? Maybe next time, you'll split your skull completely open.'"

Why are there so many reports and so much evidence around this picnic area?

"That I don't know," Don says. "Why would it come up to the girl that saw it standing by that tree line over there? Curiosity, maybe. I've learned that the creature is as elusive today as it was twenty-seven years ago. People describe it in many ways, but it's still one and the same: it walks upright like a person, it has colored hair, it's still shy, and it's still undiscovered. So, in a nutshell, that's what I have learned in twenty-seven years. Next to nothing." He laughs. "Well, I did learn to put on a good conference."

The top names in bigfoot culture, such as Bob Gimlin and Dr. Jeff Meldrum, have just spoken to hundreds of people from all over the country at the packed lodge. "But why do I keep doing this?" Don says. "Because there's an answer out there. I just have not found it. I suppose it's a learning thing. You think you have something in hand, and the idea you had in hand turns out to have a hole in it and two more questions arise as a result of it. You end up with more questions than you do answers, obviously. It's not really frustrating because I've come to a point after twenty-plus years that there's not really any hope to discover what this creature really is as long as I'm walking. So I've come to the conclusion that I can walk and examine and interview and hike the woods until I'm blue in the face and until I'm 110 years old — and I still won't have all the answers."

It's getting late, so Don decides to depart, a cue I should have taken. Instead, I linger for another hour or so, squinting my eyes to see objects that are not there and cupping my ear to hear noises that have not been made. We all talk and kibitz and eventually drive back to the lodge, where we fall exhaustedly into bed. Before

Don left, I warned him, "If you leave, we'll probably have an encounter." "Probably," he said in a tone that was both fatalistic and disdainful. But Don drove off nonetheless, looking into his rearview mirror as he departed—seeking not so much a final peek at bigfoot as a reminder of his own past.

8 WIND RIVER MOUNTAINS
WYOMING

John Mionczynski leaned against a granite rock face and peered into the valley below, about to tell me a story about the time he escaped death in Yellowstone National Park. We sat atop a ridge in the Wind River Mountains, about nine thousand feet high in the southern section of the hundred-mile range that runs southeast to northwest through western Wyoming and that boasts nineteen of the twenty-one tallest peaks in the state. Like the rest of this range, this area is covered with thick woods, pockmarked with innumerable lakes, and capped by twenty-five glaciers. Wilderness covers roughly two-thirds of the Wind River Mountains.

We had just bivouacked atop this ridge, leaving Dr. Jeff Meldrum to rest in his truck. Jeff, a professor of anthropology at Idaho State, had felt nauseous with severe stomach cramps earlier in the evening, so he had remained in the base camp located roughly a forty-minute hike below.

Earlier that morning I had deposited my wife, Betsy, and daughters, Kristen and Sarah, in a nearly empty campsite several thousand feet below. The adrenaline of driving off to meet Jeff and John had ebbed, enabling me to return to a more conventional, paranoid state where I imagined a far more deadly beast threatening my family. As a voracious news consumer, I knew that crazy people lurked everywhere—especially, I feared, in the remote campground that held my family. As is customary, I worried about all kinds of things—hungry lions, territorial grizzlies, blood-sucking ticks, encountering bigfoot, never encountering bigfoot, having rattlers slither into my sleeping bag, that John would avenge his past problems with journalists as I slept. On the trek to this ridge, John had unexpectedly announced, "I hate newspaper reporters." I had taken this as an entry into casual, light conversation, but it served as a cautionary tale for journalists.

Several years earlier, a reporter at the *Los Angeles Times* had wanted to learn why the bighorn sheep in the Rockies were dying at an unusually high rate, so he contacted the country's leading expert on these animals. John declined to speak with him, telling the reporter that he would only get in the way of his research. The intrepid reporter, though, called John's boss at the Wyoming Department of Game and Fish, who desired publicity. That meant John had to trek down from his camp in the Wind Rivers, losing a half day of research. The reporter, accustomed to living at sea level in LA, was quickly hit with altitude sickness, forcing John to nurse him back to health for two days. Ultimately the reporter used inaccurate information, stating that half the bighorn sheep population had died when the total was around one-third. "I saw him write the correct numbers down," John told me. "I asked him how he had inserted the wrong numbers. He said that he used other sources as well." But who would know more than John? John had even volunteered to verify details in the story before publication. "But the reporter laughed, saying that's not going to happen." I used to tell my journalism students never to share information before publication because sources often want quotes altered to make them look better. I've adjusted my approach through the years in light of the slashes made in newsrooms, where copy editors, once the backbone of news organizations, have been deemed extraneous instead of recognized as the nitpicking fact-checkers that save reporters' proverbial asses. Not that mistakes didn't slip into publications before. In the *Los Angeles Times* article, I also found another key error: Mionczynski's first name had been misspelled as "Jon." Newspapers are not the only ones to make factual errors, though. On the second episode of *MonsterQuest* you'll see "University of Idaho" under Meldrum's name, not "Idaho State University."

So far John had been gracious, candid, and helpful all day, so damned if I would complain about walking over tall grass that could hold packs of ticks, past cozy rock crevices that could be dens for rattlers, or up these steep inclines in fading light.

Ironically, John was the one who needed to stop a few times. At six feet two, John is sinewy, with slight shoulders, strong forearms, a thick shock of graying brown hair, and a bushy moustache. At age sixty-four, he still walks up steep mountains and leaps across stones and boulder as if he were one of his bighorn sheep. His mind is equally sharp, his gray eyes catching everything from bear scat to mushrooms to small insects, details that enable him to take meticulous field notes in his research for the U.S. Forest Service, Wyoming Game and Fish, and Interagency Grizzly Bear Study Team. Through no fault of his own, John had contracted whooping cough a few years earlier while working with Native Americans at a reservation here in the Wind Rivers. Both the Shoshones and the Northern Arapahoes reside in an area that covers roughly 2.2 million acres across this range and central Wyoming. Few Native Americans get inoculations for this highly contagious respiratory tract infection. John did not know why he started coughing uncontrollably and painfully. Thick mucus had built up in his airways, making it difficult to breath, so John finally called his physician to say he probably wouldn't make it through the night. The physician, knowing John was no hypochondriac, drove seventy miles over mostly rural, snowy roads to reach John, who was languishing in his small cabin atop a hill overlooking Atlantic City, an ironically named town that sits far from the ocean in semiarid, high plains and whose population, forty-seven, is roughly the same number of people you might find hovering around a roulette table in any of New Jersey's flamboyant casinos. The vaccination John had received as a kid had worn off. To further complicate matters, John had contracted Lyme disease six years earlier while doing research around Lake Louise, an area where ticks were so thick, John told me, that he'd sometimes pick off ten to fifteen a day. The ticks were so thick, he added, that he could see them on leaves and branches with their two front legs extended and ready to latch on to whatever ambled by—a nightmare vision if I ever heard one. At nine-thousand-plus feet, ticks are rarely found. But drop a few thousand feet to where Lake Louise resides and you'll find a virtual Lyme disease emporium. Besides showing some of the usual symptoms, which can include fever, headaches, fatigue, and rashes, John apparently suffered residual damage to his immune system.

John, though, did not need to pause long. After leaning against some crevices, we stood and continued up the ridge. By the time we reached the ridge's crest, night was rushing in. I popped up a one-person tent, barely large enough for me to slide under its paper-thin, nylon covering that couldn't stop anything much from entering or biting through it. John simply unfurled a sleeping bag across the dirt.

Below in the valleys, sheep, elk, and bears roamed, just a few of the many large mammals that live in this magnificent range. Innumerable ponds, fed by melting glaciers, hold beaver, frogs, insects, sedges—all kinds of starches, proteins, and carbohydrates to keep predators fed. This is great habitat, John said, and a primary reason why there are so many bigfoot sightings. John knows this area like some people know their backyards, having hiked, camped, and resided in the woods, meadows, and plains of Wyoming for more than forty years. He's an expert on bighorn sheep, grizzlies, and goats and even authored *The Pack Goat*, a definitive guide on how to domesticate and use these docile animals while hiking mountain trails. This mountain range also holds, he knows, more than three hundred bird species, at least two million trout, the largest herd of bighorn sheep in the United States, a small population of grizzlies that reside uncomfortably near—and at least a few bigfoot.

The sun had already peeked behind the mountain range, allowing just enough light to discern a few rock outcroppings and small lakes thousands of feet below. As the night draped distant mountain peaks, everything faded to black, leaving John to explain his traumatic experience in a Yellowstone meadow.

Brilliantly and immortally in his twenties, John absolutely knew how to determine whether grizzlies in the Yellowstone National Park area would attack humans. He would simply lie in an open meadow unprotected in a mummy bag, a polyester sarcophagus that wraps around the body and head—in this instance, creating a sort of human burrito for hungry bruins.

But that's not how John saw it. As a field biologist, he believed vigorously in his hypothesis that grizzly bears would not attack humans without provocation. John had already trapped grizzlies and attached radio collars to track them around the national park as part of the Interagency Grizzly Bear Study Team. For decades, grizzlies had been allowed to rummage through open-pit garbage dumps at Yellowstone. About ten years earlier, in 1963, the Advisory Board on Wildlife Management in the National Parks had recommended that the pits be closed and that natural ecosystems be created because the bears had started entering tents, knowing food was tucked inside. An estimated 229 grizzly died during this transition period between 1967 and 1972, which prompted the species to be listed as threatened under the Endangered Species Act of 1975. A few bears, meanwhile, had torn apart tents at the park, including several that had been set up by the bear study team. Tourists and a few anxious park administrators wondered whether grizzlies had started to associate humans with food, a theory John thought foolish enough that he put himself in harm's way.

John regretted his decision when he first heard the large grizzly moving through the field. Based on the bear's radio-collar emissions, John could tell this was the big boy who had created havoc recently. John had a revolver, but it would not provide protection against the eight-hundred-pound bear that now circled him in the moonlight unless he could insert the gun directly into the bear's palate—a daunting, improbable act.

The grizzly circled closer, eventually pressing its mammoth head against John's feet, which caused him to start imagining horrible scenarios. In his mind's eye, John saw the grizzly's jaws open widely and fiercely, crushing his ankle, and dragging his body into the thicker woods where he would be eviscerated and eaten. John shook so hard at that moment he feared he might shoot himself with the single-action revolver he held in his right hand, so he slowly released the gun's hammer and awaited his fate. The grizzly released its pressure, sniffed the air, and moved toward John's head from the side, eventually placing its nose within inches of John's face. The bear looked straight at John for a moment that seemed eternal. That's when the grizzly took in a deep breath and blew its entire lung capacity into John's face. In the cold, wet meadow, the breath hovered like fog. It also smelled an awful lot like mildewed canvas. The bear slowly backed up and moved on, leaving John traumatized and shaking for a long time. Sleep? Forget about it. He remained awake through the night.

"The worst part," John said, "was I had to do it again the next night to show this was not a one-time thing."

The next night in a different meadow another bear circled,

moved in, sniffed, and departed. That's when John realized he was prepared to get close to a bigfoot.

"It's not that I'm not going to be afraid," John told me. "But I know what it is to get that ultimate level of fear with a large animal. I'm still going to be afraid, I think, if I see one of these. But I think I'll be able to function and probably record what happens and get over it afterward."

John would test this new hypothesis very soon.

The legendary park ranger Bob "Action" Jackson chased outlaws, arrested poachers, survived harsh living conditions, and logged as many as seventy thousand miles by horse through Yellowstone's most rugged backcountry. He lived in a small cabin along the Thorofare, a trail along the upper Yellowstone River in the Absaroka Mountains first used by Native Americans and early white settlers. This is not a trail for day tourists. Jackson tracked grizzlies and tormented outfitters who sought to illegally lure elk from Yellowstone by placing large salt pits just outside the park's boundaries. Jackson knew this area like some people know their backyards. Yet the thirty-year park veteran could not identify a creature he stumbled across in the late 1970s while riding a horse through Sportsman Creek in the northwest corner of Yellowstone. Previously he saw huge footprints in remote areas, much too large to have been left by a human or grizzly, and he heard several lengthy, unusual sounds, including a twenty-six-second scream that, he said, sounded like ten thousand elk going to their death. "Whatever that thing is, it doesn't let up to take a breath," Jackson told the Colorado bigfoot curator T. E. Stein in a 2003 phone interview.[1]

Jackson had originally thought a grizzly loomed prior to his 1970s sighting. He was eleven miles up on a steep hill in a subalpine fir meadow when his horses flared their noses and snorted, causing Jackson to be especially alert. About forty yards downhill, a deer bolted from a thicket. Behind it came an animal even Jackson could not identify—black, shaggy, stocky, a little taller than six feet, furry face, arms swinging with elbows uncocked. In ten steps, Jackson watched the animal run to a thicket. It then angled through several other thickets on the way down the hill, picking up protection along the way, unlike a bear that always runs in a straight line to escape. This animal was much smarter, Jackson realized. Eventually it disappeared. Jackson heard more vocalizations and found more prints through the years, but he never encountered another creature like this.

If bigfoot exists, Wyoming seems like a squatch nirvana. The state has large swaths of remote wilderness, more than one hundred isolated mountain ranges, more than fifty rivers, and abundant wildlife, fish, and insects. Yet few people officially report bigfoot sightings across the state's 97,814 square miles. To be fair, Wyoming has few people residing within its perfectly squared-off boundaries—about 576,000 (about the same number as are crammed into Las Vegas), for an average of six people per square mile, placing the state behind only Alaska among the nation's least densely populated states. With twenty-eight reports, Wyoming ranks in the bottom quarter of states on the Bigfoot Field Researchers Organization's geographical database. Is this because a state that saw fit to grant women suffrage fifty-one years before the Nineteenth Amendment passed in 1920 has little patience for nonsense? Are independent-minded residents more likely to deal with a bothersome animal in their own way, such as the man who allegedly shot a bigfoot that was peeking in his large window and scaring his wife? Perhaps it's because few people head into these remote areas.

There's nothing extraordinary about the reported sightings in Wyoming. People see large creatures in the distance while they hike and drive, hear unusual screams, and stumble across large footprints. Many of these incidents are reported in and around Yellowstone National Park, where guides and rangers have confidentially shared stories with Jeff, knowing they'd be vilified if they did so publicly. Yellowstone spokesperson Stan Thatch, using humor unusual for a government agency, illustrated the park service's disdain for bigfoot when he told the independent online news site *Yellowstone Gate* that the park service does not track unexplained animal sightings. "We do track things like reports of wolves with sarcoptic mange, for instance. Our biologists want to stay on top of that. But there is no cryptozoologist on staff at Yellowstone, so we don't keep up with Yetis, dragons or mermaids," he said.[2] Visitors report unusual sightings, though. A family claimed they watched an eight- to ten-foot humanoid walk along a ridge near Mount Washburn, two geologists said they saw a large creature walk in front of them when they drove toward the park's east exit, and two brothers heard a large creature run past their tent but reasonably refused to investigate. I imagine the conversation went something like this: "Hey, bro, go check that out." "No fucking way, dude." In the Wind River Mountains, two backpackers had a scarier experience when, they say, a freakishly large, twelve-foot creature screamed and chased them off Sun King Mountain near Jackson Hole.

Few people spend more time in the Wind River Mountains than guides for the National Outdoor Leadership School (NOLS), housed in nearby Lander. NOLS guides lead wilderness education courses across the globe, showing students how to live off the land and treat medical emergencies and teaching them leadership skills during expeditions that last a month or more in locales such as East Africa, Scandinavia, Mexico, Alaska, and the Amazon. The original NOLS course took place in this mountain range, where students fly-fished in an attempt to land cutthroat trout, hiked 120 miles of trails, ascended peaks, and rappelled granite rock faces. NOLS guides are required to keep journals in the wild. But you won't find bigfoot references inside, even though several instructors admitted to John they had either seen one or had recognized unusual footprints. Two guides said they saw one ascending a ridge not far from where John and I had bivouacked. One instructor explained the omissions to John: "I don't want to be the crazy loon who says he's seen bigfoot." The Wisconsin outdoor guide Don Young had already learned how such disclosures can destroy one's reputation and, subsequently, one's career.

Jeff Meldrum kept his hands laced on the steering wheel, occasionally looking over to me when he made a point. We were driving on the right side of a narrow, dusty, rocky one-lane road to his base camp higher in these Wind River Mountains. Drivers zoom down these narrow paths as if their tires did not nearly scrape ledges. Jeff repeatedly checked his dashboard, stopping once to read a lighted warning. "The brakes have been acting weird since they worked on them," he said, inspiring me to reflect longingly about my wife and girls.

It was midmorning in late July. Later that night, I would make the hike up a ridge to camp overnight with John Mionczynski. Jeff was telling me about Mongolian wild men named Almas, purported to be the bigfoot of Central Asia. Unlike North American bigfoot, the Almas are smaller in height, reportedly anywhere from five to six and a half feet tall. In addition, they are often similarly reported to be covered with reddish-brown hair and have flat noses and a clearly defined brow ridge. The Almas appear in local legends, said Jeff, and drawings are also found in Tibetan medicinal books. The British archaeologist Myra Shackley, in fact, believes they are a relict species of Neanderthal that found a way to escape the leaner, more efficient *Homo sapiens.*

Jeff dismisses claims that Neanderthal and *Homo sapiens* regularly interbred. "I get annoyed by all the fanfare," he said. "There are some indicators that suggest there's a restricted gene flow between humans and Neanderthals. That gets all the attention. But, in my book, the flip side, the inverse of that, is much more interesting. Okay, there was a little bit of gene flow, but you had twenty thousand years of contact and they remained separate from one another. They didn't just blend together and lose identity. That suggests that you've got two very different types of things. So while one was driven to the verge of extinction, maybe the only ones that survived were the most primitive, the most remotely located ones in the far reaches in the most inhospitable parts of the range, which were in the mountains in the Caucasus and Outer Mongolia. That may be the underpinnings of the Almaste."

Jeff also disagrees that bigfoot rely on cognates, using the same origins or roots as human language, a theory proposed by Scott Nelson based upon a tape recording of alleged bigfoot vocalizations in the 1970s in California's Sierra Nevada Mountains. Nelson, a retired navy intelligence officer, says he recognizes language cognates and other utterances that emulate human words. For example, Nelson suggests the sound "foo" is really "food" on this tape. Two species evolving independently, though, would not have words with the same etymological origins for similar items, such as food. "He's very accomplished and I respect his work," Jeff said, "but I personally feel he's reading a lot into this [tape]."

The Sierra tape sounds like a humorous mash-up of the Tasmanian Devil, Jabba the Hutt, and Sonny the Cuckoo Bird from the Cocoa Puffs commercials. At points it sounds as though a *Star Wars* character is speaking through a static walkie-talkie. The tape, though, gives me goose bumps. The chatter sounds eerily similar to the noises I heard late in the night while in the middle of Florida's Green Swamp, when I had half-expected a band of primate warriors from *Planet of the Apes* to crash through the tree line. I'm still angry that I never hit the record button on my own digital recorder that night, but at the moment, I had been mesmerized.

Jeff turned to me and offered this aside: bigfoot have pendulous breasts like gorillas and humans. "If you look at a lactating gorilla," Jeff said, "you'll find a hominid endowed to a degree that will cause envy in quite a few human females." Had a friend told this anecdote, I would have expected a snarky comment or wry smile. Jeff stated this drily, as if he were explaining a condition to students in his Organic Evolution course at Idaho State University, where he serves as a professor of anatomy and anthropology.

No bigfoot researcher is as credentialed scientifically and academically as Jeff, a fact that draws ire from his colleagues, skeptics, and bigfoot neophytes. Jeff earned a doctorate in anatomical sciences from the State University of New York at Stony Brook, holds a master's and a bachelor's in zoology, has published an anatomy textbook with the highly respected Mosby/Elsevier (*Mosby's Dissector for the Rehabilitation Professional: Exploring Human Anatomy*), has coedited a series of books on paleontology, and has published articles in several respected journals. He teaches both upper-level and graduate courses in biology, such as human anatomy and human regional anatomy and histology and serves as affiliate curator at the Idaho Museum of Natural History. But this impressive vita is not why he struggled to earn tenure and continues to fight to retain his scientific credibility among academics. Blame his fascination with bigfoot.

Like many young boys, Jeff was intrigued by dinosaurs, perhaps playing out Jurassic fight scenarios in his young mind—a plodding brontosaurus barely escaping into a swamp ahead of a tyrannosaurus rex, a tank-sized stegosaurus trying to defend its young by swinging its spiked tail at a larger allosaurus before it could be flipped and rendered as helpless as a turtle. So when, at age eleven, he watched a large, loping, hairy beast walking through remote Bluff Creek, Jeff became fascinated, eventually listing cryptozoology as an interest on his vita for doctoral work.

Jeff started dipping into bigfoot analysis in 1995 when he was asked to analyze footage taken by a British Broadcasting Corporation crew at night in Northern California's Redwoods National

Park. This video is dark, grainy, and unfocused. People are screaming. It could almost be an outtake for *The Blair Witch Project*. In a video someone enhanced, or perhaps re-created, one can see what appears to be three large, shaggy creatures walking. Like many bigfoot videos, this one excites enthusiasts and fuels detractors. On the plane trip to Eureka to review the tape, Jeff was asked by the secretary of the International Society of Cryptozoology, Richard Greenwell, to review *Bigfoot of the Blues*, written by a journalist in Walla Walla about reported sightings in a nearby southeastern Washington mountain range.

Jeff decided to travel to interview the bigfoot witnesses Wes Summerlin and Paul Freeman, a man many considered to be a charlatan. Freeman, a former U.S. Forest Service employee, claimed to have seen bigfoot in the Blue Mountains in 1982; however, all his evidence afterward appeared fraudulent. Dr. Grover Krantz, an anthropologist from Washington State University, said that footprints Freeman found revealed ridged skin left by a primate, but other scientists disagreed. A U.S. Border Patrol tracker, Joel Hardin, subsequently declared the tracks faked. Two years later the prominent bigfoot investigator Rene Dahinden said another set of tracks cited by Freeman were also a hoax. In 1989 Freeman presented fibers found on a twisted tree branch as further evidence, but lab tests revealed them to be synthetic modacrylic fibers, similar to those used in paint rollers, rugs, and wigs.[3] So Jeff was highly skeptical when he visited Freeman unannounced in 1996.

Conveniently, Freeman said he had just found new footprints that morning. Would Jeff like to see them? Something seemed fishy, but Jeff agreed to tag along. Upon reaching the Mill Creek drainage area, they found a long line of clear tracks impressed into wet, silty soil, but the tracks took a dubious path to and from Freeman's truck. This guy must have jumped out of his pickup wearing large fake feet, Jeff thought, circled around, and then dived into the truck's bed to remove them. What kind of a chump did this guy think Jeff was?

Yet Jeff noticed that the prints revealed subtle skin ridges, texture on the sole that was detailed like a fingertip or palm on primates. He remained skeptical when he drove off to get plaster and other materials to cast the tracks. Upon his return, Jeff and his brother Michael noticed additional tracks, angled in new directions, under a spot where Freeman's truck had been parked. Jeff wondered why Freeman would not have mentioned these other tracks. Jeff and Michael found tracks that traveled through a creek drainage, near an irrigation ditch, and across a plowed field. Jeff noticed details that only a foot expert would notice—places where the toes were tightly flexed, gripping soil on a slight incline; where only three of the five toes sunk into the soil; where the ball of a foot had absorbed a protruding rock while the toes curled over it; where the foot had dragged or had slipped. The hairs stood up on the back of his neck. Jeff thought about the grief he would receive from his peers. Did he want to go down that road? As he looked at the footprints, he thought, how could he not? Jeff had officially become the bigfoot foot guy.

Because of his pursuit of bigfoot, Jeff became an outcast among professors and scientists who questioned his methods, delayed his tenure, dismissed his results, and attacked his scholarly work. Colleagues at Idaho State called his research "featherbrained," "intellectually questionable," and "a joke," saying Jeff would have a better chance of finding Santa Claus or SpongeBob than he would of finding a large primate. One professor wanted Jeff's tenure to be revoked. Said the Idaho State physicist Martin Heckworth, "Do I cringe when I see the Discovery Channel and I see 'Idaho State University, Jeff Meldrum'? Yes, I do. He believes he's taken up the cause of people who have been shut out by the scientific community. He's lionized there. He's worshipped. He walks on water. It's embarrassing."[4] Douglas Wells, another physics professor, told the *Los Angeles Times*, "One could do deep-ocean research for SpongeBob Square Pants. That doesn't make it science."[5] University of Florida anthropologist Dave Daegling said Meldrum doesn't examine doubts and interpretations about bigfoot the same way he does in his fossil and primate gait research. Meldrum's approach to bigfoot, he said, is pseudoscience that mixes belief and the scientific language. "Even if you have a million pieces of evidence," Daegling said, "if all the evidence is inconclusive, you can't count it all up to make something cohesive."[6] In addition, more than thirty Idaho State faculty signed a petition against a bigfoot symposium being held on the campus.

Jeff does have some supporters, but none more influential than Jane Goodall, the world's foremost expert on chimpanzees and one of the most recognized scientists in the world. Like Jeff, Goodall was once ridiculed for the unorthodox methods she used to study chimpanzees in Tanzania's Gombe Stream Reserve. Despite that, she set up a research center in a wilderness area considered unsafe, dismissed critics, and revealed behavior that radically transformed how we perceive both humans and chimps. Goodall shattered the belief that only humans could develop and use tools, detailing how the chimps created tools from plant stems and used them to catch termites in their mounds. Chimps, she also learned, were not vegetarians. As I've already noted, Goodall publicly supports the scientific search for bigfoot. On National Public Radio's *Talk of the Nation* in 2006, Goodall said she is certain bigfoot exists. "I've talked to so many Native Americans who all describe the same sounds," she told a caller, "two who have seen them." Later on the show she tempered her statement by adding, "Well, I'm a romantic, so I always wanted them to exist."[7] On the cover of Jeff's book *Sasquatch: Legend Meets Science*, his companion book to the popular 2003 Discovery Channel documentary, Goodall stated that Jeff has brought "a much-needed level of scientific analysis to the sasquatch — or Bigfoot — debate."[8] The book sold thirteen thousand copies, positioning Jeff as a leading expert in the search for bigfoot. Subsequently Jeff appeared on more than twenty documentaries and TV shows, such as *Unexplained Mysteries, Is It Real?*, *Destination Truth*, *Cryptid Hunt*, and *Bigfoot: The Definitive Guide*, and seven times on the cult favorite *MonsterQuest*. In addition, he has been interviewed for more than 150 news articles. In many ways Jeff has become as ubiquitous as the footprints he evaluates.

"It bothers me that there's a perception that I'm just exploiting this for gain," Jeff said as he pulled his truck off the dirt road at his camp, where John Mionczynski sat fiddling with an old Coleman stove. Jeff told me that a man who runs a website that regularly criticizes him asked, "So this has become quite a cottage industry for you. Are you making more than your regular salary as a professor yet?"

Jeff replied, "Are you joking? Are you serious?"

The blogger countered, "But you've been on all of these television shows."

"Have you ever been on one of these shows?" Jeff responded. "Do you know what they pay? Sure, I get a little compensation for spending an entire day of my time with them and for making available all of the artifacts in my lab and all of my research." So, he added, "Sure, there's a little compensation, but, my goodness, I'm not in any position to quit my day job."

In fact, Jeff was barely able to keep up with his bills after he experienced a series of personal challenges around the time he appeared in a 2007 episode of *MonsterQuest* that addressed bigfoot attacks at a remote cabin in northern Ontario. Jeff, who has six sons, had divorced earlier that year, forcing him to find a new residence and incurring legal fees and other financial obligations. Three months later Jeff was diagnosed with cancer. "I was kind of on Skid Row," he told me. "Even with insurance, I had thousands of dollars in expenses related to doctors and labs. The bills just keep coming. Just when you think you're on top of the bills, another envelope would arrive from someone else." Jeff did not share this information with the blogger, who persisted, saying, "You've also written books."

Besides *Sasquatch: Legend Meets Science*, Jeff had also written a few other books, such as *Evolution and Mormonism: A Quest for Understanding*, but few books reach bestseller status and few academic authors make more than two dollars a book, hardly enough to replace the $79,000 salary he made as a professor at Idaho State in 2011. Most authors earn a pittance from their time-consuming endeavors, which yield less money than if they had worked for minimum wage at McDonald's. My wife often jokes that I made about a buck an hour for writing the *Field Guide to Covering Sports*; however, one writes these books to contribute to an academic field.

"As a professor, I'm expected to write books," Jeff said. "It's part of my job. I wrote a book about religion and evolution. My royalty check comes every six months. It amounts to about thirty-eight or thirty-nine dollars. There's no gold at the end of the rainbow. That's what motivated Rene [Dahinden]. He wanted to do this and get paid. Roger [Patterson] did, too."

Incidentally, Jeff does not have cable television and does not follow the shows on which he appears. Unless the producers send him a DVD, he usually does not have a chance to watch. Unless someone contacts him, he usually does not know a show's primary focus. As a journalist and student media adviser, I have watched politicians, business leaders, university administrators, and athletic directors severely limit the media's access to information. A vice president at my university refuses to speak directly to *Daily Eastern News* reporters after he embarrassed himself by making several ridiculous statements about, among other things, rape on campus. Several deans, professors, and other administrators require all questions be emailed in order to control their responses.

Even professional athletes, like LeBron James, rely on agents to vet reporters before granting access. So it's refreshing that Jeff speaks freely and candidly, as he did with me in the Wind River Mountains.

Jeff sometimes gets flak, as he did for speaking on a Discovery Channel show entitled *Russian Yeti: The Killer Lives*. He did not know the title or focus of the show until right before its broadcast. On Facebook, Meldrum explained his role: "In the end, one ultimately has minimal influence and no control over the editing and spin of a particular show. The positive opportunities and potential for lending a grounding influence through most undertakings far outweigh the occasional disappointments. So if you think I have somehow compromised my authenticity, integrity or the trust of believers — get over it — and stay tuned for upcoming programs."

Jeff said he believes these shows will prime future generations for new discoveries. That's especially important today, when Americans are more likely to disbelieve proven scientific principles thanks to ultraconservative rants and a polarized political climate. Science is an ongoing, detailed, iterative process that requires observation, evidence, experimentation, review, and a little luck, right, Madame Curie? Yet today polls show that 40 percent of Americans believe the earth and mankind were created ten thousand years ago, despite overwhelming geologic, chemical, and physical evidence that the world is an estimated 4.5 billion years old. Jeff is attempting to bring science to bigfoot enquiry, even while most academic scientists believe he is doing the exact opposite. "It's going to take a whole generation of scientists retiring, or dying, before there's a more open-minded, more progressive attitude toward this subject," Jeff said.

Ultimately, Jeff says, he is simply trying to answer the question of whether there is a biological species that lies behind the legend of sasquatch.

"We don't have any ambition of a lethal collection of a specimen," he said. "It's true that there is no precedent for recognizing a new species solely on the basis of DNA. DNA has been used to differentiate sibling species. In these cases, you have physical specimens. But there have been discussions that a lethal collection is not the preferred method, that we should allow DNA sequences to establish the presence of a new species. So drawing on that literature, I think we could make a case for recognizing a unique sasquatch. Of course, this will have to be independently confirmed and corroborated. As a professional, that's my goal. On a personal level, one of my goals is to have that experience, to see such an animal. I guess it would be kind of like a tourist who pays thousands of dollars to go up to Karisoke [in Rwanda] to sit for twenty minutes across from a mountain gorilla. There's something about that kind of experience. Seeing a sasquatch would be akin to that."

John, now cooking with the Coleman stove, might agree.

John placed his .357 on his chest and waited. He lay in a large tent situated near a strand of lodgepole and limber pine roughly ninety-eight hundred feet high in the Wind River Mountains, tired from a full day investigating bighorn sheep. Before bed, he had played his harmonica, tended his fire, and then fallen asleep around 11:00 p.m. A few minutes after midnight, he had been awakened by the rumbling sounds of something breathing in a forced, gurgling manner—perhaps, he thought, a bear with a lung infection.

John figured he would attract some attention during this trip after having grabbed a tent that smelled of bacon earlier that day from the ranger station. An assistant ranger had forewarned John that he had inadvertently allowed a box of bacon to melt into the nylon floor during his own research trip, but John had impatiently waved him off, saying he was on a tight schedule.

It was 1972. Several years earlier, John had decided to leave Long Island, New York, for the more open spaces of Wyoming to become a wildlife consultant. He had already spent considerable time camping and hiking in the most remote parts of Wyoming. In all that time, he had never heard a bear breathe so slowly. John was puzzled. Black bears respired about fifteen to twenty times a minute, about half as often as a grizzly. Healthy humans, meanwhile, breathe six to twelve times a minute. This bear's breathing, now right outside his tent, was much slower. John placed the .357 in his left hand, believing he could scare off this bear by making a loud noise. When the animal pushed its head into the tent, John smacked his right hand on something soft, which felt like a nose, and yelled, causing the animal to depart into pine saplings about thirty feet behind his tent.

About thirty minutes later the animal again moved close to the tent, poked its head into the nylon to sniff the bacon, and recoiled when John smacked it on the nose and yelled. The slow-breathing animal remained somewhere near the sapling pines. John could not reconcile the breathing; it respired way too slowly for even a large grizzly. In general, larger mammals respire more slowly, and live longer, than smaller ones. Shrews, for example, take 140–170 breaths a minute and live for about a year, while mice can live two to three years longer, with a breath rate that can vary from 95 to 160. The respiratory rate for monkeys is 32, chimps 14, whales 6, and elephants 4–6. This animal was closer to a giant tortoise's 4 breaths, but it sounded way too raspy.

A half hour later the animal closed in again. Under a full moon, John could see the tall outline of an amorphous figure standing much taller than the six-foot-high tent. Lying on the tent floor, he grabbed his .357, preparing for the worst but hoping to simply fire a shot into the sky to scare off this bear. At that moment he saw another indentation in the tent, probably indicating a cub. John smacked again, this time hitting something as hard as a rock that did not budge. In the moonlight, he saw the silhouette of a hand, twice the size of his own, with an opposed thumb and hair between stubby fingers trying to brace itself on the top of the tent. The tent collapsed and the animal fell between John's legs. The animal quickly recoiled and took off. John scrambled to slip out the tent. Outside, he could not see much despite the full moon, but he heard plenty—that raspy, rumbling, deep, slow breathing in the stand of pine about a ten yards away.

John threw wood on the fire, peered into the woods, and then sat in a chair with the sleeping bag wrapped around him, adrenaline coursing through him like a racehorse and his .357 held tightly in his hands, wondering what the hell he had just encountered and, further, whether it would approach him one more time. John now knew the animal was not a bear, but damned if he could determine other possibilities. In college, a professor had shown the video of the Patterson-Gimlin film, and John had read Ivan Sanderson's article assessing its authenticity in *Argosy* magazine; however, he did not believe any of it. So John sat and looked deeply into the woods, knowing the creature watched him. But the adrenaline wore off, the night remained calm, and nothing moved, so John fell asleep.

John awoke to the sound of a pinecone hitting his toppled tent. It was still very dark. Another pinecone fell close to the campfire. Several pinecones lay by his feet. They came almost in a barrage for a while, flying over six-foot trees, traveling at least thirty feet, and landing all around him. By sunrise everything had stopped and the animal had departed.

John remained uncertain what he had seen. After he told his supervisor this story later in the morning, the ranger responded with stories of primates reportedly visiting tourists and residents in the area. The ranger's best friend, a man who served in the same capacity in another regional mountain range, saw a large animal at close range stride easily over a four-foot fence. The supervisor asked John to investigate several reported sightings. John spoke with a Native American who claimed to have shot a bigfoot that was bothering his wife by peeking in windows of their home. He brought hair samples to biologists at the University of Wyoming, who said they looked like they came from a primate. He also talked to several Basque herders who worked the high altitudes and called this animal "Old Man." "Had one here last night," one Basque herder told John. "Probably took some sheep because I heard the screams."

The area had numerous remote areas that had abundant berries, roots, and small animals. John considered the possibilities, and he started doing research on his own, which subsequently caused problems with his wilderness projects. One supervisor chewed him out for about twenty minutes, saying, "If any of you guys are ever associated with that name bigfoot or sasquatch again, I'll see to it personally that you're fired."

Years later he lost control of a bighorn sheep study he had directed for a decade when the person in charge said, "I think we'd make more progress if you weren't connected to it."

"Does this have anything to do with bigfoot?" John asked.

"This has everything to do with it," the man responded.

John stepped aside so the project could continue.

"But that's what it's like," John told me. "You're kind of black-balled in the scientific community."

John and Jeff knelt beside a large pile of bear excrement, looking through it for evidence of its diet.

"Looks like there's some pine nuts," John said, picking away with a stick. "Some sedge."

They sat over the scat for several minutes, noticing that it appeared moldy on the bottom, but I'm not sure what that could mean, besides that it was old. John, now wearing plastic gloves, put the scat in a plastic cup and then into a plastic bag. He would place this under a microscope later. The sky was powder blue and clear, the winds soft, and the temperatures cool for late July, a definite advantage of being nine thousand feet up in the mountains. Bumblebees buzzed past us. Nearby, a raven screamed, culminating a cliché. We had just hiked a ridge that inclined toward the east, away from the camping site.

So how is bear scat important to bigfoot research? "They hang out in the same restaurant," Jeff said.

Said John, "We check scat from bear because if we can tell the diet of an omnivore, we can then know what a squatch would eat."

John sees the wilderness as a giant grocery store, pointing out edible fungi, nuts, berries, and pine needles. He teaches a field study course on edible and medicinal plants for Central Wyoming College, addresses the topic in classes at the University of Wyoming, and enjoys sharing this knowledge with anyone near him. Marian Doane, a range technician for the Bureau of Land Management, said John constantly talks about plants around the campfire, usually while chewing on a root or making some tea. Said Doane, "He's constantly teaching you."[9]

John stopped under a stand of pine. He asked me, "Want to learn something about herbal medicine?" His hand was filled with thin, brown needles. "Boil these and you'll get a great tea." Pine-needle tea has about five times more vitamin C than freshly squeezed orange juice, has a high concentration of vitamin A, and serves as both an expectorant and a decongestant.

Later on the trail, John pointed to a large, white fungus spore. That mushroom, he said, was used by Native American shamans to treat wounds and ailments. At the moment, he's far more playful. This mushroom, he says, is not fresh enough to eat. So why bring it back? John smirks: "I want to see it explode in the fire."

John is resourceful in all aspects of his life—he built a motorcycle from parts of four discarded 1950s-era BMWs, built a cabin on the south ridge of Atlantic City for seventy-three dollars, and devised a system for packing goats in the mountains to provide transportation and provide fresh milk. MacGyver has nothing on John.

We walked along the ridge for a few hours, examining tracks from elk, brown bear, and smaller animals, putting up a game camera, and seeking possible locations where bigfoot might sleep, such as a cave. This is how John and Jeff investigate bigfoot in these parts, by charting areas on a topographical map John purchased from the U.S. Geological Survey for a quarter and then walking trails to record anything of significance. They also talk with rangers and camp overnight in remote locations. A year after my visit, John and Jeff would move in a new direction after finding a correlation between a berry-producing shrub that's found in particular elevations in Wyoming and throughout the Intermountain West and increased bigfoot reports in these regions after the first hard freeze, which makes the berries most desirable. After acquiring a geographic information system coverage map that revealed the plant's distribution in Idaho, they overlaid it with a map of credible sightings reported during the fall and winter. Jeff, though, said they would not identify the plant while preliminary research is underway.

Jeff and John have developed several other hypotheses. For example, they estimate that individual males have a one-thousand-square-mile home range that overlaps smaller ranges used by several females and their young. A number of times they have observed a repeated appearance of the same footprints in the same areas. Jeff has assembled a collection of more than 250 footprint casts ranging in size from four inches to nineteen inches. Plus, he cast seven fifteen-inch footprints near Walla Walla. Using all of these casts, Jeff believes bigfoot weigh seven hundred to one thousand pounds based on estimates of body segment volumes. In addition, he and John believe bigfoot are omnivores, eating fish, game both large and small, plants, and fungi. John believes bigfoot are drawn to elk gut piles left behind by hunters based upon increased sightings during elk season. John also speculates that the animals either hibernate or estivate, meaning they may spend a prolonged period dormant or torpid.[10]

Many crazy notions are posted on bigfoot listservs, blogs, and forums. I've heard several bizarre theories around campfires as well; however, few rely heavily on scientific methods. Who knows if Jeff and John are accurate, since these are just hypotheses. Still, I feel far more confident in what these two scientists postulate than in the theories of someone who's never cracked a college science text.

It was about 5:00 p.m. We'd been walking around for hours so we headed back to camp to pack in order to eat and prepare for a night trip to the ridge. Jeff, unfortunately, was already feeling ill, so it appeared John and I would make the trek up the ridge alone.

The sun had risen above the distant peaks by the time I finally awakened here atop the ridge. John was using high-powered binoculars to scan an open area amid the pine and aspen in the valley thousands of feet below. There was a slight breeze and temperatures were probably somewhere in the upper fifties to lower sixties. The sky was clear.

I walked several steps toward the rock wall John leaned against and looked down into the valley, magnificent in the early morning light. I imagined what I would see were I standing below—deer and elk nibbling at plants near the edge of the woods, birds chirping away in search of food, narcoleptic bees awakening atop flowers. If heaven does not reside in Dyersville, Iowa, it sure as hell exists in wilderness areas like the Wind River Mountains, where one's worries disappear into the sublime beauty of nature. As John peered through his binoculars, he may have been contemplating the area's elegance using his own aesthetics. Science can often reveals truths about the natural world far better than a Petrarchan sonnet or lines from Whitman or Shakespeare.

Sometimes truth is revealed in, or near, death. Even someone as courageous as Dr. Grover Krantz, a man who wagered his professional reputation to investigate bigfoot, learned something about himself at the end. Like Jeff, Krantz sought to prove bigfoot's existence based upon tracks, using casts to reveal unique dermal ridges. Like John, Krantz strenuously advocated a no-kill policy for bigfoot, even though he realized only a physical specimen would ultimately vindicate him. Like Krantz, Jeff has a large collection of cast prints. Like Krantz, John and Jeff face ridicule. Jeff and Krantz even looked somewhat alike, with full, gray beards.

But the prospect of death shook Krantz, as it does most people. As we sat overlooking the valleys, John said Krantz asked him to shoot a bigfoot after being diagnosed with pancreatic cancer. Krantz apparently did not want to be remembered as a kook. Of course, who does? But this was a man who had repudiated skeptics his entire life. Krantz first recognized the skin ridges that appear on cast prints, established that the large footprints varied from human prints, and suggested bigfoot might be a relict species of *Gigantopithecus*, a genus of ape believed to have gone extinct a hundred thousand years ago. No ape grew larger than *Gigantopithecus blacki*, which stood more than nine feet tall and weighed up to eleven hundred pounds. Despite all of this, Krantz could not reconcile his reputation, at least if the story John tells is true.

John refused Krantz's request. "But I don't want to capture or kill one," John says he told Krantz. "I just want some DNA." John said it would be like shooting the last surviving Mexican grizzly. But Krantz persisted, writing a letter further trying to persuade him. John would not relent, even for a scientist he greatly admired. He'd rather find a way to communicate with bigfoot or learn their habits, as he had with grizzly and bighorn sheep.

As John looked out over the valley, I saw a man at peace with the world, fastened to his science, his surroundings, and the good earth—a man equally at home playing Polish bluegrass on an accordion in Atlantic City's Mercantile, chatting with science students at the University of Wyoming, or effortlessly spending weeks in the wilderness, alone with his thoughts and his curiosity.

John's life, though, is tethered to bigfoot. Like Krantz, he is a sharp scientist whose mind can process ideas from many disciplines but who, ultimately, has staked his professional reputation on bigfoot existing. It is for people like John that I dearly hope bigfoot exist.

EPILOGUE

If bigfoot are real, how can they continue to elude us? We have night-vision goggles that enable us to walk through the darkest woods as if it were daylight. We have satellites orbiting the earth that can zoom in so closely that they can reveal license plate numbers. And we have GPR equipment that enables us to virtually see below the surface of the ground.

My best friend, Scott, has an explanation: God is screwing with us. Not sure whether Scott, a state's attorney who frequently argues constitutional issues related to murder cases, is unconsciously redirecting his feeling about judges to the Almighty, but the theory is as good as any other. How else can we explain perfectly fine cameras malfunctioning just when a bigfoot is within view? Or the lack of a clear, close photo? Hundreds of Americans publically claim they have seen or heard bigfoot, but nobody has undisputed evidence.

Maybe God is acting like the designer of the video game *Grand Theft Auto: San Andreas*, who has denied claims that bigfoot was inserted into the game despite evidence to the contrary. You can find bigfoot in several screenshots and videos posted online—although, in an ironic twist, these visuals mirror real-life footage by being blurry and low quality. After these rumors arose, players started adding modifications to *Grand Theft*, creating something that may not have been originally devised in the game. Ten years after the game's 2004 release, players still hunt for the virtual bigfoot and they sound just like real-life bigfoot eyewitnesses. "I do believe the creature exists," Kaleb Krimmel, a teenage player from Michigan, told the *New Yorker* in 2013. "I have encountered him more than once. I would say he is proven."[1] As in real life, video skeptics poke fun at those who believe, calling them idiots and liars: "Myth hunters are determined to believe in myths despite all evidence to the contrary. Perhaps they want the myths to be true so badly that they've managed to trick themselves into seeing things that aren't there, or they've made connections between things that aren't connected."[2] Sound familiar? This could have been ripped straight out of a comments section connected to a bigfoot media report.

Unlike us, video game players can speak with their creators. The video game company's chief executive officer said they never inserted bigfoot into the game. The game's lead designer, Craig Filshie, said there is no truth to the bigfoot rumors, but he added somewhat cryptically: "San Andreas is an extremely complex game, with millions of lines of code. It's entirely possible for strange things to happen, but none of them are intentional."[3] So perhaps bigfoot can manifest within the game's matrix, even if the game's creators had not originally planned for that to happen. Like God, the game's creators might be privately reveling in the confusion they have created.

"For all we know, God is in heaven talking to angels at a round table," Scott says. "He's laughing, telling them, 'This is the last thing I'm going to do to humans. I promise. Please, don't take this away from me. It's all I've got left to have some fun with these idiots.'"

As if God needs permission to mess with us. He's already given us the Kardashians, reality television, nipples on men, and, Christian fundamentalists might argue, dinosaurs that test our faith. He's also given us some bizarre creatures—ants that look like pandas, moles that have alien-like tentacles on their noses, and glowing jellyfish. There's also the aye-aye, a nocturnal lemur in Madagascar that has wide green, orange, or yellow eyes and long, wiry hair that sprouts in tufts around the ears, making it appear like a blend of Gollum and gremlin. There's also the jerboa, a rodent residing in arid, sandy areas within Mongolia and China, which appears as though it were created from spare parts. The jerboa has inordinately large ears like Dumbo's, long hind legs like a kangaroo's, and wide whiskers like a cat's slapped onto a tiny body that grows no more than six inches. Consider, too, the red-lipped batfish, which appears to have smudged lipstick across its face like a preteenager and which can't swim well, relying instead on stick-like feet to walk the ocean floor around the Galapagos Islands. There are also several birds that can't fly, such as penguins, emus, and kiwis. Let's not forget the yeti crab, discovered in 2005, that has white hair along its appendages. If these creatures exist, why not bigfoot?

Are premises about bigfoot any stranger than those in theoretical physics? Take string theory, for example, where some scientists posit that many universes exist parallel to ours. In these multiple universes, scientists speculate, another version of you could be doing the exact same things or doing something completely different. Laws of physics might be wildly different in these other universes, perhaps even collapsing and expanding so quickly that life never develops—or so goes this theory. One year Scott and I both read *The Elegant Universe*, a book written by a physicist, Brian Greene, who attempted to explain how multiple universes could exist. I never finished the book, my three-dimensional mind wrapped around too many enigmas and conundrums. Maybe string theory is like an idea offered in the movie *Men In Black*, where the main character, J, played by Will Smith, learns that entire universes exist in lockers in bus stations. Later, during the movie credits, viewers are shown that J's universe resides in a marble being used in a game by an alien living in another universe. "You talk about multiple universes," Scott tells me one night on the phone, "and nobody says anything. But if you say you saw a bigfoot, people say, 'Yeah, and a spacecraft captured you and probed you.' You're considered a fucking Looney Tune."

At times I feel like a seven-year-old questioning the existence of God and the creation of the universe. "Who were God's parents?" I asked my mother that night in 1971. I see her and the room as clearly as if I were still standing on that wood floor on the second level of our apartment in Finderne, New Jersey, probably because that was the first time my mind really pondered life outside of my insulated world, a conscience struggling to emerge from a self-consumed child. My mother and I were sitting by my large bedroom window and gazing at the stars hovering above the woods across the avenue. Cars rolled by periodically, but none turned into the long parking lot. My father had already left for the night, leaving my mother to deal with my second-grade logic: Wouldn't God's parents also have had parents? What existed before God created the universe? Where would he have lived? How can one create something from nothing? I knew nothing of Albert Einstein's theory of relativity or about Stephen Hawking's explanations that space and time are not fixed and therefore have no actual starting point. Or, further, that there might be an infinite number of universes, each one exhibiting a different timeline. In other words, everything that could potentially have happened in our own past, but did not, will happen in another universe. As a kid, I was naïve enough to think simple answers are out there waiting for us. At age seven, you believe a lifetime is forever and that all your questions will eventually be addressed. At age forty-eight, though, you realize hardly anything gets resolved within our short life spans. So my mother nodded, told me those were very smart questions, and continued to quietly look out at the dark skies over the woods, through the same window where she had talked me off the ledge two years earlier when my father had left us and through which I had caught a glimpse of Santa Claus flying in his sled behind Rudolph's red nose on Christmas Eve the year before, as my mother had suggested might happen if I looked long enough.

As a kid, I wanted to believe I saw Santa. That's no different than people wanting to believe they have seen a bigfoot. Take, for instance, a recently reported sighting from England. A thirty-one-year-old man snapped a photo and recorded audio of what is purported to be the first real evidence of bigfoot taken in the Friskney nature reserve near Lincolnshire, about 140 miles north of London. Newspapers teased this claim as though it were a major scientific breakthrough. In its headline, the *London Daily Mirror* blared, "Is Bigfoot in Britain? Mysterious Figure Lurking in Lincolnshire Woods Is Claimed to Be Mystery Beast." The *Huffington Post* boasted, "Is Bigfoot In Britain? Photos and Audio Prove Something Is." Exclaimed England's *Sunday-Express*, "Could these startling pictures be evidence that Bigfoot is lurking in the British countryside?" The newspapers refer to an eerie image of a menacing figure that lurks in the woods, but in reality the photo discloses nothing more than a shadowy area anywhere from thirty to sixty feet away that's partially obscured by tree limbs, trunks, and tall grass. The image could just as easily be a hollow in a distant tree, a bear, were they not extinct in the UK, or even a werewolf, a far more fantastical notion. Adam Bird, co-founder of the British Bigfoot Research Organization, also claimed to have captured a bigfoot vocalization, which was also posted online by the *Mirror*; however, the nearly inaudible recording sounds more like a fictional *Jurassic Park* creature screaming than anything. Bird, though, was adamant that the photo is compelling evidence that bigfoot exists in the British Isles. "I make no bold claims," Bird said, "but my fellow investigators think this could be genuine evidence that the British Bigfoot exists."[4] Readers of the *Mirror*, though, disagreed by a five-to-one margin, dismissing this photo as evidence through an online poll. Only 17 percent believed Bird had made a true scientific discovery.

Just to be certain, I sent this photo to several bigfoot researchers here in the United States. They scoffed at the photo's evidence.

"You're missing nothing," Tommy Poland emailed me. "As they say in the UK: Bollocks. LOL."

Wrote Harold Benny, "The photo is too far away. I enlarged it until it pixilated with Photoshop. It's another blobsquatch. There is not enough here to make a positive statement about. Maybe a good original high-resolution photo could be enlarged for a better examination. But, they should have done THAT in the first place. Of course by enhancing the photo people would yell 'manipulated photo.' A picture is either too poor or too good. We can't win."

Eric Altman, a researcher in Pennsylvania, called it bunk, adding, "According to several contacts I have in the UK, Britain is too small and doesn't have enough habitat to support a creature."

Neither Don Keating nor Billy Willard saw anything in the photo either.

Definitive proof, Don Young told me, can only come from a fresh, physical DNA sample or an actual body, dead or alive. Forget about video, photos, footprints, or thermal images.

Melissa Hovey says bigfoot will more likely be found after an old woman accidentally plows over one in an old steel Buick. Cliff Barackman, a featured host on Animal Planet's *Finding Bigfoot*, told me the odds are more in favor of a truck rolling one over while blazing down some logging road early in the morning. In other words, bet the house that pure, dumb luck will provide the best evidence, if bigfoot exists.

Still, the stories persist. A man in Kingsport, Tennessee, recently claimed a bigfoot banged against his house so hard that it knocked a picture from his wall.[5] A researcher in Ontario, Canada, claimed he played tic-tac-toe in the snow with a juvenile bigfoot.[6] And, in a case of Darwinian natural selection, a man dressed as a bigfoot walked onto Highway 93 South in western Montana, hoping to incite stories. The forty-four-year-old man stepped into the highway's right-hand lane dressed in a camouflage ghillie suit, making it hard for anyone to see him—much less the two teenaged drivers who first slammed into him and then rolled over him. According to a state trooper, "You can't make it up."[7] In light of media stories such as these, why would a reasonable person willingly face perpetual ridicule by sharing any bigfoot experience? And why, for the love of sasquatch, would people put themselves in situations where they would face a fusillade of criticism from casual observers, self-appointed experts, and digital trolls? I caught up with several people featured in this book to see what they've learned about themselves, others, and bigfoot since our first encounter.

Don Young is still desperately trying to prove that bigfoot exist. That's why he carries two arrows he designed specifically to fire into the animal. Next time, Don says, he does not plan to refrain from pulling the trigger.

After a decade in which Don said he was tracked by a bigfoot, chased up a tree by a juvenile bigfoot, and had a bigfoot in his rifle's crosshairs, he lost his livelihood as a hunting guide and his connections with people in his hometown of Phillips, Wisconsin, and has had cats taken from his property—eaten, he once told me, by a hungry bigfoot. If this all sounds crazy—and, frankly, how could it not—you'll understand why he dearly wants to find evidence of bigfoot.

When we met in Phillips, more than five years earlier, Don had planned to produce several YouTube movies on his channel reminiscent of those featured on Les Stroud's TV show *Survivorman* and Bear Grylls's program *Man vs. Wild*. Don's plans were derailed when he served nearly five years in correctional facilities for a felony charge related to child enticement, along with two misdemeanors. Don told me one November night several months after his release that his desire to find bigfoot evidence consumes him. Don walks the backwoods near his home about four days a week, looking for disturbances along paths, checking on his ten game cameras, placing double-sided tape on wires to catch hair, and hanging mousetraps at head level. He also camps in a bog about fifteen miles north of Phillips in the midst of a million acres of state and national forests along the Flambeau River, which includes two secluded lakes, for days at a time.

Before camping, Don will remove all of his clothes, slap himself with balsam or cedar boughs, roll around in dirt and leaves, and then apply mud to protect his skin and eliminate remaining odors on his body. He'll also bury his clothes in the ground before putting them back on. "Bigfoot is an animal," Don tells me. "You sometimes have to be like an animal to find an animal. You can't go out there smelling like Mennen aftershave and smoking cigars. You can't smell like a human. You have to eliminate as much civilization and human scent as possible. Every animal in the woods knows that a human is a threat. They've seen what we've done. We're the only species that destroys more than it creates."

Don, now fifty-one years old, eschews campfires, knowing the bright flames impair vision and scare off animals, so instead he lies cold in the woods listening to the world around him, enjoying the solitude of the bog as his eyes adjust to the moonlight. In these woods Don might find the only peace he knows. Even though he has tinnitus, he's able to hear the slightest movements—a night crawler slithering through the leaves, a beetle making clicks with its shell, a partridge walking, a white-faced mouse tunneling under leaves. "It's pure music to hear stuff that I would normally ignore at home," Don says. In the distance he might hear sandhill cranes hooping, crows screeching, or deer snorting. Bugs, everywhere in the summer, are not a problem in the fall or winter, but sometimes a rodent tries to run into Don's pant leg for shelter, its cold feet tickling his skin enough to force him to shake it out. Don may also hum to calm himself, play the flute, or occasionally knock against trees. "A lot of people call me antisocial," he says, "but I prefer the outdoors because animals won't stab me in the back—although they will kill you for survival." By day, he hikes. In this area, he says, he found a bigfoot burial area five years ago, but the bone he found and buried under a moss-covered rock is now lost under a thick growth of poplar trees that have replaced oak, hemlock, and maple that were clear-cut for timber. On a beaver pond, he found beaver homes that had been completely unearthed, further bigfoot evidence to Don, since black bears, the only other animal likely to do such digging, prefer not to swim. At times when he returns to camp after hiking, he'll notice small items are missing—a mirror or a stirring spoon, maybe some photos. Cameras may be knocked off trees. Sure, Don says, people can say raccoons stole these items, but he knows better. Ultimately he's hoping to coax a far larger creature to creep closer in order to prove he is not a lunatic—and, he says, he encounters them from time to time.

Before entering a bog, Don prefers to stand still at the edge, amid the trees and foliage, for thirty to forty-five minutes, just as predators do in order to make sure the area is safe. Don believes bigfoot do the same thing. By doing this, Don has watched numerous animals move about, including a six-hundred-pound black bear—and the bigfoot he saw through his rifle scope years earlier.

It's ironic that Don would now shoot a bigfoot, because he's been ordained a shaman, a healer in the Seneca tribe, who believe a visitation from a bigfoot is a blessing. Six Nations elders, including the Senecas, believe a bigfoot is sometimes a forest spirit called Genosqwa, a bulkier, larger version that is both spirit and flesh. Some Native American legends, though, describe these creatures raiding villages, decapitating prey, and killing humans. Of course, tribes like the Senecas also tell tales of two-footed, dwarf-like spirits, disembodied heads, and powerful storm spirits residing in the sky that cause thunder and lightning. So it's unclear whether one should embrace or flee a Genosqwa, since these tales can sometimes be more illustrative than factual. The elders recently taught Don sacred spirit calling ceremonies that create a bond with the Genosqwa by bringing this creature to the seeker either in the flesh or in a dream. At least, this is what Don tells me; the facts are difficult to verify. In a recent Facebook post, Don wrote of these spirits, "Harm them and they will watch over you afield." Still, Don would like to shoot one in the ass.

If anything, the design of Don's arrow is ingenious: twenty holes drilled into an aluminum spine, each opening packed with cotton, and a regular target head. About fifteen hundred feet of twenty-five-pound-strength string wraps around a spool. Ideally, Don would like to shoot a bigfoot in the meaty buttocks, sending the arrow into flesh like a giant hypodermic needle. Once the arrow enters the flesh, the cotton would absorb blood, skin, tissue, and bodily fluids. If the bigfoot pulls, dislodges, or tosses the arrow, Don could then follow the string to recover the projectile, potentially filled with all kinds of deoxyribonucleic acids that might prove the creature's existence.

Perhaps Don could send the DNA to the Oxford geneticist Bryan Sykes and his colleagues, who examined more than thirty hair samples sent to them from across the globe during a two-year study. They clearly identified each sample as coming from a common animal. The black bear and wolf/coyote/dog were identified in half the samples sent from the United States, which offered the most hair strands. Three cows were also singled out, along with one each of horse, human, deer, raccoon, sheep, and porcupine. Bears and horses dominated the nine Russian hair strands, while Indian and Bhutanese examples revealed polar bears.[8] The scientists, using rigorous methods, had no trouble analyzing the samples for an article published in the *Proceedings of the Royal Society*. In 2012 Sykes told me he doubted very much that any hair samples would reveal a new species, but he was curious where the samples derived from. "By relying entirely on DNA evidence, which cannot be easily falsified, I do not need to put myself in a position of having to believe or disbelieve accounts." Science, he said, simply interprets the world through evidence.

After receiving the hair-sample results, Sykes told me by email that bigfoot researchers are not sufficiently self-critical, entertaining only evidence that supports their beliefs. Still, Sykes won't dismiss that bigfoot exist. In the *Proceedings* article, he and his colleagues pointed out that absence of evidence is not evidence of absence. And he told me that he thoroughly enjoyed working on the project: "Although all the bigfoot and sasquatch samples turned out to be from regular creatures, I talked to so many regular people who had seen 'something,' many of whom had no axe to grind or anything to gain, that I definitely thought this was worth pursuing—though not by me. So, I guess I think it is more likely than I did that these creatures do exist. I hope I have shown how to get results that would be accepted by everyone, and encourage all enthusiasts to return to the woods and get 'the golden hair' that is the proof. But PLEASE don't let things slip and go back to the sloppy, even fraudulent, 'research,' which has been a characteristic until now. If that happens, then I really have wasted my time, and bigfoot enthusiasts will *never* be believed—and would not deserve to be either."

Until Don can fire his arrow to claim his golden DNA, he plans to keep searching for evidence—even if, as he has started to believe, science can't explain everything. "Genosqwa is not just a flesh animal," he tells me by phone. "If it were just flesh, we would have found it a long time ago. That's all mumbo-jumbo. If there is no supernatural, then why can't we explain everything? There are still many things we cannot explain, and that's what we call supernatural."

Don knows the woods intimately; he is able to identify and use plants to heal and is capable of tracking most anything. He crafts handmade fishing lures. He knows cool shit like this: putting a drop of glycerin on a teaspoon of powdered potassium permanganate, an inorganic chemical compound consisting primarily of salt ions, can start a fire. The compound can also purify water and create antiseptic solutions and works as an antifungal treatment. If a zombie apocalypse were to occur, Don would be a match for Daryl Dixon. Yet a few bigfoot enthusiasts claim Don has fabricated thermal videos, such as a clip involving Blinky, ostensibly a young bigfoot climbing a tree in his backyard. But it's as equally unequivocal as any other footage. Don says he can be an asshole, but he's been gracious to me, answering calls, responding to emails, and spending a day retracing past events in locales across northern Wisconsin. He seems earnest when it comes to having faced bigfoot, regardless of the purported evidence.

Years ago in southern Illinois, Pam Porter spoke glowingly about Don, saying he was a sweetheart. Don became terrified, she said, when they encountered something running around deep in the northern Michigan woods during a BFRO expedition, clearly not what she had anticipated from a lifelong hunting guide. You could see the fear in his eyes even in daylight among a large group of people, she told me. That does not appear to be a description of someone who's fabricating stories.

Still, I remain skeptical when he says he has photos and footage he has kept private, including footage that is far better than the Patterson-Gimlin film. Matt Moneymaker, he said, has some of this visual evidence. Eventually, Don says, he will release it all. "I'm tired of the people who say that I'm in this for a profit," Don says. "If I were in this for a profit, I would be a millionaire right now. I'm here only to prove that bigfoot exists."

Cliff Barackman sounds relaxed on the phone, speaking with me during a hiatus from *Finding Bigfoot*, Animal Planet's reality-based TV show. More than one million people regularly tune in to watch Cliff and three other investigators search for clues about bigfoot's existence on one of the network's most popular shows, which also features BFRO founder Matt Moneymaker, field biologist Ranae Holland, and bigfoot-sized California researcher James "Bobo" Fay, a friend of Cliff's before the show began. The two were featured in a *MonsterQuest* episode that focused on tribal territory near the Klamath River in northern California.

It is a few days before Thanksgiving, almost exactly two years after I spoke with Cliff in a hotel lobby in Collinsville, a city that sits about fourteen miles east of St. Louis and just a few miles from the Cahokia Mounds, once home to a large ancient settlement. The *Finding Bigfoot* crew had been in town to investigate areas in nearby Madison County, which would be shown as part of the show's third season. In fall 2012, when I first spoke to Cliff, the show was airing its third season. Tonight it's airing its sixth season, focusing on my home state of New Jersey, where the most popular monster is the Jersey Devil, which is emblazoned on the jerseys of the NHL team that plays in East Rutherford. Cliff has some time off after traveling across the United States, Nepal, China, and Indonesia during the past several years, which enables him to play his beloved jazz on the guitar, to spend some rare time in his Portland, Oregon, home, and to reflect on bigfoot. As you can imagine, he has a great deal of ideas, theories, and beliefs regarding bigfoot after having immersed himself in investigations for the past two years.

In fall 2012 he had told me, "I don't have any answers. I have questions. I'm a learner. These things [bigfoot] are cool, and I want to learn as much as I can about them. It's a good thing to fill my life with."

Two years later, here are a few things he believes might be true:

- Bigfoot are introverted just like him. More people would be surprised by the second assertion, but Cliff says he's always been shy, despite his job history. Besides serving as an investigator on the TV show, he has also sold fishing gear and bait at a tackle store and taught sixth grade at Cascade Heights Public Charter School in Clackamas County, just south of Portland. The county extends into the Mount Hood National Forest and boasts the highest number of bigfoot reports in Oregon.
- Bigfoot are not endangered, despite several efforts that seek such status. A month earlier, a New York motel operator had asked the Chautauqua County board to protect bigfoot, although this was mostly a self-serving attempt to promote his bigfoot conference. Bigfoot especially don't want to get caught in the crosshairs in Texas, where it's legal to kill bigfoot. Said L. David Sinclair, a chief of staff for the Texas Parks and Wildlife Department, "If Bigfoot did exist, and wasn't human, then it would [be legal]. Bigfoot would be a non-protected wild animal."[9]
- Eyewitness testimony is powerful. Sure, this evidence is anecdotal, Cliff realizes, but way too many people are offering the same descriptions and details for thousands of stories to be dismissed. "The strength and the integrity of witnesses is amazing," he tells me. "When grandma says she saw bigfoot in '42, people say she's crazy, lying, hallucinating. People don't believe they're real. How many people can you write off as liars or attention seekers?"
- Killing bigfoot is immoral. "It's rude to do that just to sate one's curiosity," he says. "If you shoot one, it's morally wrong. If you do actually kill one, you'd better reload." But that is the protocol of the scientific world—even if it seems like a Victorian notion. What is that? Not sure. Let's shoot it and find out. Ironically, Cliff's *Finding Bigfoot* series now has competition from a new show on Destination America entitled *Killing Bigfoot*, which follows members of the Gulf Coast Bigfoot Research

Organization as they try to track and shoot a bigfoot in the Texas and Louisiana swamps. Animal Planet and Destination America, incidentally, are both owned by Discovery Communications.

Each bigfoot area has its own culture. For example, bigfoot in Chinook Pass near Yakima, Washington, in the Cascade Range are very vocal, Cliff says, whereas the ones in Bluff Creek, California, communicate by using whistles and knocks. In Cliff's private research area in the Mount Hood National Forest, meanwhile, the bigfoot move in from the same direction each time before making quiet knocks when they get within fifty to one hundred yards. He once heard a vocalization so clear that he assumed it had been made by a nearby camper; however, the area was closed to all human traffic. He says he noticed activity six of the first seven times he hung out in this spot. Said Cliff in 2012, "It's the most outrageous spot I've ever had." He has been too busy with the show to spend much time in his favorite blueberry bog. "It [the show] has literally swallowed me up," he says.

More than anything, Cliff has learned to relax. Twenty years ago, Cliff admits, he was gung-ho to discover evidence in any way possible during extended trips into the woods. It was no coincidence that he took the teaching job in the heart of sasquatch country. Now in his early forties, Cliff no longer cares if bigfoot are proven to exist because he enjoys spending time in the solitude of the woods, regardless of whether he finds any activity. Ultimately, Cliff would like to work an area for a prolonged period in order to develop a relationship, sort of how Jane Goodall did with the chimpanzees in Tanzania. "It could be proven today and I would still be doing this," he says. "I love most everything about researching bigfoot." Eventually, he would like to buy a home in the woods near a good bigfoot location so he could go squatching by sitting on the front porch with a beer in his hand. "Over the last twenty years, this has turned more into a learning journey,"

Cliff said. "The more I've learned about sasquatches and looked at myself, the more that I see that we're all the same."

Harold Benny says that bigfoot research has kept him poor.

Since we last met in the Shawnee National Forest years earlier, Harold has lost his job as a chemist for Central Illinois Public Service Company in his hometown of Hillsboro, a town in Illinois of about six thousand people, located about sixty-five miles northeast of St. Louis and fifty miles south of Springfield in a mostly rural setting. He barely has enough money to restructure his home after he had to replace his hot-water boiler. Money is really tight. That's because he spends a great deal of money on camping, has invested a fortune on books, continues to purchase new equipment, and travels to locations all over southern Illinois to investigate sightings. He frequently goes to Murphysboro, about 120 miles straight south on Illinois Route 127, to check police records related to a creature described as a big muddy monster by several residents during the summer of 1973. His job working at a bindery, located south of Springfield, pays just enough to cover his expenses. It's pretty damned hard, he says, to find a job that would allow him to do better financially. So he manages his finances despite the loss of $9,000 a year. "I'm always buying stuff and spending money I should spend on fixing up the house," Harold tells me. "Financially, it's stretched me. When I started, I could barely pay for a trip to a BFRO expedition. Now, I spend entirely too much money on it. But I don't have a wife. I don't have anyone to keep me in control." So the house repairs can wait.

Bigfoot has cost Harold friends and a serious relationship. Several years ago he was spending time with a slightly younger woman after a hiatus from dating. He wondered, is this going to get serious? Perhaps, had she not picked up a book about bigfoot lying on a table in his house.

Did Harold really believe in such creatures? the woman asked.

Yes, he said. In fact, he spent time researching bigfoot out in the woods.

The woman laughed until she fell over. Said Harold, "She thought that was funny as hell." After that, Harold never called her again.

"We had so much fun," he said, "but I couldn't stand it that she thought that me and bigfoot were so damned funny. That was not something I expected."

Harold, who has a master's degree in zoology from Eastern Illinois University, can get equally indignant when bigfoot researchers manipulate evidence.

For example, Harold noticed that a Bigfoot Field Researchers Organization investigator saw bigfoot's eyes glowing everywhere during a 2012 expedition in Murphysboro. Harold, who stood nearby, squinted, but he could not see anything. In his early sixties, Harold knew his eyesight was not as sharp anymore, so he kept quiet and watched. That's when he made the connection. A female firefly will sit in bushes to select a suitor among the males hovering and flashing around her. The female eventually responds to a male suitor—who provides a high-protein nutritional package that she digests and uses to provision the eggs—by flashing the light in her abdomen so that it lingers a bit longer than the rhythmic flashes circling her. This guy, Harold thought, was misidentifying the females' slower flashes for eye shine. Said Harold, "He'd keep saying he saw something, but all I could see was fireflies."

Later, Harold noticed that the man also identified stars twinkling through blowing trees as eye glow. When this researcher returned three months later for a BFRO event, Harold suggested he check for fireflies before advising others he had seen eyes shining. The man neither cared about the advice nor believed him, but he was worried Harold might share this theory with others, so he found a way to get Harold ejected. "Like a fool, I had shown him my new shotgun that was stashed in the car," Harold says. "We rednecks are proud of our new shotguns." The man told the national organizers that Harold had brought a gun to shoot someone, prompting them to toss him from the BFRO. Like me, he is now a persona non grata with that organization.

Now, Harold says, that man is training others and running BFRO events in Iowa. "The new people learn from him. These things get perpetuated on and on. It's a wonder they know anything."

Harold continues on with his own group that includes more than a dozen people. He still researches the Harrisburg region where Kristen and I had explored, staying at the same campground that continues to yield strange stories. For example, Harold told me about two ATV drivers viewing a big, hairy bipedal animal walking down a hill, rocks being thrown at researchers, and something large walking through camp early one morning.

Is he glad he's still researching? "I really don't know," Harold tells me. "I think I'm on to something here. There's an animal there. I don't really know what it is and I don't know where it came from. I've read and read and read to the point that it's almost driven me crazy as to all the possibilities. I want to say bigfoot is part of wildlife. I still think part of the reason I do this is for my father, who told me as a kid that anything is possible."

Don Keating is far more interested in tracking thunderstorms and snow flurries than bigfoot these days. No longer does he spend nights hanging out in pavilions at Salt Fork State Park, nor does he regularly write reports on local sightings or produce a monthly newsletter. In fact, Don questions whether bigfoot roam the woodlands of Ohio. After thirty years, the fifty-two-year-old Ohio native has been unable to gather any scientific evidence on bigfoot in the Buckeye State. "With all I've done, experienced, encountered, discovered and all of the alleged eyewitnesses I've interviewed, I still have some doubt," he told me in fall 2014.

Don was always publically frustrated by the bigfoot community's failure to work together. He produced his newsletter to share information, invited other researchers to take part in a *MonsterQuest* episode, and desired to develop a research database. But he never received the cooperation he sought, saying others betrayed and ridiculed him through the years. These constant fights finally forced Don to halt his efforts. "If you dare disagree with someone's opinion, you'd be stoned to death," he said. "If you presented your own unique opinion on something you'd be considered a crazy person and your claims would be [considered to be] without foundation."

Don says he also lost friends over bigfoot research. Never one to hold back, Don told me, "I have learned that some others who claim, pretend, and profess to be your friend are, in reality, just leeches that cling to your coattails in hopes of learning everything you have learned over the course of many years. Furthermore, I have learned that these same friends will do everything in their power to not only make you look bad but to destroy everything you have worked so hard to create. Some people whom I held as dear friends turned out to be nothing but a wolf in sheep's clothing."

This all drove Don to replace one passion with another. Now he spends his days forecasting weather in and around Ohio. He produces a two-minute weather videocast for the *Cambridge Daily Jeffersonian*'s website, which typically gets viewed daily by a few hundred readers across several eastern Ohio communities, and two weather almanac videos of forty-five to sixty seconds that are included as part of a biweekly community television show called *Talk of the Town*, which features notable guests from southeastern Ohio. Plus, he posts his daily videocast on his Ohio Weather Facebook page, which has several thousand followers, and he regularly updates his weather website at www.ohiowx.com.

So what did bigfoot researching teach Don about himself? That he can successfully organize large events, such as the annual bigfoot conference held at Salt Fork State Park. He brought in speakers such as Bob Gimlin, who helped film the most influential video of a bigfoot, in Bluff Creek, California, and Jeff Meldrum, one of the few scientists researching bigfoot. People fill the conference and pack the hotels at the state park's resort. Bigfoot is definitely good for the local economy.

In order to get his weather career rolling, Don handed off the conference to the Ohio Bigfoot Organization for three years starting in 2012. After his three-year hiatus, Don offered a candid review of the conference. Marc DeWerth, who had organized these conferences, apparently did not agree with Don's critique, so Don decided to once again take over the conference, for his twenty-fourth year. DeWerth, meanwhile, decided to run a conference for a fourth year, pitting two large bigfoot conferences against each other within a single month in the same lodge at Salt Fork State Park in spring 2015. How popular is the topic of bigfoot in America? Unlike bigfoot themselves, squatch enthusiasts were not shy in purchasing tickets, enabling both venues to sell out four months in advance. Even overflow tickets, which offered access to closed-circuit video in another room, sold well.

So Don's faith is not completely extinguished, but don't expect him to start waxing nostalgic any time soon. Instead, he'll remain the same blunt straight shooter he's always been. "I really hope some indisputable evidence is discovered before I take my last breath, but I honestly doubt it will be."

Carolanne Solomon is a brave soul. In many ways, she reminds me of my wife, Betsy, who worked as a state biologist in Florida for nearly ten years. Betsy would walk through wetlands with little regard for aggressive water moccasins, powerful gators, or icky banana spiders — often in the middle of nowhere (and way before cell phones). Not that one could dial while being rolled by a six-hundred-pound gator. So I was surprised when Carolanne told me about an incident that terrified her.

Camping in a tract of state-managed land near the Hillsborough River State Park in 2007 with her oldest son, Timothy, Carolanne awoke to hear something she described as "the thing" circling her tent. It was so large that she could feel each step it took toward her side of the tent. She followed it with her eyes in the darkness. Then it started to walk around to the other side of the tent, where Timothy watched, wide-eyed and about to scream. Carolanne quickly covered his mouth and whispered, "Stay calm." Together, they watched the creature take a few steps, sniff the air, and turn to walk toward the table a few yards from the tent. They lost visual contact, but they heard items getting tossed about. After several minutes it stopped and walked into the woods, where it made a loud whoop. The next morning they came across a size-sixteen footprint, so they made a cast.

"I never felt scared or threatened like I did on this night," Carolanne told me. "I couldn't believe how frightened I was as it was happening." To this day, she can't explain the fear.

Yet she continues to hike game trails, waterways, and regular trails looking for signs of a bigfoot. She speaks aloud in Cherokee, saying things like hello (*O siya*), thank you (*wado*), friend (*u-na-li*), and good-bye (*do na do go vi*). At her base camp, Carolanne frequently plays flutes and powwow drums and burns sage, sweetgrass, and cedar, sometimes as part of a smudging ceremony intended to cleanse negative energy from a person, place, or thing. This can be done by rubbing one's hands in the smoke, scooping the smoke, and then bringing it to the head, eyes, throat, ears, and heart. "I have experienced over the years that when I smudge, play Native American music, or speak in Cherokee that I tend to get more activity," she said.

Carolanne says she learns something new each time she investigates, even if she refuses to state anything factual about bigfoot. For example, she believes that bigfoot are like kids in that they won't perform on cue. "I have gone into some of my sites on an almost daily basis where I have had some sort of activity every time," she says. "But many times when I bring someone with me all we experience is crickets chirping."

As she hikes, Carolanne hears whoops, whistles, tree knocks, coyote sounds, monkey chatter, whispering, and loud screeches like those I heard with her several years earlier in the Green Swamp, which she attributed to (wink) a four-hundred-pound owl—although not all at once or all the time. Sometimes, she'll hear limbs break, find limb structures, see red eye shine, and smell nasty, overwhelming odors. Once a stick was tossed at her; another time she heard a deep growl. Carolanne says she can never quite catch up to the sounds, which is certainly the exact opposite of the behavior of any sane person. Once she heard a baby crying.

More than anything, Carolanne says, she has learned to distrust other researchers after seeing so much misinformation and hearing so many lies and hoaxes being spread by fame-seekers. Several years ago a Florida researcher asked her for help in salvaging his reputation. Carolanne agreed to show him how to conduct research more accurately and more truthfully. They met twice. Both times this person blogged and posted videos about events that never happened. She called, emailed, and eventually posted corrections in the website's comments section, which were quickly deleted. By the third scheduled meeting, Carolanne planned to tell him she would no longer help, except the man never arrived at the meeting location. Instead, she met two people at the campground who reported that this man had departed after doing some strange things: tossing sticks in front of his camera and speaking to the camera about being deep in the woods, when these people never saw him leave the campground. "I have learned that it's all about who can be the most famous and getting their names known," Carolanne said. "Egos run rampant and so do backstabbers and two-faced people. I have learned that I am back in middle school when it comes to the mentality of most. You're considered a top researcher because you put up a million videos and pictures of blurry stumps and noises of things running through the woods. I have learned that if you write a book or are in one or on a TV show or are overly opinionated, you are considered an expert. There is no respect for your fellow researcher. It just seems that most are out for themselves instead of working together. It seems that doing good, honest research is a thing of the past."

Carolanne, though, is too intrigued by whatever lies in Florida's wild, so she'll keep hiking, camping, and investigating. Like Albert Einstein said, "If we knew what we were doing, it wouldn't be called research."

NOTES

3. SOUTHERN ILLINOIS

1. Ann Schottman Knol, "Reliving the Tale of the Big Muddy Monster," *Southern Illinoisan*, December 7, 1985.

2. Andrew Malcom, "Yeti-Like 'Monster' Gives Staid Town in Illinois a Fright," *New York Times*, November 1, 1973.

6. EASTERN KENTUCKY

1. Ian Urbina, "In Kentucky's Teeth, Toll of Poverty and Neglect," *New York Times*, December 24, 2007.

2. Richard J. Jensen, "United Mine Workers of America," in *Encyclopedia of U.S. Labor and Working-Class History*, ed. Eric Arneson (New York: Routledge, 2007), 1:1434.

3. "Wolf Attacks Dog North of Anchorage," *Alaska Dispatch*, November 20, 2011.

4. Ben Leach, "Ozzy Osbourne's Pet Dog Eaten by Coyote," *London Telegraph*, July 9, 2009.

5. Ron Coffey, "Kentucky Bigfoot," Examiner.com, January 16, 2012, http://www.examiner.com/article/kentucky-bigfoot.

6. Vera Matson and Lionel Newman, "Daniel Boone," theme song from the TV series.

7. Hugh Trotti, "Did Fiction Give Birth to Bigfoot?" *Skeptical Inquirer*, September 22, 1994.

275

8. "Hairy Man Attacks," *Hillsdale (MI) Standard*, January 26, 1869.

9. Jane Goodall, interview by Ira Flatow, *Talk of the Nation*, National Public Radio transcript, September 27, 2002.

10. U.S. Centers for Disease Control and Prevention, "Carbon Monoxide–Related Deaths, United States, 1999–2004," *Morbidity and Mortality Weekly Report*, December 21, 2007, http://www.cdc.gov/mmwr /preview/mmwrhtml/mm5650a1.htm.

11. Robin Lloyd, "Out There: Billions and Billions of Habitable Planets." Space.com, February 19, 2009, http://www.space.com/4272-billions-billions -habitable-planets.html.

12. "Carl Sagan on Alien Abduction," *NOVA*, PBS.com, February 27, 1996, http://www.pbs.org/wgbh/nova/space/sagan-alien-abduction.html.

13. "Carl Sagan on Alien Abduction."

7. SALT FORK STATE PARK

1. "Ohio Grassman," *MonsterQuest*, season 2, episode 5, June 18, 2008.

2. "10 Great Places to Walk in the Shadow of Bigfoot," *USA Today*, January 11, 2013.

3. Jasmine Rogers, "In Search of Bigfoot," *Marietta (OH) Times*, October 20, 2012.

4. Ohio State University Extension, "Forests of Ohio," http://ohioline .osu.edu/forests/forst_5.html.

5. Kelly Pickerel, "What Goes Stomp in the Night," *CyBurr*, May 4, 2009, http://theburr.com/archives/Spring_09/what_goes_stomp_in_the_night .php.

6. "BFRO Database History and Report Classification System," Bigfoot Field Researchers Organization, http://www.bfro.net/gdb/classify .asp?PrinterFriendly=True.

7. Innocence Project, "Eyewitness Identification Reform" fact sheet, January 31, 2007, http://www.innocenceproject.org/free-innocent /improve-the-law/fact-sheets/eyewitness-identification-reform.

8. Report no. 4837, "Geographic Database of Bigfoot/Sasquatch Sightings and Reports," Bigfoot Field Researchers Organization, www.bfro.net.

9. William Henry Venable, *A Buckeye Boyhood* (Cincinnati: Robert Clarke, 1911).

10. Kirsten Stanley, "Bigfoot Burial Ground Identified in Ohio?" *Portsmouth (OH) Daily Times*, May 5, 1999.

11. Mark Hume and Eff Vinnick, "Trail Ends for Legendary Bigfoot Researcher Rene Dahinden," *National Post*, April 27, 2001.

8. WIND RIVER MOUNTAINS

1. Report no. 12302, "Geographic Database of Bigfoot/Sasquatch Sightings and Reports," Bigfoot Field Researchers Organization, www.bfro.net.

2. Ruffin Prevost, "TV Crew to Follow 'Bigfoot Hunters' in Yellowstone This Summer," YellowstoneGate.com, April 1, 2014, http://www.yellowstonegate.com/2014/04/tv-crew-to-follow-bigfoot-hunters-in-yellowstone-this-summer/.

3. Jeff Meldrum, review of *Bigfoot of the Blues*, by Vance Orchard, BigfootEncounters.com, 1995, http://www.bigfootencounters.com/reviews/blues.htm.

4. Jesse Harlan Alderman, "Scientist Is Big on Bigfoot, Serious about Sasquatch," Associated Press, November 4, 2006.

5. Associated Press, "Idaho State Professor Publishes Research on Sasquatch," September 5, 2012.

6. Marguerite Holloway, "Bigfoot Anatomy," *Scientific American*, November 19, 2007.

7. Goodall interview.

8. Jeff Meldrum, *Sasquatch: Legend Meets Science* (New York: Forge, 2006).

9. Emilene Ostlind, "John Mionczynski: A Biologist Revered and Ridiculed," WyoFile.com, September 20, 2011, http://www.wyofile.com/2011/09/john-mionczynski/ (page no longer available).

10. Margaret Matray, "Take to the Woods and You Might Find a Hidden Neighbor—with Size 25 Shoes," *Casper (WY) Star-Tribune*, October 24, 2010.

EPILOGUE

1. Simon Parkin, "The Hunt for One of Gaming's Most Mythical Creatures," *New Yorker*, August 26, 2013.

2. Parkin, "Hunt for One of Gaming's Most Mythical Creatures."

3. Parkin "Hunt For One of Gaming's Most Mythical Creatures."

4. "Is Bigfoot in Britain? Mysterious Figure Lurking in Lincolnshire Woods Is Claimed to Be Mystery Beast," *Mirror*, December 2, 2014, http://www.mirror.co.uk/news/weird-news/bigfoot-britain-mysterious-figure-lurking-4731307.

5. Rain Smith, "Police Blotter: Bigfoot Roams Bloomingdale Road, Bangs Up House," *Johnson City (TN) Press*, December 9, 2014.

6. "A Profound Truth," Sasquatch Ontario YouTube Channel, December 25, 2014.

7. Associated Press, "Man Trying to Create Bigfoot Sighting Killed in Montana," FoxNews.com, August 27, 2012, http://www.foxnews.com/us/2012/08/27/man-trying-to-create-bigfoot-sighting-killed-in-montana/.

8. Bryan C. Sykes, Rhettman A. Mullis, Christophe Hagenmuller, Terry W. Melton, and Michel Sartori, "Genetic Analysis of Hair Samples Attributed to Yeti, Bigfoot, and Other Anomalous Primates," *Proceedings of the Royal Society B* 281 (March 27, 2014).

9. Terrence Henry, "Is It Legal to Kill Bigfoot in Texas?" StateImpact Texas, May 10, 2012, http://stateimpact.npr.org/texas/2012/05/10/is-it-legal-to-kill-bigfoot-in-texas/.